EDUCATION
Where It's Been,
Where It's At,
Where It's Going

Edited by

Frank R. Krajewski
Gary L. Peltier

EDUCATION

Where It's Been
Where It's At
Where It's Going

EDUCATION

Where It's Been
Where It's At
Where It's Going

Edited by

Frank R. Krajewski
Gary L. Peltier
Both of the University of Nevada, Reno

Charles E. Merrill Publishing Company
A Bell & Howell Company
Columbus, Ohio

Published by
CHARLES E. MERRILL PUBLISHING COMPANY
A Bell & Howell Company
Columbus, Ohio 43216

ISBN: 0-675-08940-9

Library of Congress Catalog Card Number: 73-75505

1 2 3 4 5 6 7 / 78 77 76 75 74 73

Printed in the United States of America

CONTENTS

TRANSITIONAL PERSPECTIVES 91

RADICAL PERSPECTIVES 151

PREFACE

In an era of unprecedented youthful activism, not enough can be said about the vast changes, both real and sought, occurring in our educational institutions. It would be presumptuous to believe that any anthology could be so comprehensive as to encompass all considerations regarding potential and actual changes on the educational scene, but there is a point at which one can begin to sense the enormity of the problem. This book affords that opportunity. It is not designed to answer all questions, in fact it may not answer any questions, but this is more by design than by accident. A colleague once remarked that asking the right question is far more vital than providing a quantity of unfit answers. Hopefully these readings will encourage the asking of those "right questions" and lead ultimately to the exploration of alternatives rather than the pursuit of mediocre solutions.

The division of the text into three general areas is arbitrary. The significance of the material lies in the quality of the readings and more than just cursory attention to the categories should be considered wasteful. We have purposely avoided some of the more standard ways of organizing materials in this rather large area of study and concern. On the other hand, the categories of traditional, transitional, and radical may provide a useful structure for those of you who prefer structure, labels, and categories. Our real concern is for the messages in the readings and the applications found within the case studies.

As is the case with most anthologies of similar stature, the authors felt the urgency to fill a need left by the omission of the included material in other volumes. Designed primarily for use by undergraduates in social foundations of education classes, the text does not assume to identify any particular dogma as a panacea for the nation's academic ills. The categories of traditional, transitional, and radical serve only as an attempt to clarify the material produced by the authors therein. It is by no means intended to characterize any of the authors with labels that have proved to be as meaningless as many of the myths they seek to dispel. The traditional section includes articles that seek to clarify present issues within the context of currently available means. On the other hand, there are articles included in this section which point out the futility of employing existing means for the solution of problems. The intent here is to encourage professional educators and the few potentials among the masses of fledging education majors to consider very critically the nature of the task which they are about to undertake. If the volume serves no function other than providing an awareness of how things are to a relatively minor portion of the population of educators, then the task will indeed have been worthwhile.

As should be the case in a pluralistic society there are those among us with neither the intense faith in the present system nor the complete lack of same to find cures in the current educational scene. The articles in the transitional section concern themselves, although not exclusively, with some specific charges that provide the basis for new designs that are described in the radical section. Criticism serves a very real and legitimate function despite the cries by some that unless you can provide answers you shouldn't pose the questions. It would be sad to learn that the utilization of socratic dialogue in classroom teaching is obsolete. The authors in this section largely raise questions to which they provide no answers. Fortunately there are those among us who rally around the expositions of the critics and suggest added dimensions to an already lengthy list. It is the authors' feeling that an agenda of educational alternatives can never become too crowded, lengthy or in any way obsolete.

It is the function of the third and final section to acquaint those unacquainted, and to encourage those already familiar to re-familiarize themselves with innovative, some new and some not-so-new programs, ideas, and frequently random thoughts of sincere, dedicated human beings. If the time ever comes that we cease to consider thoughtfully and painstakingly the pleas of these social and educational reformers, then so will any need for texts of this nature.

If the writings in these pages can further help to enlighten or motivate one to become unsettled about a highly unsettling educational system then this labor will not have been in vain.

No published volume, despite its enormity or lack of it, becomes reality without the incursion of numerous debts. To attempt to list all to whom the authors are indebted would perhaps require an additional volume. At least the entire staff of the Department of Educational Foundations of the College of Education at the University of Nevada in Reno must be included. The departmental secretary Annette Martin, graduate assistants Betty Gailband and Susan Ripley, and undergraduate assistant Mike Calabrese are but a few who have contributed to the creation of this volume. The numerous authors and publishers whose works are contained herein are also deserving of a large share of gratitude, for without their cooperation there would be no completed effort.

Case Study Rationale and Suggested Procedure

The case studies provided in this volume are designed to relate the often theoretical discussions of the college classroom to the actual practice and situations which occur in many public schools.

It is our contention that case studies aid students in understanding the complexities of the educational process, encourage students to develop a consistent and justifiable philosophy of education as a framework with which to approach educational problems, as well as foster empathy and insight on the part of the students for the type of situations they must ultimately meet and solve.

The case studies in this book have been rather arbitrarily assigned to one of the three major sections of the book. Most of the case studies contain elements of the traditional and transitional and radical views of education and can therefore be used wherever deemed appropriate.

There are several possible approaches which might be employed with these case studies. The authors have found them useful in stimulating classroom discussion; as problems which the students must solve in a formal written paper; and as a beginning point for role-playing sessions.

If the case studies are to be "solved," either orally or in writing, the following procedure is recommended:

1. *Define the Problem.*   A careful delineation of the immediate problem(s) presented and the philosophical issues raised. Is there available research or additional information which is applicable to the situation presented?

2. *Criteria for a Good Solution.*   What would happen if the case were to be successfully solved? What is valued in the situation? The student, the school, the teacher, democratic principles, expediency, convenience, etc.?

3. *Possible Solutions.*   Alternative courses of action should be offered and the probable consequences of each explored.

4. *Choose the Best Solution.*   The best solution should be selected and defended by the student. If possible, the student should indicate how the proposed solution would result in the achievement of the criteria for a good solution (2 above).

TRADITIONAL
PERSPECTIVES

The first major section of this book provides a glimpse at most of the major educational philosophies which could be classified as traditional in approach and emphasis. In addition, many of the selections are illustrative of conservative educational practices.

In this time of vociferous and polemic educational controversy one is tempted to ask, "Why bother with tradition?" There are several reasons which might be offered. First, tradition is perhaps the one most important factor in determining present educational practices. Second, it is extremely difficult to understand the present without some knowledge of the past and the continuing strength of the subject-centered tradition in American education. Third, a traditional survey can inspire one both to see the need for educational change and innovation and to become skeptical about the possibility of making such changes. Both of these insights can be illuminating to the teacher.

This section provides some basic definitions and concepts which undergird the remainder of the text: What is culture? What is the school's role in our society? The articles by Havighurst and Neugarten, Stanley, Heald and Keats provide some basic definitions of culture, society and the school's role in our contemporary society; Lee deftly outlines some of the basic conflicts in our schools.

We are also assuming that one cannot fully comprehend an educational system unless one understands the society of which it is a part. Therefore, we have attempted to provide a fairly representative sample of selections which illustrate important and influential philosophical, and in some cases, political views. The more radical views are found in part 3 of this text, but we do offer Michael Harrington portraying the enormous problem of poverty in rebuttal at this early stage of the battle. The crisis situation of the culturally different in our urban schools is explored by Brookover and Bel Kaufman. Bickel offers a perspective on school desegregation—perhaps the number one societal and educational dilemma of our time.

Another general question of this traditional perspective is what are the problems and aspirations of today's teachers? The selections by Calisch and Dorey air various issues and concerns of the profession.

Pittenger and Gooding examine the unique mixture of educational philosophies and mutated learning theories which characterize the common educational practices in today's schools.

Then, more specifically, you will find a number of selections which point up educational problems: the misuse of records in "Cry the Bitter Fruit"; and the crippling effects of education graphically illustrated in the poems, "The Little Boy," and "Unlikely to Succeed." Reavis and Romano help us to see the ridiculousness of some of our educational assumptions and practices, while Corey explains the dilemma of the "poor scholar" in our public schools.

Increasingly the American school is emerging as one of the few remaining avenues to a successful life, i.e. good jobs, high standard of living, sound families, an active citizenry and dependable taxpayers. Youngsters who grow up outside the schools often become juvenile delinquents; later in life they tend to exhibit marital irresponsibility and become a drain or burden on the society as they swell the welfare rolls. If we are to break the cycle of poverty, poor home—poor education—poor job—poor home—poor education—poor job, it must be done through the schools.

Our schools have established an impressive record over the last sixty years as the table below indicates. Most of those who presently do not graduate from high school are from the lower classes of our society. The twenty-five percent dropout group which remains constitutes one of the major challenges to education in the 1970s.

THE SCHOOL AS A SELECTING AND SORTING AGENCY

Robert Havighurst
Bernice L. Neugarten

The American educational system provides opportunity for social and economic mobility by selecting and training the most able and industrious youth for the higher-status positions in society. Insofar as the school system does this job efficiently and fairly, it equips youth to be qualified for career opportunities and contributors to the success of democracy.

CHANGE IN THE AMERICAN EDUCATIONAL SYSTEM AS A SELECTING AGENCY

Number Out of Every Thousand of a Given Age who Reach a Given Educational Level	YEAR				
	1910	1938	1960	1965	1969[*]
First year high school (age 14)	310	800	904	937	961
Third year high school (age 16)	160	580	746	810	864
Graduation from high school (age 18)	93	450	621	710	759
Entrance to college or a similar educational institution	67	150	328	370	454
Graduation from college (Bachelor's degree)	22	70	170	180	220
Master's degree	1.5	9	34	42	
Doctor of Philosophy degree	0.2	1.3	4.7	6.7	

Source: Robert Havighurst and Bernice L. Neugarten, *Society and Education* (Boston: Allyn and Bacon, 1967).

[*]*Digest of Educational Statistics,* USOE, 1970.

Reprinted by permission from Robert Havighurst and Bernice Neugarten, *Society and Education,* 3d edition (Boston: Allyn and Bacon, 1967), pp. 71-73.

The degree of selection can be observed in the table which shows the number of boys and girls out of a thousand born in a given year who reach various levels of the educational ladder. It will be seen that the high school is much less selective than it was forty or fifty years ago, but that the college, while graduating increasing numbers, still operates as a highly selective agency.

The process of selection is not carried on in a formal sense by the school alone. Several factors determine how far a boy or girl goes in school: The parent's wishes, the individual's aspirations and ability, the financial status of the family, as well as the school's system of encouraging some students and discouraging others. The end result, however, is selection, with the school playing a major part in the process.

ON A SMALLER SCALE

For every 10 students entering the 5th grade (1961)
> 9.6 enter high school (1965)
> 8.6 third year high school (1967)
> 7.6 graduate high school (1969)
> 4.5 enter college (1969)
> 2.2 likely to earn four-year degrees (1973)

This brief selection attempts to resolve the eternal plea of the students for more "practicality" and less "theory" in their education courses. Stanley simply introduces the notion of value clarification as an objective of philosophical study. If you have ever been plagued with wondering "why philosophy," this selection will be able to provide you with a fundamental rationale as well as interest you in engaging in more subtle forms of introspection.

WHY
PHILOSOPHY

William Stanley

Frequently when we disagree with others about vital matters we are inclined to think our opponents are either knaves or fools, or at least that they are grossly ignorant of the facts. But consider two statements, one from the pen of a distinguished president of a great university and the other the work of a committee of outstanding scholars representing a great organization of American historians.

Education implies teaching. Teaching implies knowledge. Knowledge is truth. The truth is everywhere the same. Hence education should be everywhere the same. ... I suggest that the heart of any course of study designed for the whole people will be, if education is rightly understood, the same at any time, in any place, under any political, social, or economic conditions.[1]

Being a form of social action, education always has a geographical and cultural location; it is therefore specific, local, and dynamic, not general, universal, and unchanging; it is a function of a particular society at a particular time and place in history; it is rooted in some actual culture and expresses the philosophy and recognized needs of that culture.[2]

Could two statements disagree more sharply? Yet who would wish to impute knavery or ignorance either to the President of the University of Chicago or to the committee of eminent scholars representing the American Historical Association? How then may we account for such diametrically opposed ideas as to the very nature of education coming from such impeccable sources?

This puzzle leads to an interesting and significant conclusion. Many have claimed that all would be well if we could just make men good, while others have insisted that if we could just get the facts all disputes would be settled and men would at least agree. But it is doubtful, even if we should attain both of these very important objectives, that there would result even approximate agreement in the major disputes between men over grave questions of policy. For there is a third factor involved, in many ways more fundamental than either of the above, for it furnishes the very standards by which both the good and the true are judged.

Back of education, as of all other significant activities, are basic conceptions of the nature of man and the world, of mind and of knowledge, of the good life and of value.

Reprinted by permission from William Stanley, "Why Philosophy," *Madison Quarterly* 2 (November 1942): 145-47.
[1]Robert M. Hutchins, *The Higher Learning in America,* p. 66.
[2]American Historical Association, *Report of the Commission on the Social Studies: Conclusions and Recommendations.*

All of us, while we may not have a conscious and consistent system of philosophy, have opinions and views about these great matters.

They profoundly color our acts and inevitably mould the contours of our decisions. But with most of us this philosophy is not the result of careful thought and deliberate choice—rather, like Topsy, it just "growed." We have absorbed it from the culture around us. Hence it is not really ours; it is our master, not our servant. For it has made us, and holds us in thraldom by its invisible and unconscious chains.

Moreover, since our culture contains fragments of many philosophies, it is more likely than not a confused and contradictory mass of opinion and prejudice that leaves us at the mercy of the waves of popular propaganda that surge about us.

So we study philosophy, not to attain a point of view, for we have that already: but to become conscious of our point of view and thus break the spell of its silent mastery over our minds. By contrasting it with other philosophies we shall gain the power of choice and thus make it our own. By criticism we shall prune it of its inconsistencies and confusions and thus make it a useful intellectual tool, our servant and not our master. Then we shall have gained something indeed precious and priceless, for only by the aid of this tool may we locate ourselves intellectually in the world around us and by it alone may we effectively and without divided minds and purpose attack the problems which confront us. Critical thinking is ever the high road to freedom and true individuality; while contrast and conflict are always preconditions of thought.

It has been claimed that to attempt to change the values of lower-class youth tends to alienate them from their familial and cultural milieu. On the other hand it is charged that to identify lower-class values and construct a school curriculum consistent with them serves to betray the purposes for which the educational institution exists. The dilemma is a serious one, not only for teachers of the culturally different, but for each one of us concerned about developing meaningful teaching-learning situations within the context of a system that to many symbolizes only tyranny and oppression. Heald argues convincingly for the right of "middle-class values" to provide the trail along which we ought to proceed. What are your feelings? Perhaps this article will help you to identify more clearly the values you do possess and, as Stanley implies in the preceding article, understand the need for value identification and clarification. Keep in mind that your behavior as a teacher is largely a manifestation of a deep-seated value system.

IN DEFENSE OF
MIDDLE-CLASS VALUES

James E. Heald

Increased educational concern for the culturally deprived child has been attended by innuendoes to the effect that something is inherently wrong with middle-class values. From pens of scientists, sociologists, and educators have come charges that teachers with middle-class values must change them in order to succeed in educating the lower-class child.

The values held by middle-class teachers have been castigated, convicted, and condemned. However, before condemnation through allegation becomes final, middle-class values deserve a defense.

The Allegations

1. ". . . if we want to help lower-class children we will have to reorient our thinking and philosophy. We will have to adopt fundamental reforms, radical and crucial in nature, so that the school as an institution will be more nearly in conformity with the cultural and behavioral patterns of this [lower] class."[1]

2. ". . . Allied to this general problem is the need in many cases to retrain teachers who, used to one type of pupil from middle-class families, suddenly find themselves engulfed with slum-area children whose values run directly counter to those of teachers. Unless such teachers re-adjust their thinking, an impossible situation is at hand."[2]

3. ". . . Hasn't our middle-class culture produced a society with more than its share of tensions, anxieties, neuroses, and psychoses? How many souls have been blighted, twisted, and distorted by its impossible demands?"[3]

Reprinted by permission from James E. Heald, "In Defense of Middle-Class Values," *Phi Delta Kappan* 46 (October 1964): 81-83.

[1]Samuel Tenenbaum, "The Teacher, the Middle Class, the Lower Class," *Phi Delta Kappan,* Vol. 45, November, 1963, p. 86.

[2]James B. Conant, *Slums and Suburbs.* New York: McGraw-Hill Book Company, 1961, p. 68.

[3]Tenenbaum, *loc. cit.*

The reader of these and similar allegations must conclude that only by laying aside middle-class values can the slum-area teacher expect to become effective. In fact, all society might be better for the loss of such a restrictive set of values![4]

OPENING STATEMENT FOR THE DEFENSE

When teachers with middle-class values "re-orient," "readjust," or in fact deny their value system in order to become more effective, what will the substitute value system look like? The plaintiffs, in preparing the allegations, fail to define a new value structure for teachers which would assure effectiveness. Several logical possibilities seem to exist: 1) Teachers may accept the values of another class; 2) teachers may reject values of the middle class without substituting a new value system (this would seem a psychological impossibility); and 3) teachers may replace their current value system with a new one, nature yet undetermined.

Therefore, the defense will build its case by refuting the first possibility and by supplying some determinants for the third.

THE CASE FOR THE DEFENSE

Acceptance of a value system from a society other than middle-class has been suggested as an alternative. Tenenbaum[5] suggests the lower class, and he has also suggested that schools "be more nearly in conformity with the cultural and behavioral patterns of this class." Before adopting these proposals, it now seems appropriate to revisit the value structures of the classes as determined by Havighurst and Taba[6] in order to recall the values supporting their cultural and behavioral patterns.

Exhibit I

Members of the middle class value:[7]
1. civic virtue and community responsibility;
2. cleanliness and neatness;
3. education as a potential for solving social problems;
4. education as a preparation period for adulthood;
5. good manners;
6. honesty in all things;
7. initiative;
8. loyalty;
9. marital fidelity;
10. responsibility to church;
11. responsibility to family;
12. self-reliance;
13. sexuality, morality;
14. thrift.

---

[4]Tenenbaum also suggests that a non-middle-class culture might have "something . . . to alleviate our own sickness." (p.86)

[5]*Ibid.*

[6]Robert Havighurst and Hilda Taba. *Adolescent: Character and Personality.* New York: Wiley and Sons, 1949.

[7]*Ibid.,* pp. 31-35. (Compilation includes both "upper-middle class" and "lower-middle-class" values.)

Members of the lower class value:
1. honesty, when friends and neighbors are involved;
2. responsibility, when friends and neighbors are involved;
3. loyalty, when friends and neighbors are involved.

Members of the lower class:
4. overlook or condone stealing and dishonesty;
5. are less restrained in acts of aggression;
6. are less restrained in sexual activity;
7. view juvenile delinquency as normal behavior;
8. feel little compulsion to stay in school.

These, then, are the value systems under consideration. Teachers holding the first set have been warned to "reorient" or "readjust," and it has been suggested that movement toward the second would indeed be desirable if education for the culturally deprived is to be improved.

What needs to be considered in making a judgment?

1. Serious examination of Exhibit I should leave little doubt about the folly of abandoning middle-class values for those of the lower class. Such a movement would place schools in the position of attempting to stand for the moral and the legal while condoning the immoral and the illegal. Only the unthinking would contend that morality can best spring from a society if its leaders are immoral or that the "means" would justify the "ends." The hypocrisy of such a position would make teaching an even more impossible and uninviting profession than it currently is.

2. Human behavior tends to improve as expectations improve. To condone dishonesty, unrestrained sex activity, and juvenile delinquency as acceptable behavior is to establish conditions conducive to such behavior remaining normative. To expect humans to rise above such behavior is to offer hope for changing behavior which is considered immoral and judged illegal. Unfortunately, the teacher trying to change behavior away from the immoral and the illegal may find herself in the unenviable position of having knowledge which makes her an accessory both before and after the fact. In this position, what does represent moral and legal behavior on the part of the teacher to whom society has not yet granted the legal protection of privileged communication?

3. One of the most serious indictments made about the values of the middle class concerns the inflexibility and rigidity associated with the structure itself. A member of the middle class *must* be of a particular value pattern to be acceptable, and deviation from the perceived pattern of acceptability is cause for peer rejection. The cause is not just and deserves its criticism.

However, rigidity of structure *per se* is insufficient evidence for rejecting the values attached thereto, despite the entreaties of the moral relativists. It may be recalled that the same arguments were used by the relativists as they begged for release from the rigid Victorian concepts about sex on grounds that the rigidity itself was responsible for the guilt feelings contributing to much mental illness. With the campaign successfully concluded, the relativist is embarrassed by the increased number of neuroses arising from the lack of a stable structure in a changing society. The individual has nothing to which he can attach his personal anchor and from which strength of conviction can be derived.

Rigidity alone cannot be inherently evil unless one accepts as a basic tenet that every good is flexible. To carry moral flexibility (relativity) forward is to remove guilt, and simultaneously to destroy human conscience. No description is available of the society which would arise from the ashes of the pyre for the human conscience, but I believe the description would be frightening beyond comparison.

4. To assess the merits of the value systems under consideration, a comparison might be drawn against an older system so secure that "whatever may have been the original source or sanction, the insights have been thoroughly validated by the long experiences of mankind."[8] Such security resides in the Hebraic-Christian ethic. It is offered as Exhibit II with the hope that it will subsequently serve a benchmark function.

Exhibit II

Precepts embodied in the Hebraic-Christian ethic, as offered by Counts, are:

1. "Every man is precious . . . because he is unique." Therefore, "All institutions and social arrangements . . . are to be judged, accepted or rejected, preserved or modified, as they affect the lives of individual beings."

2. Man is a "moral creature in a moral order." He is to fulfill his nature by "striving to do good and make[ing] the good prevail in the family, the community, the nation, and the world."

3. There shall be a brotherhood of equality and essential unity among the races of mankind.

4. There shall be no privileged castes or orders and no man shall exploit another or his property.

5. For the perfection of human society, man is:

    a. to do justice;
    b. to be generous;
    c. to show mercy;
    d. to be honest;
    e. to be truthful;
    f. to cultivate a humane spirit;
    g. to love his neighbor;
    h. to be accountable for his actions;
    i. to be true to his conscience.[9]

Counts concludes his analysis of the ethic by stating,

These ethical insights are both simple and profound. Even a skeptical and cynical generation must know that the teachings and practices which flow from them are the essence of any good society. Only as we introduce them more fully into the closer relationships of our American community and into the wider relationships of nations can we hope to build a better country and a better world. *In the measure that we ignore or violate them we open the door to savagery and barbarianism.*[10] (Italics are added.)

The defense rests!

SUMMATION

Professional educators seeking to help the culturally deprived have been deluged with helpful hints for solving the learning problems of impoverished children. Among the

---

[8]George Counts, *Education and American Civilization.* New York: Teachers College, Columbia University, 1952, pp. 226-27.
[9]*Ibid.,* pp. 222-26.
[10]*Ibid.,* p. 226.

solutions has come the suggestion that movement away from a middle-class value structure by teachers would be desirable—in fact, necessary. The defense has denied this contention and has asked that the values of the middle classes be weighed, examined, and scrutinized before final judgment is pronounced.

When examined in the time-honored light of an older ethic, the values revered by the American middle class take on new luster because of the numerous similarities. However, the fact remains that the values do not emerge completely untarnished, and the defense, now denied a perfect case, must enter a new, three-part plea in behalf of the defendant: 1) Middle-class values are acceptable as guides to the conduct of teachers engaged in the education of the culturally deprived; but 2) middle-class values are not all-encompassing, and their weakness lies not in what they include but what they omit; therefore, 3) the new value structure proposed for consideration by the jury encompasses all of the middle-class values and the high expectations attached thereto.

But in addition, new values of even higher order should be gleaned from the older *ethic:* 1) There shall be value in treating all persons as beings of supreme worth; 2) there shall be value in living as a brother to men of all races, creeds, and social positions; 3) there shall be value in actively working for improvements in all social arrangements affecting the lives of men; and 4) there shall be value in striving to make good prevail in the family, the community, the nation, and the world.

Such a value structure might spawn a profession of teachers who would overlook the grime and pox of poverty, who would see beyond the impoverishment of the unenriched intellect, and who could come to dwell in the hearts of the lowliest children. Teachers with these new values would love children more than they hate dirt, and no child could be relegated to genus *subhomo.* As a member of the family of man, his worth would be inherently supreme and independent from social class, economic condition, or ethnic membership.

Condemn middle-class values? No, be proud of them! "Readjust" or "reorient" them? No, but recognize their lack of inclusiveness and expand them to the point where the entire class, including its teachers, can find value and pleasure in improving the culture, the education, the morality, and the social usefulness of the deprived, the impoverished, the destitute, and the abandoned.

The case is remanded to the profession.

Many of the problems facing education today emerge from societal conditions over which teachers have little or no control. It therefore becomes incumbent on each of us to familiarize ourselves with the nature and extent of these problems. Some of our most pressing problems lie outside of the arena in which we operate and our effectiveness can be enhanced only if we begin to address ourselves more directly to these problems at their sources. Foremost among the plethora of issues troubling us is that of poverty. It transcends racial and ethnic barriers and touches many members of our society in a nondiscriminating manner. Michael Harrington is among the few who crusade actively on behalf of the poor. As the author of The Other America *in the early sixties, his influence is reputed to have been a significant factor in motivating President Kennedy to institute the poverty program. How much do you really know about this terrible affliction from which we can find no escape? Of what value is this knowledge to you as a teacher and a human being?*

THE BETRAYAL OF
THE POOR

Michael Harrington

In the seventies the poor may become invisible again. And even if that tragedy does not occur, there will still be tens of millions living in the other America when the country celebrates its two-hundredth anniversary in 1976.

This prediction should be improbable. Lyndon B. Johnson declared an "unconditional war" on poverty in 1964, Congress agreed, and for the next four years the White House recited awesome statistics on the billions which were being spent on social betterment. The sixties was a time of marches and militancy, of students and churches committing themselves to abolish want, and of documentary presentations of the nation's domestic shame by all the mass media. Indeed, the impression of frenetic government activity was so widespread that Richard Nixon campaigned in 1968 with a promise to slow down the pace of innovation. So how, then, argue that poverty will persist in the seventies and perhaps once again drop out of the society's conscience and consciousness?

The fact is that society has failed to redeem the pledges of the sixties and has taken to celebrating paper triumphs over poverty. Thus in August of 1969 the Department of Commerce announced that the number of the poverty-stricken had dropped from 39.5 million to 25.4 million in a matter of nine years (1959 to 1968). The only problem, as will be seen, is that the numbers prettied up the reality.

When Lyndon Johnson declared his social war in the State of the Union message of 1964, the Council of Economic Advisers defined poverty as a family income of less than $3000 a year. This was a rough measure, since it didn't take into account family size or geographic location, yet it was extremely useful in identifying the groups which were particularly afflicted.

In the next few years the criteria were made much more sophisticated. In a brilliant attempt to define poverty objectively, the Social Security Administration took the Department of Agriculture's Economy Food Plan as a base figure for the poverty level. This was about 80 percent of the Low Cost Plan which many welfare agencies had used to estimate budgets; it consisted in a temporary emergency diet. In 1964, the Economy

Reprinted by permission from Michael Harrington, "The Betrayal of the Poor," *Atlantic Monthly,* January 1970, pp. 71-74.

Plan had provided $4.60 per person a week, or 22 cents a meal, and the poverty income "line" was $3100 a year. In 1969, it was $4.90 a week, and a four-member family was said to be poor if its income was below $3553 a year.

These definitions were drawn up by concerned public servants, some of them with a deep personal commitment to abolish the outrage they were defining. But note an extraordinary fact. Between 1964 and 1969, the poverty level was raised by only $453 a year, or about 14 percent for the five years. Yet during this same period, union workers, with an average increase in wage settlements in 1968 of 6.6 percent, were not making any substantial gains in purchasing power. In other words, the statistics enormously underestimate the disastrous impact of inflation upon the poor. And this problem was not simply a matter of personal income, for some of the most dramatic inflationary increases took place in the area of medical services and thereby canceled out all of the increases in Medicare benefits and forced some people out of Medicaid.

But there was another optimistic assumption in the official definition. When the Economy Food Plan was taken as the base figure, it was assumed that all other needs would cost twice the amount of the grocery bill. But, to keep up with changes in the economy and society since then, one should compute the other items at three times the price of food, not two. By using the erroneous assumptions of the Eisenhower fifties, the government abolished the poverty of 12 million Americans who were still poor.

If it seems extreme to suggest that honest, and even concerned, experts could thus overlook the anguish of 12 million of their fellow citizens, consider the famous Census undercount in 1960: almost 6 million Americans, mainly black adults living in Northern cities, were not enumerated. Their lives were so marginal—no permanent address, no mail, no phone number, no regular job—that they did not even achieve the dignity of being a statistic. Again the extent of misery was underestimated.

In 1967 there were roughly 12 million citizens whom the Council of Economic Advisers called the "near poor" (with incomes between $3335 and $4345 for families of four). If these numbers were underestimated in the same way as were the poor, there are 16 million Americans who are but one illness, one accident, one recession away from being poor again. If, as now seems so possible, America in the seventies should reduce its social efforts, this group will lose almost as much as the poor.

And there is another, and even larger, segment of the population whose destiny is related to that of the other Americans. In late 1966, the Bureau of Labor Statistics figured that it would take $9191 for a "moderate standard of living"—you could buy a two-year-old used car and a new suit every four years. It should be remembered that raising the minimum wage for the lowest paid workers tends to help raise the take of those who are organized and much better off, but turning our back on the poor creates a political and social atmosphere in which the needs of an increasing number of people can be overlooked.

Perhaps the simplest way to get a summary view of the dangerous trends is to examine one generation of broken promises in the area of housing.

The government promised every citizen a decent dwelling in 1949. Under the leadership of a conservative Republican, Senator Robert A. Taft, the Congress agreed that the private housing market was not serving the needs of the poor. They therefore pledged to build 810,000 units of low-cost housing by 1955. In 1970, one generation later, that target has not yet been achieved. But the problem is not what the government did not do, but what it did instead. For while Washington was providing cheap money and princely tax deductions for more than 10 million affluent home builders in suburbia, it was taking housing away from the poor. As the President's National Commission on Urban Problems, chaired by former Senator Paul Douglas, reported in January, 1969, "Government action through urban renewal, highway programs, demolition on public housing sites, code enforcement and other programs has destroyed more housing for the poor than government at all levels has built for them." In 1968 a law was passed pledging the United States to do in the seventies what it had pledged to do in the fifties. Within a year it became clear that it was unlikely that the nation would redeem this second promise. To build 26 million new housing units in ten years, 6 million of them low-cost, would require speeding up the production of dwellings for the poor to twenty times the present rate. And as George Romney, the Secretary of Housing and Urban Development, admitted in 1969, it is quite possible that we will fall 10 million units behind the goal.

What this means for the seventies is the further decay of the central cities of America, an increase in the already massive level of housing poverty which afflicts a third of the people—and the emergence of ghost towns in the middle of metropolis.

For the plight of the cities is becoming so grievous that even slums are not as profitable as they used to be. As a result, the Real Estate Research Corporation told the *Wall Street Journal* in 1969, between ten and fifteen thousand buildings are being abandoned in the course of the year.

When Richard Nixon was elected President he told the people that the federal government had tried to do too much and that he would therefore decentralize social programs and set more modest goals. There was a half-truth and a dangerous falsehood in his analysis, which bodes ill for the poor in the seventies.

Under Lyndon Johnson the Administration talked as if it were undertaking and accomplishing prodigies. One of the reasons why a disturbing number of white workers turned to George Wallace in 1968 was that they were under the impression that Washington had done so much for the poor, and particularly the Negroes. They confused the bold rhetoric with action and did not understand that life in the ghettos had changed very little. Insofar as Nixon taxes Johnson for having talked too loudly, he is right. But the rest of his thesis—that the federal government was too activist, and that efforts must be cut back and turned over to the states—is wrong.

In order to destroy this myth of the favored pampered poor, one need only consider official figures. In 1968 the National Advisory Commission on Civil Disorders—the "Riot" Commission—reported that in Detroit, New Haven, and Newark, the cities where the violence was the most destructive in 1967, the median percentage of those eligible who were actually covered by any one of the major social programs was 33 percent. In other words, in the United States, a majority of the poor are not on welfare at all. And, the Commission showed, the national average for welfare payments is "a little more than one half of need," and in some cases one fourth of need. In January, 1969, a special Cabinet committee reported to Lyndon Johnson that the existing domestic programs were already underfunded by $6 billion and that a moderate expansion of civilian efforts along lines already suggested by various commissions and study groups would cost another $40 billion by 1972. So the government by its own standards is falling billions of dollars behind what should be done.

To many citizens, people who receive welfare are regarded as a burden upon the hardworking common man. But what is really happening is that many of the poor are being undercompensated for humiliations which the government and the economy, or both, have visited upon them. The most dramatic case in point is the rural poor who were driven into the cities in recent years. Billions of dollars in federal subsidies were paid to rich individuals and corporate farmers—including hundreds of thousands to Senator James O. Eastland, the impartial plantation owner who sits on the Senate

Agriculture Committee and helps determine his own rewards. These handsome welfare payments to the wealthy allowed them to make a profit by reducing the land under cultivation and also provided them with funds for mechanization. Productivity in the fields increased twice as fast as in the factories, but millions of the rural poor became economically superfluous.

Between 1950 and 1966 federal monies helped to force 5.5 million black farm workers into the cities. They came from areas where education for Negroes was substandard, and these black migrants were required to relate to a bewildering, complex urban environment and compete in a sophisticated labor market. They brought with them, as Harold Fleming has said, "the largest accumulation of social deficits ever visited upon an identifiable group."

In short, it is not that Washington has done too much but that it has so often done the wrong thing. And the central thesis of Mr. Nixon's 1969 welfare message—"a third of a century of centralizing power in Washington has produced a bureaucratic monstrosity, cumbersome, unresponsive ineffective"—is not an accurate description of what happened. Moreover, Mr. Nixon's major welfare proposal to establish a minimum income for families contradicts his own analysis, for it proposes to federalize welfare benefits at a certain level. Mr. Nixon was quite rightly disturbed that Mississippi pays an average of $39.35 a month to support an entire family while New York has much higher standards. He therefore wants to use the federal power to force Mississippi from abusing its states' rights in such an inhumane way, which is hardly decentralization.

One of the most disturbing facts about the poor is that roughly half of them are young. They will be flooding the labor market so fast in 1975 that the Department of Labor expects 25 percent more sixteen-to-nineteen-year-olds looking for jobs than in 1965—and 50 percent more black youths. This will happen at a time when blue-collar positions for which they will be competing will be opening up at a rate of about 15 percent a year. In other words, there is a very real possibility that many, even most of the children of the poor will become the fathers and mothers of the poor.

These dangerous trends did not explode in the sixties, but two of the reasons were Vietnam and inflation. The nation's tragic commitment to the horror in Southeast Asia created 700,000 new "jobs" in the Armed Forces and a million new openings in defense industry. Since 80 percent of the draftees had high school diplomas, the Army did not actually take the poor in but removed some of their competition from the labor market. Then with inflation after 1965—which was triggered by a $10 billion " mistake" in federal spending based upon optimistic assumptions about a victory in the war in 1966 —the labor market tightened up even more. But with peace in Vietnam, what are the acceptable substitutes for the employment generated by war and inflation?

In his message to Congress on population problems in the summer of 1969, President Nixon attacked a sweeping proposal made by the National Committee on Urban Growth Policy for not being sufficiently daring. The Committee, which included Democratic regulars like Hale Boggs and John Sparkman and even a Goldwater Republican, John Tower, had said that the nation must build ten new cities for one million citizens each and ten new towns for 100,000 inhabitants. After noting that there will be 100 million additional Americans by the year 2000, three quarters of them living in urbanized areas, the President said of the Committee's suggestion, "But the total number of people who would be accommodated if even those bold plans were implemented is *only* 20 million—a *mere* one fifth of the expected thirty-year increase." (Emphasis added.)

As the seventies open there is every indication that housing poverty will become even more acute, and that the children of the last decade's poor will, as parents in an economy without enough decent jobs, increase the size of the other America. To avoid such tragedies, certain things must be done.

First of all there must be planning. There should be an Office of the Future attached to the presidency and a Joint Congressional Committee on the Future which would receive, debate, and adopt or modify annual reports from the White House.

Suburban home builders, automobile manufacturers, and trucking companies all pick up their huge federal subsidies without a thought of pollution. And now—not simply if poverty is to be abolished, but if the quality of life in America is to be kept from deteriorating—we must consider the "side effects" of new technologies even more scrupulously than we do those of new drugs. A year before his death, Dwight Eisenhower urged the building of new cities, racially and socially integrated and with new jobs. Mr. Nixon apparently agrees. But the enormously complex planning needed to accomplish such a task is not going to be done by the invisible hand of "Adam Smith."

Second, there must be billions of dollars in social investments. President Nixon, like President Johnson before him, hopes that private enterprise can do the job. His first version of this philosophy was called "black capitalism," and he ordered the concept extended to all the impoverished minorities when he took office. But the blunt economic facts of life are that costs in the slums are twice as high as in the suburbs, congestion much more serious, the labor market relatively untrained, and the neighborhoods unprofitable for big business. Minority enterprises can, of course, make a contribution to their areas and should be helped generously, but for the vast majority they offer no real hope.

As the sixties were ending, there did seem to be one area in which the cooperation of the public and private sector worked: employment. The National Association of Businessmen, with strong federal help, is trying to put poverty-stricken and minority workers into good jobs, and the measurable gains have been highly publicized. However, a 1969 analysis by the *Wall Street Journal* was not so sanguine. The main reason for the hirings, Alan Otten wrote, was the tight labor market, and any increase in unemployment—which is inevitable given the Nixon strategy against inflation—would turn these people back out on the streets. Yet when the Automobile Workers Union proposed to the Ford Corporation that its older members be permitted to take a voluntary layoff so that the new men could stay on, the company refused. The reason was simple: the supplementary unemployment compensation for a veteran is costlier than for a new worker. The profit motive was stronger than social conscience.

Early in the seventies the gross national product of the United States will pass the $1 trillion mark. As an article in *Fortune* calculated this trend, there would be a fiscal "dividend"—the automatic increase in government income without any rise in taxes which takes place when the GNP becomes larger—of $38 billion in 1974 and around $80 billion by 1980. The problem under these circumstances is not finding the resources but being intelligent enough to use them democratically and creatively.

In his 1969 welfare message, President Nixon made a sharp attack on the unevenness of the present states' rights welfare system. But in his proposals he urged Congress to delegate even more power to the very local administrations which had previously abused it, and he came out for a federal minimum which would leave people well below the poverty line. In the Nixon program, Washington would provide the funds to bring family payments up to $1600 a year, and the twenty states which now pay less than that would be required to contribute only half of their present welfare spending up to the total.

Instead of thus institutionalizing a federal minimum which is less than 50 percent of the way to the poverty line, the United States should adopt the principle that all of its citizens are legally entitled to a decent income. Lyndon Johnson's outgoing Cabinet computed that one version of such a social involvement, a negative tax, would cost between $15 and $20 billion a year. Given the *Fortune* prediction of an $80 billion dividend by 1980, that amount is clearly within the country's means.

Such a program should have a work incentive. Instead of the typical American practice of taxing the earnings of the welfare recipient 100 percent (by reducing his benefits by the amount of his wages), the individual should be allowed to keep a decreasing proportion of his income supplement as his pay goes up. But this also means that there must be a vast increase in the number of decent jobs. In New York City, where Aid to Dependent Children payments approximate the level of menial jobs in the economy, there is no motive for the mothers to look for work, and they haven't. So a guaranteed income with a work incentive means a commitment to genuine full employment.

And that is where the notion of a guaranteed income ties in with the right to work. It was Franklin Roosevelt who first urged, in the campaign of 1944, that if the private economy does not provide jobs for the people, then the public economy must. If the promises of the Housing Acts of 1949 and 1968 were carried out, there would be a labor shortage and the country would discover that it really needs the unused work potential of the poor and the near poor. The effect of such a program would not be inflationary because workers would be producing valuable goods and services for their wages.

As the seventies begin, the nation needs planned long-range social investments to provide a decent home for every citizen and to guarantee either a living income or a good job for all. If the cities continue to sprawl and technology revolutionizes the land in a casual, thoughtless way, polluting our natural resources, it is the poor who will be the most cruelly used, but the entire nation will suffer as well.

At any point in your formal schooling did you begin to wonder on what grounds the institutions concluded that you belonged in a particular group or section of a class while your friends were scattered throughout several other sections? Undoubtedly you will find yourself teaching classes which have been so divided. Do you feel this is the way to effect a more palatable learning environment, or is administrative expediency to be desired above the concerns of the students? Brookover makes a rather convincing argument not only against the practice of ability grouping but also the criteria by which one gets "grouped."

A SOCIOLOGICAL ANALYSIS OF
ACADEMIC SELECTION AND ACHIEVEMENT

W. B. Brookover

One hundred years ago on July 2, Abraham Lincoln signed the Morrill Act authorizing the establishment of the land-grant colleges "for the liberal and practical education of the industrial classes" as distinguished from the professional education of doctors, lawyers, and ministers. The resulting pattern of higher education and the concurrent development of universal secondary schooling had made formal education an integral part of our complex social system. Education for constantly extended periods of years provides the foundation upon which our whole occupational structure is based. The development of highly industrialized societies in Europe, without the extended mass education characteristic of the United States demonstrates that the two are not inseparable, but their parallel development in our society has made education the major agency for occupational and status allocation. As increased division of labor and mechanization reduced the proportion of low-skilled laborers, educational prerequisites have been established for almost all occupations.

This allocation function begins in the early elementary grades and continues through the child's school career. The accumulation of teacher evaluations and student performance largely determines the level and type of education which each child will receive. This in turn structures the range of social statuses in which a person may perform as an adult.

This function of the educational system is complicated by the fact that the composition of the labor force in American society is changing rapidly. During the past few years professional, technical, and managerial people have become the largest group in the American working population. This highly skilled, educated group is now larger than the blue collar, manual workers group. All signs point to even greater growth of this group in the future. The large pool of unemployed persons today is predominantly composed of those with little formal education. Job opportunities are readily available in many areas for people with higher levels of education. Our economics progress, our defense strength, and our position in the world depend on an increasing supply of highly educated people, both in quantity and in quality.

All this means that the complexities of the allocation functions expected of education have increased. Not only must the school assist in selecting mechanics and doctors by grading, promoting or failing, and counseling, but a much higher proportion must be directed into the college and graduate levels of education and allocated to various positions requiring such education.

Reprinted by permission from W. B. Brookover, "A Sociological Analysis of Academic Selection and Achievements," material attached to presidential address given to the Ohio Valley Sociological Society.

The overpowering need for highly educated personnel, increased by the cold war fear, has put much pressure on the educational system to improve its effectiveness in the production of such persons. Numerous responses to this demand can be identified. The National Defense Education Act's support for science, guidance, new media, and graduate education programs is one of the most evident. Others are numerous curriculum changes, special programs for the gifted and culturally deprived, return to homogeneous ability grouping, and higher standards of achievement in evaluation and admission to various curricula. All such changes are intended to increase quantity and improve the quality of highly talented people. Certainly some gains have been and will continue to be made, but I fear the prevalent assumptions about human learning which underlie our educational practice will unnecessarily limit the level of achievement in the society.

Most educators recognize the importance of non-genetic factors such as motivation and sub-cultural differences in educational norms on the nature and extent of academic achievement, but we still base many educational policies on the assumption of a restrictive, organic theory of ability. A brief look at American educational practices to which most sociologists as well as educationists subscribe will illustrate such a genetic conception of learning. We use intelligence and related tests to classify students into a wide range of categories, from the presumably superior biological organisms identified as gifted or talented to the several categories of mentally handicapped. Educational programs are then designed to fit the presumed limits of ability identified by these measures. Contemporary literature on the education of the gifted is almost exclusively devoted to the methods of discovering or identifying those people who have such endowments. One looks in vain for methods of developing such abilities. Using similar devices, we classify retarded children into custodial, trainable, and educable categories which describe the presumed genetic limits of ability to learn desired types of behavior. Between these two ends of the distribution, we postulate a normal curve of essentially fixed biological abilities or capacities.

Although mental test and measurement scholars have long recognized the fact that current instruments measure only a sample of achievement, we still use them as if they were measures of innate capacity as Terman insisted.

In a discussion of methods of identifying gifted, Robert Havighurst says, "Educators now have on hand a remarkable array of technical aids in the discovery of talent. We have a variety of adequate and practical tests and other such features for identifying talented youth." He later cautions that "a large group of economically underprivileged but able boys and girls are likely to go through life with their talents underdeveloped unless they are stimulated and aided to get education of good quality." The impressions left by the paper, however, are that "gifts" or "talent" are a fixed endowment to be discovered.

In an analysis of social factors in academic achievement, Peter Rossi tacitly assumes that I.Q. scores are measuring something unaffected by these factors when he says, "We found that between 40-60 per cent of the variation (in achievement) could be accounted for by variation in I.Q. level. . . . Yet despite the importance of intelligence a considerable portion can be accounted for in other terms." He then discusses occupation and educational level of the family, motivation, teachers, school environment, and other related factors. As an afterthought at the end of the paper, Rossi states that I.Q. is not innate but affected to some extent by environment. His earlier use of I.Q. as an explanation gives the contrary impression.

Rossi and Havighurst, like most teachers and professors, continue to discuss I.Q. and related tests as if they measured some genetically limited capacity, with full knowledge of the effect which a whole range of social factors have on such measures. I suspect most sociologists like these men have been socialized by the genetic I.Q. complex in our culture to the extent that they accept many test results in the same manner. In a similar fashion, I suspect many of us have accepted the decision about the limits of our children's musical talent based on Seashore's test of pitch discrimination even though it has been amply demonstrated that such behavior is readily modified by teaching.

Recent studies of creativity raise another question about traditional mental tests. Getzels and Jackson at Chicago and McKinney and others in California have found negative correlation between indexes of creativity and I.Q. scores, at least in the upper ranges of the latter, and no evidence of any positive correlation in the total range. Highly creative people are apparently found at most any point in the mental test range.

Perhaps this is part of the explanation for the intelligence characteristics and social origins of advanced graduate students. Strauss, in a recent study of the background of Ph.D.'s at the University of Maryland and Johns Hopkins from 1952-57 found that their high school I.Q. scores ranged from 91-165. The mean was approximately 120 with humanities and social science Ph.D.'s slightly higher than natural scientists. Gottlieb's studies of graduate students indicate that those in natural science are more likely to finish their Ph.D. and do it faster than those in the humanities and social sciences. A recent national study of advanced graduate students in the United States reveals that two-thirds come from families in the lower socio-economic strata. It is unlikely that their high school test scores are superior to their upper strata cohorts. Apparently, factors are operating in the success of graduate students which are not measured by I.Q. scores.

In our efforts to improve educational efficiency in the last decade, we have developed numerous new educational curricula and institutions to provide varying types of education for different classifications of students. Selection for and placement in the various groups, curricula, and schools is generally largely based on some combination of mental tests. Children identified as custodial, are treated as such and no effort is made to teach them the types of behavior normally provided in school. The trainable are given a limited range of instruction which should make it possible for them to function at some low level of occupational skills. The educable are provided an opportunity to learn a limited range of academic skills and knowledge usually in special schools or classes where not too much is expected to them, but it is hoped that they may become able to live useful lives.

For the normal range of presumed abilities, we have established a variety of homogeneous groups based on I.Q. and achievement scores. Paul Woodring, an educational spokesman for Ford Foundations, in *A Fourth of the Nation* advocates that grouping with differential curricula be established by the third grade or before. Few schools officially do this so early in the school career, but such placement in differentiated programs in junior high school and high school is now common in school units with sufficient enrollment to make it feasible. In such systems, only the groups with higher test scores are given the curriculum designed to lead to high levels of education and sorely needed occupations requiring such education.

Frequently, a very small proportion of the students with presumably great capacity are placed in separate programs on the assumption that their learning will be retarded by more conventional classroom procedures.

At the college level, other forces have supplemented the desire to improve efficiency as causes for increased selectivity and differentiation of institutions. The pressure of increased enrollments on facilities and the traditional use of selective admission as a criterion of college prestige have contributed to the current pattern. Like many others, the land-grant colleges and universities are no longer dedicated to the education of the industrial classes but concentrate on the education of those born with a battery of mental tests in their bassinets.

Where formerly we had only highly selective institutions, we now have a whole hierarchy of college and university categories ranging from the junior colleges and Ferris Institute in Michigan who take all high school graduates to Harvard, Yale, and Princeton who admit only those with high test scores and the proper alumni stamp of approval. The system of high education in California has now officially confirmed a system of segregated colleges and universities wherein the elite twelve or fifteen per cent may enter the University of California system. The next group go to the state colleges and the lower group must go to junior colleges, if at all.

As a side, but relevant, issue, it is doubtful in my mind whether the selection practices in California colleges and elsewhere and secondary curricula placement are any more defensible under the constitution than Negro-white segregated schools. Both practices are based upon a classification of presumed biological differences and both now place students in different institutions on the basis of mental test scores. I doubt that any one would maintain that the education in junior college and the University of California are equal even though separate.

Although many educators believe that pupil placement in differentiated programs and selective admission to college and universities increase overall achievement, this conclusion may hold up under careful analysis. In previous periods, when the society needed large numbers of manual workers and few highly educated, such practices no doubt were useful in screening out all but the few. Unless the various types of colleges are of equal quality the selection practices are likely to reduce our total supply of much needed personnel. If not, they only enhance the prestige of the elite institutions.

Similar questions must be asked about homogeneous grouping and separate schools for different ability levels at the elementary and secondary level. Do such practices increase the total level of achievement and the supply of highly educated for our society? On the basis of current evidence, I would hypothesize that the opposite is true, when placement is based on the assumption of differential fixed capacity to learn. Children placed in a lower ability group will not be given the opportunity to learn that which is necessary for higher levels of education. Although many would not have done so in any case, there is ample evidence to demonstrate that some with low scores will master the hard academic materials if given the opportunity. Unfortunately the system contains a self-fulfilling prophecy. To the extent that school programs are tailored to fit the presumed capacity limits of the different groups, future tests will demonstrate that the former tests were accurate predictors. There is no substantial evidence, however, from carefully designed studies to support the contention that homogeneous grouping enhances achievement, except among retarded students for limited periods. In view of this, the maximization of the collective achievement is more likely to occur when all are given the opportunity to learn the desired behavior with no assumptions about limited genetic ability.

This latter specification requires a different conception of human learning than characterizes American education today. Sociologists have long understood and proclaimed the basic tenets of such a conception, but have seldom applied it to school achievement. We all recognize that practically all children in any society learn the common behaviors as defined in its cultural norms. As the society and culture change from one period to another, the children learn to behave differently. In applying this sociological principle to human ability Robert Faris, in his presidential address for the American Sociological Association, uses the concept of collective ability. He says, "A high level of collective ability produces not only science and machinery, but also efficient organizational behavior; this in turn allows effective complex governmental, economic, and social organizations . . . The present argument is that in a literal sense and to an important degree, a society generates its level of ability, and further that the upper limit is unknown and distant, and best of all that the processes of generation of ability are potentially subject to intentional control." When one considers the tremendous increase in the level of achievement both quantitatively and qualitatively as reflected in American educational systems, this conception of ability is not unsupported. Only a few decades ago, approximately one-fourth of the students completed high school, compared with approximately three-fourths today. Three decades ago, one in five persons of college age was enrolled in college, but now over one in three is enrolled. A wide variety of criteria indicate that the average level of performance has increased among those attending high school and college. My children have learned the basic principle of rocketry and space science as readily as I learned to operate an internal combustion gasoline engine. There is a difference, however. They learned this currently important knowledge in school where many ask, "Does he have the ability?" I learned the important behavior, in my youth, at home where no one asked any questions about my limited ability.

In the light of the great need for new abilities and our understanding of the social factors producing differential types of behavior, sociologists have a major responsibility for developing a new conception of learning which will enhance the collective ability of a society. Faris pointed out a series of promising areas of research derived from our basic sociological frame of reference. He summarizes his comments as follows. "The central implication of the present argument is that attractive potentialities of increased collective ability are possible if we advance our knowledge of the sociological influences which stimulate and limit aspiration and achievement and find strategic points with which we may establish some control over them . . . It appears that we only need to apply massive research effort in the field of the relation of social factors to abilities. Fortunately there exists today a nationwide enthusiasm for the development of talent resources; a milling crowd is stirring into action even in advance of academic sociological leadership."

As some of you know from papers given in these and other meetings, my colleagues and I were started on a project in this field before President Faris' call. A brief report of our efforts is in order here.

From a general sociological framework, I have previously stated four basic postulates.

1. Persons generally learn to behave in ways that each considers appropriate to himself.
2. Appropriateness of behavior is defined by each person through the internalization of the expections of significant others.
3. The functional limits of a person's ability to learn are determined by his self-conception of his abilities as acquired in social interaction.
4. A person learns what he believes significant others expect him to learn in the classroom or in any other situation.

From this basic theoretical orientation, my collegues and I have designed a series of research projects, supported by the U.S. Office of Education, to test the hypothesis that an individual's self-concept of his ability to learn is the functionally limiting factor in his school achievements. The first phase of the research was designed to determine whether or not self-concept of ability could be identified and isolated as a variable in behavior and whether or not it was related to school achievement.

We have developed a simple Guttman-type scale which is correlated with school grade point average of seventh graders at about 0.57. When the effect of whatever it is intelligence tests measure is partialled out, self-concept of ability is correlated with school grades at about 0.40. With this evidence that self-concept of ability is a relevant variable in achievement, we are now launching three experiments designed to change the self-concept of low achieving junior high school students and thence, their level of achieving. In what is perhaps the most crucial of these, we propose to modify the general level of expectations which parents hold for their children. We hypothesize that these enhanced expectations will be internalized as increased self-conceptions of ability and that higher levels of achievement will follow. Parents are selected as the significant others for two reasons: First, this group of junior high school students have, in one hundred per cent of the cases, identified one or both parents as important in their consideration of school affairs. Second, although teachers are also identified to design an experiment in which other variables in a teaching situation would not be contaminated by changing the teachers' expectations of low achieving students. The other two experiments are designed to introduce a counselor and an expert on learning into the low achieving child's realm of interaction to determine if such personnel may become significant others or counteract the impact of the established significant others who hold low expectations for the student. If this affects a change in the self-concept, we hypothesize a subsequent change in the achievement of these students.

In these experiments we postulate as Faris does that the biological limits are unknown and rarely, if ever, reached. We, therefore, propose to modify the functional limits which are derived from the social interaction of the student. If the results of these and other studies of self-concept now underway are positive a decidedly different orientation to academic selection and achievement may be appropriate. Instead of seeking to identify the limits of biological capacity and differentiate educational programs in line with such criteria, we would focus our attention on devising social groups and patterns of social interaction which would enhance the ability of children to acquire whatever types of behavior may be needed in the society.

Such a perception of academic ability would free us from the theories of inadequate talent which now pervade American society. The limits of achievement would be determined only by the limits of our facilities to provide the kind of social norms and expectations which would nurture high achievement in the necessary areas of behavior. A social environment in which children are expected to learn algebra, calculus or sociology would produce such behavior quite as readily as the current environment leads to the acquisition of an adolescent vocabulary and the pattern of romantic love. As Jerome Bruner says in *The Process of Education,* "Any subject can be taught effectively and in some intellectually honest form to any child at any stage of development."

In the light of world events dominated by the struggle for the maintenance of a free society, it is high time that social scientists devote their energies to the devising of such learning environment rather than operate according to the doctrines of infant damnation imposed by the concept of organic limitations implied in our testing complex. For doctrinal reasons, which we do not accept, the Russians have long since accepted the basic thesis that any child can learn whatever the environment can provide for him and expects of him. If we are to compete in this expanding world of interaction which demands higher and higher levels of technical skill and achievement, we must find means to expand our horizons of learning rather than limit them. Our contemporary doctrine of organic limitations does not provide the foundation for such achievement. Sociologists have the theoretical orientation and the know-how to lead the way in opening the doors for expanded academic and social achievements, but they must cast off the chains inherited from Darwin and Terman.

School desegregation has been both a success and a failure, says Alexander Bickel, a professor of law and legal history at Yale. The success was mainly in the South, the failure nationwide.

The major problems are resegregation—the fleeing of whites from a school district, leaving an all white school which then becomes all black; and the attempts of Negro leaders in the North to decentralize the neighborhood schools with their present racial makeup and to bring the neighborhood schools under the control of its surrounding black community.

Reflecting an attitude now widespread among liberals and even among black radicals who once unreservedly supported desegregation efforts, Bickel is reluctant to advocate gambling major resources on a chase after integration. These resources might be better spent, he thinks, in consolidating the gains desegregation has made thus far, and then improving the neighborhood school in all parts of our land.

"DESEGREGATION: WHERE DO WE GO FROM HERE?"

Alexander M. Bickel

It [was] 16 years this May since the Supreme Court decreed in *Brown* v. *Board of Education* that the races may not be segregated by law in the public schools, and [it will be] six years in July since the doctrine of the *Brown* case was adopted as federal legislative and executive policy in the Civil Rights Act of 1964. Yet here we are apparently struggling still to desegregate schools in Mississippi, Louisiana, and elsewhere in the Deep South, and still meeting determined resistance, if no longer much violence or rioting.

The best figures available indicate that only some 23 percent of the nationwide total of more than six million Negro pupils go to integrated public schools. About half the total of more than six million Negro pupils are in the South, and there the percentage of Negroes in school with whites is only 18.

What has gone wrong? The answer is, both less and a great deal more than meets the eye; it is true both that the school desegregation effort has been a considerable success and that it has not worked.

The measure of the success is simply taken. Sixteen years ago, local law, not only in the 11 Southern states but in border states, in parts of Kansas, in the District of Columbia, forbade the mixing of the races in schools, and official practice had the same effect in some areas in the North, for example portions of Ohio and New Jersey. Ten years ago, Southern communities were up in arms, often to the point of rioting or closing the public schools altogether, over judicial decrees that ordered the introduction of a dozen or two carefully selected Negro children into a few previously all-white schools. There are counties in the Deep South that still must be reckoned as exceptions, but on the whole, the principle of segregation has been effectively denied, those who held it have been made to repudiate it, and the rigid legal structure that embodied it has been destroyed. That is no mean achievement, even though it still needs to be perfected and completed, and it is the achievement of law, which had irresistible moral force and was able to enlist political energies in its service.

Reprinted by permission from Alexander M. Bickel, "Desegregation: Where Do We Go from Here?" *The New Republic*, February 1970, pp. 518-21. Copyright © 1970, Harrison-Blaine of New Jersey, Inc.

The achievement is essentially Southern. The failure is nationwide. And the failure more than the achievement is coming to the fore in those districts in Mississippi and Louisiana where the Supreme Court and a reluctant Nixon Administration are now enforcing what they still call desegregation on very short deadlines. In brief, the failure is this: To dismantle the official structure of segregation, even with the cooperation in good faith of local authorities, is not to create integrated schools, anymore than integrated schools are produced by the absence of an official structure of school segregation in the North and West. The actual integration of schools on a significant scale is an enormously difficult undertaking, if a possible one at all. Certainly it creates as many problems as it purports to solve, and no one can be sure that even if accomplished it would yield an educational return.

School desegregation, it will be recalled, began and for more than a decade was carried out under the so-called "deliberate speed" formula. The courts insisted that the principle of segregation and, gradually, all its manifestations in the system of law and administration be abandoned; and they required visible proof of the abandonment, namely, the presence of black children in school with whites. The expectation was that a school district which had been brought to give up the objective of segregation would gradually reorganize itself along other nonracial lines and end by transforming itself from a dual into a unitary system.

All too often, that expectation was not met. The objective of segregation was not abandoned in good faith. School authorities would accept a limited Negro presence in white schools and would desist from making overt moves to coerce the separation of the races, but would manage nevertheless to continue operating a dual system consisting of all black schools for the vast majority of Negro children and of white and a handful of nearly white schools for all the white children. This was sham compliance —tokenism, it was contemptuously called, and justly so—and in the past few years the Supreme Court, and HEW acting under the Civil Rights Act of 1964, determined to tolerate it no longer.

ɪ HEW and some lower federal courts first raised the ante on tokenism, requiring stated percentages of black children in school with whites. Finally they demanded that no school in a given system be allowed to retain its previous character as a white or black school. Faculties and administrators had to be shuffled about so that an entirely or almost entirely black or white faculty would no longer characterize a school as black or white. If a formerly all-Negro school was badly substandard, it had to be closed. For the rest, residential zoning, pairing of schools by grades, some busing, and majority-to-minority transfers were employed to ensure distribution of both races through the school system. In areas where blacks were in a majority, whites were necessarily assigned to schools in which they would form a minority. All this has by no means happened in every school district in the South, but it constitutes the current practice of desegregation. Thus among the decrees recently enforced in Mississippi, the one applicable in Canton called for drawing an east-west attendance line through the city so that each school became about 70 percent black and 30 percent white. Elsewhere schools were paired to the same end.

It bears repeating that such measures were put into effect because the good faith of school authorities was in doubt, to say the least, and satisfactory evidence that the structure of legally enforced segregation had been eliminated was lacking. But whatever, and however legitimate, the reasons for imposing such requirements, the consequences have been perverse. Integration soon reaches a tipping point. If whites are sent to constitute a minority in a school that is largely black, or if blacks are sent to constitute something near half the population of a school that was formerly white or nearly all-white, the whites flee, and the school becomes all, or nearly all, black; resegregation sets in, blacks simply changing places with whites. The whites move, within a city or out of it into suburbs, so that under a system of zoning they are in white schools because the schools reflect residential segregation; or else they flee the public school system altogether, into private and parochial schools.

It is not very fruitful to ask whether the whites behave as they do because they are racists or because everybody seeks in the schools some sense of social, economic, cultural group identity. Whatever one's answer, the whites do flee, or try to, whether in a Black Belt county where desegregation has been resisted for 16 years in the worst of faith and for the most blatant of racist reasons; or in Atlanta, where in recent years, at any rate, desegregation has been implemented in the best of faith; or in border cities such as Louisville, St. Louis, Baltimore, or Washington, D.C., where it was implemented in good faith 15 years ago; or in Northern cities, where legal segregation has not existed in over half a century. It is feckless to ask whether this should happen. The questions to ask are whether there is any way to prevent the whites' fleeing, or whether there are gains sufficient to offset the flight of the whites in continuing to press the process of integration.

To start with the second question, a negative answer seems obvious. What is the use of a process of racial integration in the schools that very often produces, in absolute numbers, more black and white children attending segregated schools than before the process was put into motion? The credible disestablishment of a legally enforced system of segregation is essential, but it ought to be possible to achieve it without driving school systems past the tipping point of resegregation—and perhaps this, without coming right out and saying so, is what the Nixon Administration has been trying to tell us. Thus in Canton, Mississippi, a different zoning scheme would apparently have left some all-black and all-white schools, but still put about 35 percent of black pupils in schools with whites.

We live by principles, and the concrete expression in practice of the principles we live by is crucial. *Brown* v. *Board of Education* held out for us the principle that it is wrong and ultimately evil to classify people invidiously by race. We would have mocked that principle if we had allowed the South to wipe some laws formally off its books and then continue with segregation as usual, through inertia, custom, and the application of private force. But substantial, concrete changes vindicating the principle of the *Brown* case were attainable in the South without at the same time producing the absurd result of resegregation.

This argument assumes, however, that the first of the two questions posed above is also to be answered in the negative. Is there, in truth, no way to prevent resegregation from occurring? Approaching the problem as one of straight feasibility, with no normative implications, one has to take account of an important variable. It is relatively simple to make flight so difficult as to be just about impossible for relatively poor whites in rural areas in the South. There is little residential segregation in these areas, and there is no place to move to except private schools. State and local governments can be forbidden to aid such private schools with tuition grants paid to individual pupils, and the Supreme Court has so forbidden them. Private schools can also be deprived of federal tax exemption unless they are integrated, and a federal court in the District of Columbia has at least temporarily so deprived them. They can be deprived of state and local tax aid as well. Lacking any state support, however indirect, for private schools, all but well-to-do or Catholic whites in the rural and small-town South will be forced back into the public schools, although in the longer run we may possibly find that what we have really done is to build in an incentive to residential segregation, and even perhaps to substantial population movement into cities.

On a normative level, is it right to require a small, rural, and relatively poor segment of the national population to submit to a kind of schooling that is disagreeable to them (for whatever reasons, more or less unworthy), when we do not impose such schooling on people, in cities and in other regions, who would also dislike it (for not dissimilar reasons, more or less equally worthy or unworthy)?* This normative issue arises because the feasibility question takes on a very different aspect in the cities. Here movement to residentially segregated neighborhoods or suburbs is possible for all but the poorest whites and is proceeding at a rapid pace. Pursuit of a policy of integration would require, therefore, pursuit of the whites with busloads of inner-city Negro children, or even perhaps with trainloads or helicopter-loads, as distances lengthen. Very substantial resources would thus be needed. They have so far nowhere been committed, in any city.

One reason they have not is that no one knows whether the enterprise would be educationally useful or harmful to the children, black and white. Even aside from the politics of the matter, which is quite a problem in itself, there is a natural hesitancy, therefore, to gamble major resources on a chase after integration, when it is more than possible that the resources would in every sense be better spent in trying to teach children how to read in place. Moreover, and in the long view most importantly, large-scale efforts at integration would almost certainly be opposed by leading elements in urban Negro communities.

Polls asking abstract questions may show what they will about continued acceptance of the goal of integration, but the vanguard of black opinion, among intellectuals and political activists alike, is oriented more toward the achievement of group identity and group autonomy than toward the use of public schools as assimilationist agencies. In part this trend of opinion is explained by the ineffectiveness, the sluggishness, the unresponsiveness, often the oppressiveness of large urban public school systems, and in part it bespeaks the feeling shared by so many whites that the schools should, after all, be an extension of the family, and that the family ought to have a sense of class and cultural identity with them. And so, while the courts and HEW are rezoning and pairing Southern schools in the effort to integrate them, Negro leaders in Northern cities are trying to decentralize them, accepting their racial character and attempting to bring them under community control. While the courts and HEW are reassigning faculties in Atlanta to reflect the racial composition of the schools and to bring white teachers to black pupils and black teachers to white ones, Negro leaders in the North are asking for black principals and black teachers for black schools.

Where we have arrived may be signaled by a distorted mirror image that was presented in the Ocean Hill-Brownsville decentralized experimental school district in New York during the teachers' strikes of the fall of 1968. A decade earlier, black children in Little Rock and elsewhere in the South were escorted by armed men through white mobs to be taught by white teachers. In Ocean Hill-Brownsville in 1968, white

---

*For instance a UPI dispatch from Oklahoma City dated January 20 as follows:

"Mrs. Yvonne York, mother of a 14-year-old boy taken into custody for defying a federal desegregation order, said today she will take the case to the Supreme Court. US District Judge Luther Bohanon last week ordered the Yorks to enroll their son Raymond at Harding Junior High in compliance with desegregation rulings. The boy had been enrolled at Taft Junior High a few blocks from his home. Harding is four miles from his home. Raymond was taken into custody yesterday by federal marshals when Mrs. York tried to enroll him at Taft. He was detained for a few hours." A city councilman is quoted as saying, "The people of Oklahoma are fed up with forced busing and federal court orders running our schools. We demand an end to this madness."

teachers had to be escorted by armed men through black mobs to teach black children.

Can we any longer fail to acknowledge that the federal government is attempting to create in the rural South conditions that cannot in the foreseeable future be attained in large or medium urban centers in the South or in the rest of the country? The government is thus seen as applying its law unequally and unjustly, and is, therefore, fueling the politics of George Wallace. At the same time, the government is also putting itself on a collision course with the aspirations of an articulate and vigorous segment of national Negro leadership. Even if we succeed, at whatever cost, in forcing and maintaining massively integrated school systems in parts of the rural South, may we not find ourselves eventually dismantling them again at the behest of blacks seeking decentralized community control?

There must be a better way to employ the material and political resources of the federal government. The process of disestablishing segregation is not quite finished, and both HEW and the courts must drive it to completion, as they must also continually police the disestablishment. But nothing seems to be gained, and much is risked or lost, by driving the process to the tipping point of resegregation. A prudent judgment can distinguish between the requirements of disestablishment and plans that cannot work, or can work only, if at all, in special areas that inevitably feel victimized.

There are black schools all over the country. We don't really know what purpose would be served by trying to do away with them, and many blacks don't want them done away with. Energies and resources ought to go into their improvement and, where appropriate, replacement. Energies and resources ought to go into training teachers and into all manner of experimental attempts to improve the quality of education. The involvement of cohesive communities of parents with the schools is obviously desired by many leaders of Negro opinion. It may bear educational fruit, and is arguably an inalienable right of parenthood anyway. Even the growth of varieties of private schools, hardly integrated, but also not segregated, and enjoying state support through tuition grants for blacks and whites alike, should not be stifled, but encouraged in the spirit of an unlimited experimental search for more effective education. Massive school integration is not going to be attained in this country very soon, in good part because no one is certain that it is worth the cost. Let us, therefore, try to proceed with education.

The above article brought a number of comments from New Republic *readers, and Mr. Bickel was moved to write further. Here is further explication of his position, taken from the March 21* New Republic:

A great deal of the critical response to my article on schools has substance as well as fervor, but is not properly addressed to me. Many of my critics see only two positions —theirs, and another that I am supposed to share with Senator Stennis. They are mistaken. They come to their error out of the experience of a decade and a half of fighting Southern segregationists, and out of the memory of how an earlier Reconstruction was defeated and nullified in 1877 by the politically motivated capitulation of the North. The experience is mine also, and I deeply respect those, lawyers and others, who fought and are still fighting as foot soldiers in the trenches, rather than, like myself, as support troops. I recognize, moreover, the danger of another Compromise of 1877. But those who read me more calmly will know that I proposed no capitulation and advocated no equivalent of the notorious Compromise. I had and have distinctly in mind the need to avert both.

Desegregation of Southern schools reached a turning point, I said, about two years ago, when courts and HEW made the transition from the effort to disestablish dual school systems to the active promotion of integration. The Supreme Court has not yet told us that total integration of pupils of both races, in disregard of neighborhood lines and other considerations, is the law of the Constitution. The law is in flux. The question is what it ought to become. The question that I discussed, whatever Senator Stennis may have in mind, is not whether we ought to renege on the desegregation that has been accomplished, or let up in the effort to accomplish it in parts of the South where it is not yet a reality, but where do we go from there?

I agree with Mr. Panetta, with Professor Tyack, with the less temperate Professor Orfield, and with others, whose comments have yet to be published, that desegregation has worked in the South and has produced many stable situations. I would do nothing to disturb this achievement, and I would, as I said, carry the task of desegregation to completion in the South. I agree also that some hopeful attempts at integration—racial dispersal—have been made in special places elsewhere in the country, and I would not disturb these either. But I question any generalization drawn from these few hopeful attempts.

Obviously I make a distinction, as many of the replies to my article fail to do, between segregation and racial imbalance, and a corresponding one between desegregation and integration or racial dispersal. Segregation is the separation of children of different races in the public schools by law or intentional administrative action. Desegregation is the disestablishment of segregation. Racial imbalance is just what it sounds like, and its causes are found in conditions that school law and school administrators have not created and cannot help. Integration, aimed at curing racial imbalance, is the mixing of children of different races in the public schools by law or intentional administrative action. In order to be satisfied that segregation has been honestly disestablished in a place where it has in the past been imposed by law, it may be necessary to require some visible mixing of the races in the school. But it remains true that to require integration is quite something else.

I have argued that integration is, under present circumstances, impossible of achievement on a national scale; that attempts to impose it, in the South as elsewhere, often produce the perverse result of resegregation; that a rising segment of Negro leadership no more wants it imposed than do many whites; that it often amounts to the mixing of the black lower class with the white lower class, which is educationally useless, so far as we know, even though the mixing of the lower and middle classes might have some uses; and that, therefore, integration ought not to have the highest priority in the allocation of our human, political, and material resources. That is what I have tried to say—about integration, not desegregation—and I do not believe I have been successfully contradicted. I may add that I am not alone among students of the problem in saying what I do, and that I have myself been saying it for nearly a decade.

I realize that the debate about where to go from here may somehow—any straw will do—enspirit certain unreconstructed Southerners who would like to return to where we started from 15 years ago, and may consequently dispirit Southern moderates, whose fidelity to law in arduous conditions over the same period has been a tremendous national asset. I think, therefore, that the law of desegregation should be reaffirmed by Congress. I believe also that the continuing process of desegregation would benefit from an attempt to stabilize the law and clarify it, so that those who would still resist desegregation cannot make allies by claiming that what will ultimately be imposed is necessarily racial dispersal. To these ends, I have cooperated in drafting a bill with Representative Richardson Preyer of North Carolina, a former federal judge, and one of those Southerners whose career has been marked by fidelity to law and by personal commitment to the moral precepts that the law embodies.

As Professor Charles Hamilton wrote in these pages, government ought to support —not merely permit—the education of children in desegregated situations. And it ought to exert itself to improve the quality of education. The bill I speak of would create a national right for any public school pupil to transfer from a school in which his race is in a majority to one in which his race is in a minority. Transportation, if needed, would be provided at public expense. Secondly, the bill would commit the federal government to the equalization of educational opportunities and facilities. Thirdly, without disturbing the authority of federal courts and of HEW to measure the good faith of a desegregation performance, the bill would define the end result, which, in a term used by the Supreme Court but left by it undefined, is called a unitary school system.

In general, a unitary school system would be achieved either by a genuine neighborhood zoning of school attendance areas or by mixing the races in the schools in a ratio that, within a substantial permissible range, bears a relation to the proportion of one race to the other in the total school population in a district. Voluntary efforts by school boards to achieve better racial balance would, of course, be permitted, as would efforts to forestall resegregation of the schools, and the concomitant hardening of the lines of residential segregation. North or South, once a school system has reached—or has for a half century been in—a unitary state, federal courts and HEW would retain jurisdiction to pursue and cure any measure, however covert, to achieve in whatever degree any forced separation of children in the schools solely on the basis of race.

Segregationists, says Professor Hamilton, "must be fought at every turn. But in our determination to defeat them, let us not devise plans that are dysfunctional in other serious ways. The principle is a free and open society, and we can pursue several realistic routes to its achievement." That is what I believe.

The age-old question of who should control the schools remains as yet unresolved. Teacher militancy, once unheard of, has come to be a fact of educational life. The lines are sharply drawn between the power of a school board and the authority of the professionals and soon you will be thrust into the fray and called upon to take your position. Do you know where you stand? Have you given careful thought to which group should have the power? Is it an either-or situation? Some have likened it to the class struggle of the Russian revolution. How well prepared are you to defend your perspective?

AUTHORITY

John Keats

If we (the citizens of the community) wish to run our schools, are not *all* the basic policy decisions ours, in teacher qualification as in anything else?

Perhaps we have been reluctant to think about teaching jobs in this light because we laymen are so often advised by our professional educators to keep our crude hands off their sacred profession. When you read our educators' books, you will find many of them again and again comparing themselves to physicians. If your child has appendicitis, they say, you give it a surgeon, but you don't try to tell the surgeon how to operate. Therefore—kindly keep out of the classroom, and stop trying to tell us what and how to teach. At the same time, they say we may, however, raise their salaries and buy another school bond, just as we are asked to pay the surgeon's bill.

And to all this, we can say: Suppose we give our child to the surgeon. Suppose this child dies on the operating table. Suppose we discover the surgeon has used a shovel instead of a scalpel, and has removed the healthy liver instead of the burst appendix. What then? Are we not entitled to know the difference between a liver and an appendix? Are we not sufficiently qualified to entertain some legitimate doubts as to the surgeon's command of his carft? And as for that bill. . . .

And so it would seem that the doctor analogy could be used two ways, and I submit the only way we can find the teachers we want is first to know exactly what we want the courses we offer to be and to do, and then try to find the men and women willing to do the job we want done. It is important to understand that we won't get what we want from people *unwilling* to do the job our way. At any rate, we certainly cannot allow our educators to tell us what the job should be, any more than we'd let the sheriff tell us what laws he had suddenly decided to enact and enforce. We should by all means listen to our schoolmen's advice, and get as much advice as possible, but in the matter of what is taught, and how and why, as in the matter of teaching qualifications, as in all other public school matters, the basic policy decisions must be ours.

Our pluralistic society has never come to any uniform agreement upon what our schools should or should not do. Thus, our public schools have often been the subject of criticism and spirited debate because of the contradictory beliefs held by influential people and groups about the role and purpose of the school.

The selection which follows indicates some of the contradictory beliefs presently held about our schools. You probably have strong beliefs on some of these issues. What are your beliefs based on? Do you have any objective evidence other than your own experience which supports your views?

CONTRADICTORY POSITIONS IN AMERICAN EDUCATION

Gordon C. Lee

1. The curriculum of the modern school is sterile, lacking in inspiration or challenge, because it clings to outmoded matters irrelevant to the real world and to the actual life of contemporary American youth.

   But: The curriculum of the modern school is overloaded with triviality, with "fads and frills," while the fundamental theoretical studies, the basic intellectual skills, are grievously slighted.

2. Modern education is excessively, if not preponderantly, utilitarian and practical in its aims and its content; it is far too concerned with "vocational" training and the immediate application of learning.

   But: Unemployment and juvenile delinquency are seriously on the increase because we fail to teach our youth to *do* anything.

3. We pay altogether too little attention to the gifted child in today's schools.

   But: The curriculum at all levels is increasingly dominated by academic, college-preparatory studies.

4. The school today is too "soft" and "easy"; it is a place where children gather to enjoy life and to play rather than to engage in genuine learning.

   But: Learning is most effective when there is interest in what is being studied and when happiness and the absence of anxiety pervade the process.

5. The modern school is an irreligious, godless, or at least agnostic, institution suffused by an unqualified secularism threatening the moral foundations of American life.

   But: The public school is no place for the promulgation of sectarian dogmas; it must adhere to a scrupulous neutrality in matters of faith. Moreover, when schools undertake to cultivate honesty, tolerance, and unselfishness, they *are* religious in the best sense of the word.

6. A broad, liberal education is indispensable for effective living in the contemporary world.

   But: Ever narrower technical specialization and professional skill are mandatory if one is to survive in an increasingly complex technological civilization.

7. In America, the schools are "everybody's business."

   But: The general public should not attempt to tell professionals—whether doctors or lawyers or teachers—how to manage their affairs.

Reprinted by permission from Gordon C. Lee, *Education and Democratic Ideals* (New York: Harcourt Brace Jovanovich, 1965), pp. 4-5. © 1965 by Harcourt Brace Jovanovich.

8. The modern school is too involved in "activity," the encouragement of self-expression and freedom; it makes small contribution to the development of true discipline.

   But: We must provide schooling which prepares youth to participate actively in a democratic society.

9. The education of teachers overstresses pedagogical technique and child "adjustment"; it is generally weak in providing the prospective teacher with the substance of material to be taught.

   But: The main job of a teacher is to help children to develop their own unique potential, to promote the growth of stable, well-balanced persons—history, French, or mathematics is but a means to those ends.

10. Education must show the way to social progress and prepare youth to live in an ever changing world.

    But: It is not the school's job to represent and advocate the particulars of a new social order; in education the questioning or minimizing of basic, time-tested assumptions is hazardous in the extreme and all too frequently robs young people of an acquaintance with crucial elements in their heritage.

Mr. Calisch provides us with a spirited version of what a real teacher should be. Writing from the viewpoint of the subject-centered traditional philosophy of education, he disparages the child-centered teacher. Compare his ideas on the role of the teacher with those of Ronald and Beatrice Gross and Paul Goodman in part 3 of this text. Who is right?

SO YOU WANT TO BE
A REAL TEACHER?

Richard W. Calisch

Over the years, literally thousands of young people have neglected to write and ask my advice as to whether they were making a mistake in preparing to be teachers. By now, hundreds and hundreds of them (many no longer quite so young, of course) are moving about in the world of the classroom. With more brashness than modesty, I have finally decided to speak out to them, and to all teachers and would-be teachers everywhere. Although I'd run for cover if anyone started deciding just how qualified I am to be a career teacher, I'm prepared to list what I think those qualifications ought to be. Many people will undoubtedly disagree with one or several items on my list, but here goes, anyway.

In the first place, if you're not a brainy, top-level, creative student, consider doing something else. Good teaching is done by good students, by people who themselves are compulsive about learning. It takes intelligence; it takes the ability to read and write well.

Good teaching takes the kind of person who wants to know just about all there is to know about his subject and who tops everything off with a strong desire to help his students acquire knowledge. You can't be content to keep just a few pages ahead of them. You must really know the field, whether it be mathematics or physical education, literature or cooking. (This calls for even greater emphasis on subject matter courses in college.) You need to be an expert, a specialist, a scholar, a consistent learner, in order to be a teacher. Teaching is, after all, primarily an intellectual art.

Being an intelligent specialist isn't enough, however. You must also have a wide range of adult knowledge and interests. It goes without saying that a teacher of any subject should be well-versed in the literature, music, art, and history of his world, as well as alert to the newest of the new. He should be hip to the world around his eyes and ears—knowledgeable about the latest cars, movies, fashions, books. You may not be able to answer all your students' questions or participate in all their discussions, but at least you should know the terms they use. A teacher who can't rap with the guys on their ground isn't going to educate them on his.

But—and this is important—never forget that you are there to bring young people up the educational ladder, not to bring yourself down.

A teacher must understand students' likes and dislikes, hopes and fears, but at the same time, he must teach as an adult. Sometimes it takes courage to tell a youngster he is wrong; but when he *is*, pretending he *is not* is a grave sin, in my mind. I guess what I am saying here is that I wholeheartedly endorse the client concept of education,

Reprinted by permission from Richard W. Calisch, "So You Want to Be a Real Teacher?" *Today's Education: NEA Journal* 58 (1969): 49-51.

in which the teacher has the obligation to know his subject and much more besides; in which the student comes to the teacher as a client to absorb what he can, to learn what the teacher has to teach.

Your responsibility is to make your teaching relevant to your students, but you must not succumb to the pressure to tell them only what they want to hear because that way is easier.

Treating children childishly produces childish grown-ups. To avoid doing this, you must use all of the intelligence, knowledge, and expertise that you possess. You must be in command, and this takes that added combination of confidence, wit, maturity, and strength of character. If you lack these attributes or are satisfied with your present attainment of them, there is another occupation for you.

I have stressed the teacher's need to have knowledge and intelligence. Hand in hand with these attributes go two others: creativity and imagination. A teacher needs to be an idea person. You must be able to make use of any idea, from any source, and turn it to a thought-producing teaching technique.

When Georgy asks, "Why?" when Suzy says, "What for?" when Mary says, "Are you kidding?" you've got to be able to come up with answers, and they aren't always in the book. Answering a question, such as "What good is this ever going to do me?" from a belligerent, bored, boorish troublemaker is going to take creativity and imagination, as well as a conviction on your part that whatever it is *will* do him some good. This conviction can arise only if you yourself are an expert in whatever field you teach.

In summary, a teacher, first and foremost, must be intelligent, knowledgeable, creative, and imaginative. I know that's not the standard definition, but if Mr. Binet doesn't complain, I won't knock his test. Score yourself one point each for intelligence, expertise in your subject matter, creativity, and imagination. If you don't have four points now, quit here.

My next bit of advice will seem strange, but take it anyway. Sometime when you're feeling up to par, find a quiet, secluded room with no books, no TV, no transistor radio, no cokes, no tasty snacks. Go in, sit down, and stay for an hour. Ask a friend to let you know when the time is up. If the hour seems like a year or if you fall asleep, forget about teaching.

If your inner resources are not enough to keep you interested in yourself for one class period, imagine how you will affect your students. Your subject matter is only subject matter until you add the vital ingredient to it—you. And if your *you* isn't enough to make that hour of solitude pleasant and interesting, it is going to be hell for the 30 or so squirming students who have just straggled in after an hour's ordeal with some other dull pedagogue.

That hour you spend alone in the empty room may be the most eye-opening hour of your life. You'll find out whether someone could possibly spend 60 minutes in your company without going out of his mind from simple boredom.

If you've read this far and still think you want to teach, test your weirdo quotient. Every good teacher has in him the confidence and self-reliance to be a weirdo. From Socrates to "Sock it to me!" the memorable lessons have been taught by showmen who knew the value of a vivid performance. The classroom is a stage and the teacher is the player: hero, villain, clown, and the whole supporting cast of the greatest long-run, hit show ever to play off Broadway or on. And it's a show whose script changes daily, without notice, and usually without consultation with the cast.

In every good classroom personality, there is some of P.T. Barnum, John Barrymore, Ringo Starr, and Houdini. Are you afraid to stand up and sing with a wastebasket over your head, to demonstrate the various qualities of sound? Can you be King Richard bawling "A horse! A horse! My kingdom for a horse!" or act out photosynthesis, playing all parts yourself?

Think back to your own teachers. From which did you learn the most? Certainly not from the sit-behind-the-desk mumblers who read their lectures from neatly typed notes. Teaching involves a great deal of showmanship and salesmanship, and the great teaching personalities are those that are not afraid to be different, unusual, or what the current jargon styles "weirdo." Classroom spontaneity and showmanship take confidence and a degree of cool that the average person doesn't possess; but, then, a teacher isn't an average person.

Have you ever tried to talk a died-in-the-wool Democrat into voting for a Republican, or a vegetarian into eating meat, or a Card fan into cheering for the Cubs? How did it come out? Probably it produced a humdinger of an argument—one with sparks, flames, daggers, and music played by the brasses. Or else the person you were talking to just turned you off, wouldn't even listen.

Those two responses to persuasion are most typical, because people just don't like to have their cherished beliefs challenged and will protect them from attack in any way they can. Yet teaching involves challenging the sacred beliefs of the student and asking him, forcing him if necessary, to examine them.

Each student brings to the classroom a whole complex of his own folk beliefs about those aspects of life of which he is ignorant. Typically, his attitude will be that if he has never heard of it, it either isn't true or is unimportant. He will cling to his preconceptions like the proverbial drowning man to the proverbial log. Your job is to push him off the log and see that he stays afloat. Don't expect him to be overjoyed about it. Don't expect him to love you for it. If he learns from you, if he matures and gains confidence under your direction, then you have achieved success. If you also want love, get married.

I tell my pupils that if I can't send them home muttering darkly at least once a week, I've failed. And I mean that. An exasperated student will think, ask, read, search for answers—and that is education. Even though he may come up with answers that disagree with your beliefs, you have done your job as a teacher if he has arrived at those answers through intelligent thought.

What students need is some answers and a lot of needling questions. So I agree with Socrates that a teacher must try to be the most irritating person for miles around. (You can expect hemlock as your reward.)

Most books I've read about teaching indicate that the prime requisite for a teacher is a "love of children." Hogwash! That bit of misinformation has probably steered more softhearted and softheaded Mr. Peeperses and Miss Brookses into our art than any other deception ever practiced on the mind of man. What you must love is the vision of the well-informed, responsible adult you can help the child become.

Your job as a teacher is to help the child realize who he is, what his potential is, what his strengths are. You can help him learn to love himself—or the man he soon will be. With that kind of understanding self-love, the student doesn't need any of your sentimentality. What he needs is your brains, and enabling him to profit from them calls for decisive firmness. "I must be cruel only to be kind," say Hamlet and many a good teacher. Discipline and firm guidance are often called meanness by those subjected to them, but in my experience they are the kind of loving care most likely to produce intelligent, knowledgeable, perceptive adults who can do a better job of coping with the problems of the world than did those who taught them.

The fact that real teaching is an art is too often pooh-poohed. Some critics place teaching in the same category as baby-sitting; and far too many people enter the field because it seems like an easy way to earn a fair living. Girls may look on it as a pleasant way of biding their time until they capture husbands.

But the kind of teacher I have been talking about is a dedicated person who plans to stay in teaching despite its drawbacks. He looks upon his work with individual children as an art to which he brings his talent, his craftsmanship, his experience, learning, intelligence, and that indefinable something called inspiration.

I hope, prospective teachers, that as you take an honest, searching look at yourselves you can sense that you have the potential for being this kind of teacher.

A 1915 California teacher's contract provided for the following thirteen conditions of employment:

—not to get married

—not to keep company with men

—must be home between the hours of 8 p.m. and 6 a.m. unless in attendance at a school function

—not to loiter downtown in ice cream parlors

—not to leave town at any time without permission of the chairman of the school board

—not to smoke cigarettes

—not to drink beer, wine or whiskey

—not to get in a carriage or automobile with any man, except her brother or her father

—not to dress in bright colors

—not to dye her hair

—must wear at least two petticoats

—must not wear dresses more than two inches above the ankles

—must keep the school room neat and clean

—must sweep the floor at least once daily

—must scrub the floor at least once weekly with hot water and soap

—must clean the blackboards at least once daily

—must start the fire at 7 a.m. so the room will be warm by 8 a.m.

It wasn't until 1925 that the California State Supreme Court ruled that the loss of tenure because of marriage was unconstitutional.

If there is agreement that financial considerations do and should prevail over other types then perhaps we can justifiably view the teaching profession as unlike other business-type professions. Does Dorey belittle the role of the teacher by subjugating it to a level of dollars and cents or is it just the opposite? What is his real position in relation to the everyday work-world standard of established time schedules and salary rates? Can it actually be applicable to education?

IS TEACHING
A PROFESSION?

J. Milnor Dorey

(Harry Parsons, teacher of a general business course in a high school, was correcting papers at his home one evening when the doorbell rang. He admitted Parker McGowan, a prominent attorney of the city and president of the school board.)

Parsons: Well, this is an honor, Mr. McGowan.
McGowan: I wouldn't say that. I've come to ask a favor.

(A favor! And for the man who had squelched the teachers' request for an increase in salaries!)

Parsons: Won't you sit down? What can I do for you?
McGowan: Thanks. It's about my boy Henry. You have him in your classes, I believe, and in your home room. He finishes high school in June—I hope—and I haven't made up my mind whether to send him to college or put him to work. I want your advice.
Parsons: I see. You assume that because of my personal contacts and professional training I can understand him better than you?
McGowan: Well, not exactly that. As parents, we know what his good and bad traits are; but you have a professional equipment that should help us decide whether college is the right thing for him.
Parsons: Yes, I understand Henry's aptitudes and skills; and I can give you advice. But my fee will be ten dollars.
McGowan: Your what?
Parsons: My fee. You're familiar with fees, Mr. McGowan. You'll recall that when I had to sell a bit of property left to me, in order to meet an insurance premium, you drew up the deed—rather, your clerk did. Your fee was twenty-five dollars. I'll be more conservative and charge you only ten dollars.
McGowan: But, man, you're a teacher! You're paid a salary by the taxpayers!
Parsons: Certainly, but for a seven-hour day and a five-day week.
McGowan: Ridiculous! You're not paid on a set time basis.
Parsons: But you forget, Mr. McGowan. When the school board, of which you are president, turned down our request for an increase in salaries to meet the higher cost of living, you defended your refusal on the basis that we were paid for a seven-hour day and a five-day week, and therefore were paid all we earned.

Reprinted by permission from J. Milnor Dorey, "Is Teaching a Profession?" *Business Education World* 35 (November 1954): 18-19. Reprinted courtesy of McGraw-Hill, Inc., copyright November 1954.

No, my fee for professional services is ten dollars. If you don't want them, I'm afraid you'll have to excuse me. I have a pile of papers to correct that I don't seem to be able to get done in a seven-hour day, what with extracurricular work after school, student conferences, and faculty meetings.

Incidentally, you seem to create the impression through the newspapers that taxpayers are a special class of the public and teachers are exempt.

McGowan: But—but, even so, you're not in a profession like ours where fees are the established method of payment!

Parsons: Not in a profession? Teachers spend as much time, money, and cerebration acquiring the knowledge of the subject matter they must teach, and the techniques and skills in teaching, as you lawyers, doctors, and engineers. The trouble is, you people look down on teaching as a profession—you think anyone can do it. Teaching is a science and an art. Even if one is a born teacher, he must acquire an understanding of psychology, methods, vocational guidance principles, and a special skill in handling adolescents. That's what you're asking me to give you. It's high time that this condescension on the part of the business and professional world stop or there will be more teacherless schools.

McGowan: It seems to me you're uttering dangerous sentiments.

Parsons: Too dangerous for my own good, you mean? I'm quite well aware of it. However, if you should choose to decide that I am not needed in the high school, I could step into National Utilities tomorrow at twice the salary you're paying me.

McGowan: Why don't you do it then?

Parsons: Because I'm fool enough to believe I ought to stick, considering this general exodus. Someone has to stick. Besides, I love to teach and work with young people.

But, to come back to Henry: if you want my advice about him, my fee is ten dollars.

McGowan: Not from me, you won't get it!

Parsons: Suit yourself. Dr. Erwin paid, though.

McGowan: Erwin? What did he want?

Parsons: He came to see me the other night about his boy, too. But that was a different problem. You may know John. His parents are just plain helpless. But I understand John and his emotional disturbances, and he listens to me. So, I told Dr. Erwin that if he would give me a free hand I believed I could handle the situation.

At first, he took the same arrogant position you did when I suggested a fee. But, in the end, he paid. You see, he gave me a checkup last year and charged me twenty-five dollars. This fall I had him go over me again. His fee this time, for the same job, was thirty-five dollars. I asked him why, and he said it was the increased cost of living. You see, you so-called professionals have the advantage over teachers. When prices go up, all you do is raise your fees, and your net stays the same. We teachers have to take what's handed out to us.

McGowan: I still say you have no license to charge for professional services when you are paid a salary. The professional service of lawyers and doctors is of quite a different value to society.

Parsons: I'm glad you mention that. You mean that lawyers and doctors are rendering services to society greater than those of teachers. Let's see. The whole town knows that, as a corporation lawyer, you got Sintex Limited out of a jam with the Government. I'll bet you that your fee for just that one case was as much as the average salary for our elementary teachers for a whole year.

I can see you don't want to take me on. So, would you say that that sort of business is serving society better than the work of a teacher who is trying to rear a generation that will conduct business under a better code of ethics? Or, would you say that the lawyer who makes much more than the teacher merely by drawing up wills, deeds, mortgages—a skill that does not take profound erudition or time to learn—is more worthwhile to society than the teacher?

And, while we're on the subject, would you say that publishers who make a fortune with magazines that appeal to people of sixth-grade intelligence are doing society a greater service than the teachers who are trying to weed out the morons from society, and to improve the tastes and standards of those who want their help? They have an uphill job in the face of much of the so-called literature fed the public. And there's always shouting about the over-burdened taxpayers when increases in salaries for teachers come up.

No, if the public won't recognize the dignity and caliber of the teaching profession as quite on a par with any other profession, we'll have to charge fees for our professional services. Parents come to us all the time for advice and information on their problems. Our outside time is taken up with them. So, Mr. McGowan, how about Henry? Want my advice for ten dollars?

McGowan: Well—I do admit I'm stumped as to what to do for the boy's good. You ought to be able to throw light on the vocational angle.

Parsons: That's not the only angle I can throw light on—angles that, as a parent, you ought to know. How about it?

McGowan: All right. Want your fee in advance?

Parsons: No, I'm not a lawyer. I don't ask for a retainer.

Most teachers fall into a habitual pattern of teaching. This pattern of behavior becomes the actual educational philosophy of the teacher as applied in the classroom. In the selection which follows, Owen E. Pittenger and C. Thomas Gooding describe ten of the most common educational beliefs and practices found among teachers everywhere. They point out that these widely accepted and common-sense beliefs and practices are often distortions of once sound educational philosophies and are unreliable and highly questionable guides for the beginning teacher to follow.

PROCRUSTEAN PREDILECTIONS OR POPULAR HANGUPS IN EDUCATION

Owen E. Pittenger
C. Thomas Gooding

Contemporary American educational practice is a composite of classical and modern forces sometimes amalgamated in highly unlikely permutations. A number of contemporary ideas in education have developed from the bowdlerization of cogent formal philosophies and theories. Perhaps all the more insidious because these beliefs and practices can be stated as reasonable common-sense interpretations, each of the following sets of assumptions fails to meet the criterion of being consistent with compatible theory and philosophy.

1. TREAT THEM NICELY

One of the most pleasant distortions of an educational philosophy is found in some nursery and elementary schools in which the stated or implied function of education is to treat the children nicely so that they may grow up free of restriction or inhibition. This "rosebud" school of thought sees each child as a perfect miniaturization of an adult, who only needs the opportunity to unfold into the full flower of adulthood.

2. MAKE THEM DO IT

From the very distant past comes a point of view that has often become separated from the rationale that made it fit other cultures at other times. The present statement would be: "It is important for children to learn to do certain things irrespective of their interests and regardless of whether they see any reason to learn them because these are the things that everyone ought to know." Tallying the number of identical sunsets painted by second grade children, or for that matter the number of educational surveys and canned experiments passively conducted by college students, would tax the capacity of the largest computers we have. However, we may relax because the teachers involved know these are the best things to do and all will be better for having done them.

Reprinted by permission from Owen E. Pittenger and C. Thomas Gooding, *Learning Theories in Educational Practice: An Integration of Psychological Theory and Educational Philosophy* (New York: John Wiley, 1971), pp. 181-203. Copyright © 1971 by John Wiley & Sons, Inc.

3. MAKE THEM DO THE RIGHT THING

In effect this is the same type of approach as "Make Them Do It," except that it adds the teacher's private interpretation of what is Godly and righteous. The privately moralistic teacher determines on a personal basis that it is the duty of children to learn certain modes of behavior, that it is wicked to have independent thought, naughty to disagree with the teacher, or proper to be passive and accepting of the teacher's authority. Such teachers are most easily detected when their values and teachings are at odds with community mores and values. Usually they do not concern themselves with what others think of their missionary work and seldom modify their actions in terms of new information about children or the society in which they live.

4. MAKE THEM DO THE HARD THING

The learner ought to do that which is difficult because hard work is better for him. To avoid the risk of doing easy things, most teachers who rely on this "philosophical" position also eliminate pleasant activities and hold in great suspicion that which students grasp easily. A most common practice that must have "hardness" as a prime component is that of giving students lower marks at the beginning of the semester so that they will work harder. No matter how effective his performance the learner must adopt the notion that learning is not easy under any circumstances, that he is in jeopardy of failure unless he tries harder. Many teachers defend this practice by stating that they can later give more high marks and thereby increase motivation as material becomes more difficult. Students, however, develop some extremely intelligent defensive techniques to circumvent the impact of this approach.

5. MAKE SCHOOL A PLEASANT EXPERIENCE

Fortunately, education has an antidote to the teacher whose purpose it is to make students learn— the teacher who is committed to joyous expression. All school experiences must be the free expression of personal emotional satisfaction. The motto emblazoned on the social programs that serve as curriculum guides for teachers of this order must be, "Let them have fun." If it is not fun then it is too real and earnest to be a part of the experience of the young. Ultimate success resides in the child's opportunity to experience the real or imaginary benefits of being happy all the time. The teachers in this category must be distinguished from the group of early childhood educators who use the child's present interests, problems, and developmental tasks as the basis of the curriculum. The latter group uses play as a focal point in a series of learning experiences. The "fun" teachers emphasize the emotional responses to activities that do not accentuate the academic responsibility of the learner.

6. LET THEM EXPERIENCE LIFE AS AN EXPERIMENT

Providing a relief if not a balance for the "happy" school of thought is the modern teacher who has taken up the mantle of the earlier day religionists and tries to save the world and society and children by insisting that children be taught to do things the right way. The right way in this case is the SCIENTIFIC way. The assumption seems to be either that all truth can be discovered with science and in science or that anything not amenable to analysis with the present methods of science is unknowable and therefore insignificant. Often the most capricious behavior is disguised as an experiment. Two hallmarks separate this false prophet of science from the gentlemen and scholars of science. The first is the rally call, "Let's see what happens." The second indicator is the extent to which the "experiments" are left unreported, unwritten, unanalyzed, and unshared. Instead of contributing to a growing body of knowledge the experience seems to satisfy only irrational curiosity. Perhaps the comment, "Wasn't that interesting?" is a suitable substitute for scholarship, but it would not satisfy those who believe more systematically in philosophies of science or scientific educational philosophies.

7. TELL THEM AND TEST THEM

This is probably the most widely practiced teaching technique based on the unexamined assumption that one learns by listening. It is broadly applied in school, home, church, and elsewhere as a formal and informal method of instruction. If this is a "bad" method then most of us have been subjected to an endless stream of bad teaching. Inherent in such an approach, however, is the notion that when we tell a person something he ought to remember it because it is good for him, or because he is a recipient of everything that is presented to him, or because we believe it is important and presume the learner will so perceive.

8. HAVE THEM LOOK, SEE, AND SAY

This is a form of simplistic approach which has been espoused as being a "natural" approach to education. In this type of classroom the emphasis seems to be on getting everybody to talk about their personal experiences or common activities. Talking is expected to cause or promote worthwhile learning. Structure is virtually absent. Some typical justifications are: This is the way we learned before education became such a formalized process. This is a free and spontaneous way to learn. It is the natural way children learn before they come to school. The learner is given an opportunity to express himself.
There are problems with this technique. What does the teacher do when the spontaneity breaks down? Is any endeavor allowable? If not, what are the limits of acceptable behavior? How would personal and social limits be structured in a supposedly free and natural classroom?

9. PRAISE THEM AND PUNISH THEM

A time-honored technique of teaching. If it were not for the fact that we have direct evidence that punishment techniques result in very little positive change in behavior, this technique would be compatible with some of the educational philosophies and theories of learning. There is, however, a much more common distortion of this approach, which is malignant beyond compare because of its subtlety. The teacher uses praise and punishment to indicate his personal pleasure with the learner's performance.

This use is tantamount to emotional blackmail and is contrary to the spirit or outcomes of research on human learning.

Until teachers will take the time to represcribe the daily goals of education and develop techniques of measuring how well children are meeting these goals one can expect teachers to continue in the pattern of saying, "I like it," or "I don't" instead of properly evaluating student performance.

10. SUBTLY PERSUADE THEM

Get students to do what you have already decided they should learn. If you can make students believe that the activity is their idea you will have them in the palm of your hand.

This approach appeals to certain pseudopsychologically oriented instructors, because it *appears* to take into account the motivational state of the learner.

The next selection is typical of many public educational practices. We are forever working against the accomplishment of laudable goals by the means we select to achieve them. As illustrated below, we want to foster ethical standards in schools, yet the administration does not trust the teachers, neither the administration nor the teachers trust the students and the students are warned not to trust each other! Obviously we must trust youngsters, give them some responsibility and then *expect high standards from them if we really want trustworthy and responsible students. Do we?*

FROM
UP THE DOWN STAIRCASE

Bel Kaufman

Circular #4
TOPIC: ETHICAL STANDARDS

PLEASE KEEP ALL CIRCULARS ON FILE, IN THEIR ORDER

TO PROTECT OUR STUDENTS FROM THE TEMPTATION OF FRAUDULENT PRAC-TICES AND TO ASSURE TEACHERS OF THE AUTHENTICITY OF ALL DATA, THE FOLLOWING PRECAUTIONS MUST BE TAKEN:

1. SUBJECT TEACHERS ARE TO SIGN STUDENT PROGRAM CARDS IN INK, WITH THEIR FULL NAME, AS PROOF THAT STUDENT HAS APPEARED IN CLASS. NO INITIALS, PENCIL OR NAME-STAMPERS ARE ACCEPTABLE.
2. THE ABOVE IS ALSO TRUE OF ALL PASSES SIGNED BY THE TEACHER.
3. CHECK THE ROLL BOOK FOR NON-EXISTENT ADDRESSES AND NON-AUTHENTIC PARENT OR GUARDIAN, TO FACILITATE WORK OF TRUANT OFFICER.
4. IN MAKING ENTRIES ON RECORDS, DO NOT ERASE, SCRATCH OUT, OR USE INK ERADICATOR. CORRECTIONS ARE TO BE MADE ONLY WITH THE SIG-NATURE OF THE PRINCIPAL OR ADMINISTRATIVE ASSISTANT WHO WILL APPROVE THE CORRECTION.
5. DURING FIRE, SHELTER AREA OR OTHER EMERGENCY DRILLS, INFORM STUDENTS TO BE PARTICULARLY CAREFUL ABOUT THEIR VALUABLES. BOOKS AND NOTE BOOKS ARE TO BE LEFT BEHIND, BUT POCKETBOOKS AND WALLETS ARE TO BE HELD ON TO. WE HAVE HAD AN EPIDEMIC OF UNFORTUNATE INCIDENTS.

WITH THESE PRECAUTIONS IN MIND, WE CAN HELP OUR STUDENTS ACHIEVE THE HIGH ETHICAL STANDARDS WE EXPECT OF THEM.

James J. McHabe
Adm. Asst.

Reprinted by permission from Bel Kaufman, *Up the Down Staircase* (Englewood Cliffs, N.J.: Prentice-Hall, 1964), pp. 24-25. © 1964 by Bel Kaufman.

A serious dilemma facing most educators stems from an inability to reconcile the personal differences between what a student values and what a teacher values. You have, no doubt, given some thought to this whenever decisions regarding attendance, test scores, assignments, etc., were felt to be of serious consequence by someone whose power exceeded your own. How do you propose to mediate these differences when you are "in control"? In this selection by Lamper, did Billy deserve the liberties denied him by the teacher? Was the teacher correct in denying these things to Billy? What you decide may hold significant implications for the future you anticipate as a classroom teacher.

CRY
THE BITTER FRUIT

Neil Lamper

There was a day in the vineyard of youth when the fruit was ready for sun and rain and well-tilled soil to make it grow full, juicy, and sweet.

That was the day Billy found the robin's nest. Cautious and quiet, he crawled higher in the tree and looked into the nest, woven of weeds, straw, and bits of fuzz. It was intricate and a thing of beauty.

Billy knew the bird had been a robin because tiny pieces of blue egg shell were left in the nest. Careful not to crush his treasure, he ran to school with it. All of his friends in the second grade were impressionable youngsters who could be awed, and they spoke in whispers about the nest.

The second-grade room was a pleasant place, bright with cheerful colors, books, and drawings. Each window ledge had some rock, bit of wood, or plant brought in by the pupils. There were tall tables for standup work, and low tables just right for elbows when children were seated.

All day long the boys and girls investigated the world. It was fascinating, and the people in it were strange and interesting. Questions were fuses that led to the dynamite of knowledge. Birds' nests, turtles, and even sand compelled the curious to the book shelves, or to the outdoors that was the home of an endless variety of mysteries.

There was delight and ecstasy in the knowledge of *why* the nest, and *how* the turtle and *when* the sand. Billy was rewarded; his nest was treasured; his contribution was immense.

It was about this time that Billy's second-grade picture was taken. It shows a blond boy, smiling and making no attempt to hide a missing front tooth. His shining eyes bespeak a great capacity to be interested in everything around him.

Billy himself was amazing and amusing. He was seldom sick. He was happy in learning about nature. He was fueled by a burning curiosity and enthusiasm that proceeded sometimes slowly, sometimes rapidly, but always surely.

But as the years passed, the vineyard became a desert land and the boy, its bitter fruit.

There is, at the school, a file on Billy, who is now in the ninth grade. One of the first entries in this educational record is a report on a reading test, duly entered in the third

---

Reprinted from Neil Lamper, "Cry the Bitter Fruit," *Today's Education: NEA Journal* 47 (May 1958): 282-83.

year of Billy's quest for knowledge. This report shows that Billy is a poor reader, but it does not show that after the test he spent hours watching a black ant struggling across the face of the land, carrying a dead ant bigger than itself. Nor does it show that Billy's thoughts, as he watched the ant, were cosmic and considered the infinities.

Similar insufficiencies accompany the intelligence test (short form) that gives Bill an IQ of 89. Indeed, it is the short form. It ignores Bill's health, his love of nature, his wonder, his persistency, his undeviating honesty, his loyalty, warmth, and spontaneity.

All of these aside, Billy's mental age was divided by his chronological age, multiplied by 100, and Billy's reward was a number. Subsequent teachers would classify Billy as belonging to a slow-learning group.

Also in the file are achievement tests without number, giving each year irrefutable evidence that Billy should be somewhere else. Some said, in a lower grade; some said, in a trade school; some said, on the farm. And each year Billy's marks kept indicating that he did not possess the facts contained in the books which he still had difficulty in reading.

In the file, too, are report cards with marks that slid from Bs to Cs, from Cs to Ds, and then, allowing Billy no place to hide, completed his shaming with the finality of the glaring red Es. Throughout these years, Billy had asked fewer and fewer questions.

When he wanted to draw his idea of a man, he was given a pattern and told to cut around it. All the silly little identical patterns were placed in the windows so at open-house time the scrubbed and sterile school shone with consistency.

When Bill came rushing to school and enthusiasm tumbled his words as he tried to describe the polliwog that grew legs or the music of the cicada, he was taken even more firmly in hand and told that his communication was terrible. His participles dangled; his objectives replaced his nominatives. Confused by doesn'ts and don'ts, finally he was silenced.

There was no more rushing. There were no more questions. There was no more enthusiasm. Curiosity became an invitation to trouble, wonder a web to entrap, awe a sin, and questions were for others to ask.

In the second grade the record notes no absences; in the ninth grade, he was absent more often than he was present.

The record of his retrogression is told, too, in the notes on his "citizenship," made during the years by his teachers, always kindly, increasingly baffled:

Billy is full of life and vigor. Everyone likes him. He is a good worker, but he must be kept busy.

Billy is a lovable child. With help and attention, he can do average work.

With direction and challenge, Bill may improve.

Bill is nervous, but I hope he is headed in the right direction.

Bill tries so hard to learn, but he must be held to a consistently high level of achievement. Bill seems a little immature.

William is inclined to be lazy unless you keep after him. It is a continual battle to make him finish anything he starts.

William is a fair student in everything but reading. He still needs lots of work on phrasing. He is nervous and moody, and he will have nothing to do with the group. It is his way of getting attention. But he does like sports.

Bill is still a very slow child, but since he has already repeated the sixth grade once, there is no point in retaining him. He is nervous and is becoming a discipline case.

William refuses to read or cooperate in a group and is a general nuisance. He is far below grade level.

There isn't much to say about William except that I haven't been able to help him much. He does little in school except misbehave. He has very poor work habits, little natural motivation, and a terrific desire for recognition, which he satisfies by doing unkind things, such as kicking and pinching others.

William has many tensions behind his retrogressive behavior.

William is usually very uncooperative and discourteous. He does little or nothing in class. He is his own worst enemy.

In short, the record shows that William did not fit well into the pattern and progression of grades, classes, and groups of alikes.

What William had become shows clearly, too, in his ninth-grade picture. Now the shoulders sag, and the face is sullen, with bold eyes but a blank expression. The hair is trimmed in accordance with the local "hoods," and he wears a black leather jacket trimmed with chrome. What happened between the robin's nest and the black jacket?

Why has the soil in the vineyard become hard and unproductive? Are there no warming rains that can revive the withered vine?

So cry the bitter fruit. The vineyard has not fulfilled the promise of the land.

HANDY "ALIBIS" FOR STUDENTS

F. J. McDonald

What to say—

When you are given an objective test: "It doesn't let you express yourself."

When you are given an essay test: "It's so vague. You don't know what's expected."

When you are given many minor tests: "Why not have a few big ones? This keeps you on edge all the time."

When you are given a few major tests: "Too much depends on each one."

When you are given no tests: "It's not fair. How can he possibly judge what we know?"

When every part of the subject is taken up in class: "Oh, he just follows the book."

When you are asked to study a part of the subject by yourself: "Why we never even discuss it."

When the course is in lecture form: "We never get a chance to say anything."

When the course consists of informal lecture and discussion: "We never cover any ground."

When the students present reports: "He just sits there. Who wants to hear the students? They don't know how to teach."

When detailed material is presented: "What's the use? You forget it all after the exam anyway."

When general principles are presented: "What did we learn? We knew all that before we took the course."

Taken from Dr. F. J. McDonald, Educational Testing Service, Princeton, N.J.

18 WAYS TO MAKE CLASS INTERESTING FOR STUDENT AND TEACHER

Frank R. Krajewski

1. Seldom, if ever, attend class.
2. If you do attend, find fault with the professor.
3. Never accept responsibility in a class. It's much easier to criticize than do anything.
4. If asked for your opinion in class, tell the prof you have nothing to say but after the class really let loose.
5. Do no more than is absolutely necessary. When other students roll up their sleeves and make the class interesting, complain that the class is run by a few students.
6. Never, but never, exercise your voting privilege when given on class issues, but do shout that your opinion is never asked for.
7. When readings are assigned or a special assignment given, tell everyone that a lot of time and money has been wasted on an assignment that accomplished nothing.
8. When no special readings or assignments are made, say the class is dull.
9. Don't ever suggest how the class might be improved—and if it doesn't, drop the course.
10. If you can pass a class without really participating, don't participate.
11. Be sure to look out for something wrong—when you find it, be sure to scream.
12. At every possible opportunity, complain about the course and encourage your friends to complain.
13. When you do happen to attend class, vote to do one thing; then complain that you are not allowed to do the other.
14. Agree to everything said in class but be sure to disagree with it outside of class.
15. When asked for an opinion or information, don't give it.
16. Cuss out the prof for his informality in running the course.
17. Cuss out the prof for his formality in running the course.
18. Get all the information you can from the course and hoard it. Don't do anything that might make the class more interesting for anyone else.

   Self-analysis will tell you if you are guilty of any of the above.

THE LITTLE BOY
WHO DIDN'T PASS

Don McNeill

A sad-faced little fellow,
sits alone in deep disgrace;
There's a lump arising in his throat,
and tears drop down his face.
He wandered from his playmates;
he doesn't want to hear
Their shouts of merry laughter,
since the world has lost its cheer.
He has sipped the cup of sorrow
He has dripped the bitter glass
And his heart is fairly breaking—
the boy who didn't pass.

In the apple tree the robin sings
a cheery little song
But he doesn't seem to hear it,
Showing plainly something's wrong.
Comes his faithful little Spaniel
for a romp and a bit of play,
But the troubled little fellow
bids him sternly "go away!"
And alone he sits in sorrow
with his hair a tangled mess
And his eyes are red with weeping—
the boy who didn't pass.

Oh, you who boast a laughing son,
and speak of him as bright;
And you, who love a little girl
who comes to you at night,
With shining eyes and dancing feet
with honors from her school,
Turn to that lonely lad
that thinks he is a fool
And take him kindly by the hand,
the dullest of his class
He is the one who most needs love—
the boy who didn't pass!

Reprinted by permission from *Don McNeill's Favorite Poems,* 1951.

Again the question of children's interests becomes a crucial factor in a teacher's decision. Is it at all possible to infuse the traditional subject materials with new life? Can learning traditional material ever become a pleasant learning experience? Under what conditions is this possible? Must all teachers reach the pinnacle of creativity in order to be effective? What about those among us who don't feel we have this capability? Are we to be excluded from the profession on this basis?

THE POOR SCHOLAR'S SOLILOQUY

Stephen M. Corey

No I'm not very good in school. This is my second year in the seventh grade and I'm bigger and taller than the other kids. They like me all right, though, even if I don't say much in the schoolroom, because outside I can tell them how to do a lot of things. They tag me around and that sort of makes up for what goes on in school.

I don't know why the teachers don't like me. They never have very much. Seems like they don't think you know anything unless they can name the book it comes out of. I've got a lot of books in my own room at home—books like *Popular Science Mechanical Encyclopedia,* and the Sears' and Ward's catalogues, but I don't very often just sit down and read them through like they make us do in school. I use my books when I want to find something out, like whenever Mom buys anything secondhand I look it up in Sears' or Ward's first and tell her if she's getting stung or not. I can use the index in a hurry to find the things I want.

In school, though, we've got to learn whatever is in the book and I just can't memorize the stuff. Last year I stayed after school every night for two weeks trying to learn the names of the Presidents. Of course I knew some of them like Washington and Jefferson and Lincoln, but there must have been thirty altogether and I never did get them straight.

I'm not too sorry though because the kids who learned the Presidents had to turn right around and learn all the Vice Presidents. I am taking the seventh grade over but our teacher this year isn't so interested in the names of the Presidents. She has us trying to learn the names of all the great American inventors.

KIDS SEEMED INTERESTED

I guess I just can't remember names in history. Anyway, this year I've been trying to learn about trucks because my uncle owns three and he says I can drive one when I'm sixteen. I already know the horsepower and number of forward and backward speeds of twenty-six American trucks, some of them Diesels, and I can spot each make a long way off. It's funny how that Diesel works. I started to tell my teacher about it last Wednesday in science class when the pump we were using to make a vacuum in a bell jar got hot, but she said she didn't see what a Diesel engine had to do with our experiment on air pressure so I just kept still. The kids seemed interested though. I took four of them around to my uncle's garage after school and we saw the mechanic, Gus, tearing a big truck Diesel down. Boy, does he know his stuff!

I'm not very good in geography either. They call it economic geography this year. We've been studying the imports and exports of Chile all week but I couldn't tell you what they are. Maybe the reason is I had to miss school yesterday because my uncle took me and his big trailer truck down state about two hundred miles and we brought almost ten tons of stock to the Chicago market.

He had told me where we were going and I had to figure out the highways to take and also the mileage. He didn't do anything but drive and turn where I told him to. Was that fun! I sat with a map in my lap and told him to turn south or southeast or some other direction. We made seven stops and drove over five hundred miles round trip. I'm figuring now what his oil cost and also the wear and tear on the truck—he calls it depreciation—so we'll know how much we made.

I even write out all the bills and send letters to the farmers about what their pigs and beef cattle brought at the stockyards. I only made three mistakes in 17 letters last time, my aunt said—all commas. She's been through high school and reads them over. I wish I could write school themes that way. The last one I had to write was on, "What a Daffodil Thinks of Spring," and I just couldn't get going.

I don't do very well in school in arithmetic either. Seems I just can't keep my mind on the problems. We had one the other day like this:

If a 57 foot telephone pole falls across a cement highway so that 17 3/6 feet extend from one side and 14 9/17 feet from the other, how wide is the highway?

That seemed to me like an awfully silly way to get the width of a highway. I didn't even try to answer it because it didn't say whether the pole had fallen straight across or not.

NOT GETTING ANY YOUNGER

Even in shop I don't get very good grades. All of us kids made a broom holder and a bookend this term and mine were sloppy. I just couldn't get interested. Mom doesn't use a broom anymore with her new vacuum cleaner and all our books are in a bookcase with glass doors in the parlor. Anyway, I wanted to make an end gate for my uncle's trailer but the shop teacher said that meant using metal and wood both and I'd have to learn how to work with wood first. I didn't see why but I kept still and made a tie rack at school and the tail gate after school at my uncle's garage. He said I saved him $10.

Civics is hard for me, too. I've been staying after school trying to learn the "Articles of Confederation" for almost a week because the teacher said we couldn't be good citizens unless we did. I really tried, because I want to be a good citizen. I did hate to stay after school, though, because a bunch of us boys from the south end of town have been cleaning up the old lot across from Taylor's Machine Shop to make a playground out of it for the little kids from the Methodist home. I made the jungle gym from old pipe and the guys made me Grand Mogul to keep the playground going. We raised enough money collecting scrap this month to build a wire fence clear around the lot.

Dad says I can quit school when I'm fifteen and I'm sort of anxious to because there are a lot of things I want to learn how to do and as my uncle says, I'm not getting any younger.

THE ANIMAL SCHOOL

G. H. Reavis

(A fable of the administration of the school curriculum with special reference to individual differences.)

Once upon a time, the animals decided they must do something heroic to meet the problems of "a new world," so they organized a school. They adopted an activity curriculum consisting of running, climbing, swimming and flying and, to make it easier to administer, all the animals took all the subjects.

The duck was excellent in swimming, better in fact than his instructor, and made passing grades in flying but he was very poor in running. Since he was slow in running, he had to stay after school and also drop swimming to practice running. This was kept up until his web feet were badly worn and he was only average in swimming. But average was acceptable in school, so nobody worried about that except the duck.

The rabbit started at the top of the class in running, but had a nervous breakdown because of so much make-up work in swimming.

The squirrel was excellent in climbing until he developed frustration in the flying class where his teacher made him start from the ground up instead of from the tree-top down. He also developed charlie horses from over exertion and then got a C in climbing and a D in running.

The eagle was a problem child and was disciplined severely. In climbing class he beat all the others to the top of the tree, but insisted on using his own way to get there.

At the end of the year, an abnormal eel that could swim exceedingly well, and also run, climb, and fly a little had the highest average and was valedictorian.

The prairie dogs stayed out of school and fought the tax levy because the administration would not add digging and burrowing to the curriculum. They apprenticed their child to a badger and later joined the ground-hogs and gophers to start a successful private school.

Does this fable have a moral?

Reprinted by permission from G.H. Reavis, "The Animal School," *Missouri Schools* 13 (January 1948): 16.

In an earlier article by Brookover the question of grouping received serious consideration. One of the single most important factors in ability grouping is the teacher's personal assessment of each student in his class. How much do you really know about each of the students that has been described in this article? Does it tell you more about the teacher than the student? Although the reading appears to take a humorous twist, do you feel the teacher's interest was a comedic one when he wrote these anecdotal comments?

LOTS OF PEOPLE THINK
THEY SEE FLYING SAUCERS

Ralph P. Romano

I've been in guidance (and I'm *not* apologizing) in an inner-city school for the past 15 years. The heart of our traditional approach to discipline is an intricate demerit system. Technically, demerits are supposed to be given for M.D.O.'s (Major Disciplinary Offenses). At one time nine unconscionable areas of aberrant behavior were all carefully spelled out, in the manner of the Seven Deadly Sins. But most of our teachers now rely on their own versions of what constitute "crimes" against school and society.

Long before the Rise of Student Power, I saw the day coming when demerits would be no more. Painstakingly, like a squirrel hoarding nuts (now there's a simile fraught with possibilities), I collected and preserved for posterity a raft of revealing anecdotal writeups. They speak for themselves:

"Changed 4 F's on his report card to 4 B's. Then had the unmitigated gall to add this comment over his father's forged signature: 'Mrs. H. and I couldn't be happier about this. Michael is a delight.' "

"Please remove him from my class—posthaste: The crassness of his cranium renders him impervious to even a token assimilation of ideas."

"He threw my unabridged dictionary out of a second-story window."

"Listening to earphone radio in class. For about the first half-hour, I thought he was listening rapturously to me!"

"Flashing dirty words to the girl behind him by writing on the bottom of his shoe."

"Out of his seat at beginning of biology class, handling skeleton without permission, while singing loudly, 'Knee-bone connected to the calf-bone.' "

"Warned about eating lunch on the sly during class. After I issued a demerit, he declared that he intended to make it a test case. He's sure to be upheld by the Supreme Court. I have a hunch that all of those justices were once disgruntled last-lunch kids!"

"Raiding the home economics refrigerator. Caught red-handed, he said, 'Crime certainly doesn't pay, Miss B. These sandwiches were terrible.' "

"When I asked her name, she refused to give it; claims that her *hearing* is impaired. I'm sure her mind is also."

"Firecracker."

"Threw a lighted cigarette directly at Tommy S., who claims not to have asked for it."

Dated April 16: "*Chewing, chewing, chewing.* I think she's had the same piece of gum since September the 9th . . . of last school year."

Reprinted from Ralph P. Romano, "Lots of People Think They See Flying Saucers," *Phi Delta Kappan* 51 (April 1970): 444-45.

"She came to school in a skirt so short I had to look twice to see if she had any skirt on at all. . . . How do you expect a Latin teacher to compete with something like this?"

"Called me a *mean* S.O.B. P.S. I never thought of myself as *mean.*"

"Swearing while making a recording in the language lab."

"Talk, talk, talk, talk, talk."

"Striving to make a general ass of himself—and not stopping until the job was completed."

"He threw a small bottle of acid in class, yelling, 'Don't mess with the Mafia!' "

"Deliberately angled sun's rays into my eyes most of the period. I can just see well enough to write this."

"Misconduct during study. Was found holding desk above his head, aiming it in the direction of another student. When I reminded him that body-building classes were held *after* school, he sassed back, 'How would *you* know?' "

"Sat in front of me all period—*scratching.*"

"Threatened to jump out of the window. I would have called his bluff if my room were on the third floor—instead of the first."

"While teaching *Ethan Frome,* I happened to mention that I was once stepped on by a horse. This imbecile wisecracked, 'My, Miss F., you *have* lived a *full* and *interesting* life, haven't you?' "

"His limitations are—limitless."

"Plagiarism. Handed in lines from 'Barbara Fritchie' as his own original verse."

"*Asinine Behavior*—nine times!"

"This rogue lacks any sense of decency, honesty, or self-control. He should do very well in politics."

"Open insubordination. He made this remark in class: 'Are you *that much* of a louse that you'd give a person a zero?' From here on in, he'll *know* that I am."

Three demerits to the same offender: Sept. 26—"Breaking paper bag in cafeteria." Oct. 17—"Breaking paper bag in cafeteria." Nov. 1—"Trying to pull railing out of the wall. I advised him to go back to breaking paper bags."

"Clipping a girl lightly on the derriere and declaring that she was his *sister.*"

"Asked for a corridor pass to see the nurse. I checked. He didn't show. I caught him out of bounds. He kept *insisting* that he mistook the boys' room for the nurse's office."

"Vincent emptied contents of two wastebaskets into another pupil's desk. When pupil opened desk, Vincent roared, 'Some kids live like pigs!' "

"Rolling marbles from the back of the auditorium during assembly. I suspect he doesn't have *all* of his."

"Reprimanded about being a nuisance in class, he wiseacred, 'I'd behave better if you made me feel wanted.' I assured him that he would soon be among the 10 most wanted men in the country."

"I'm sending her out of my class to forestall an emotional disturbance—mine."

"I told the class to get to *work.* He accused me of using a dirty four-letter word."

"Repeatedly skips my fourth-period class. Claims to suffer from attacks of amnesia."

"I told you last year that he didn't belong in my academic division. Don't you counselors have a test for sanity? If so, *take it!*"

"Passing a note to the girl seated beside him in study hall. The note read, 'If you are *pregnant, smile.*' "

"Using the library photocopier to reproduce *photographs* of nudes."

"I looked up and saw a purplish-colored object being thrown by him. It sailed high in the air and landed several rows back. Of course he denied everything. '*Lots* of people *think* they see flying saucers,' he said."

THE LITTLE BOY
(A LESSON IN CREATIVITY)

Author Unknown

Once a little boy went to school.
He was quite a little boy.
And it was quite a big school.
But when the little boy
Found that he could go to his room
By walking right in from the door outside,
He was happy.
And the school did not seem
Quite so big any more.

One morning,
When the little boy had been in school awhile,
The teacher said:
"Today we are going to make a picture."
"Good!" thought the little boy.
He liked to make pictures.
He could make all kinds:
Lions and tigers,
Chickens and cows,
Trains and boats—
And he took out his box of crayons
And began to draw.

But the teacher said: "Wait!
It is not time to begin!"
And she waited until everyone looked ready.
"Now," said the teacher,
"We are going to make flowers."
"Good!" thought the little boy,
And he began to make Beautiful ones
With his pink and orange and blue crayons.

But the teacher said: "Wait!
And I will show you how."
And she drew a flower on the blackboard.
It was red, with a green stem.
"There," said the teacher,
"Now you may begin."

The little boy looked at the teacher's flower.
Then he looked at his own flower.
He liked his flower better than the teacher's,
But he did not say this,
He just turned his paper over
And made a flower like the teacher's.

On another day,
When the little boy had opened
The door from the outside all by himself,
The teacher said:
"Today we are going to make something with clay."
"Good!" thought the little boy,
He liked clay.

He could make all kinds of things with clay:
Snakes and snowmen,
Elephants and mice,
Cars and trucks—
And he began to pull and pinch
His ball of clay.

But the teacher said:
"Wait! It is not time to begin!"
And she waited until everyone looked ready.

"Now," said the teacher,
"We are going to make a dish."
"Good!" thought the little boy,
He liked to make dishes,
And he began to make some
That were all shapes and sizes.

But the teacher said, "Wait!
And I will show you how."
And she showed everyone how to make
One deep dish.
"There," said the teacher,
"Now you may begin."

The little boy looked at the teacher's dish.
Then he looked at his own.
He liked his dishes better than the teacher's
But he did not say this.

He just rolled his clay into a big ball again,
And made a dish like the teacher's.
It was a deep dish.

And pretty soon
The little boy learned to wait,
And to watch,
And to make things just like the teacher.
And pretty soon
He didn't make things of his own anymore.

Then it happened
That the little boy and his family
Moved to another house,
In another city,
And the little boy
Had to go to another school.

This school was even bigger
Than his other one,
And there was no door from the outside
Into his room.
He had to go up some big steps,
And walk down a long hall
To get to his room.

And the very first day
He was there,
The teacher said:
"Today we are going to make a picture."

"Good!" thought the little boy,
And he waited for the teacher
To tell him what to do.
But the teacher didn't say anything.
She just walked around the room.

When she came to the little boy
She said, "Don't you want to make a picture?"
"Yes," said the little boy.
"What are we going to make?"
"I don't know until you make it," said the teacher.
"How shall I make it?" asked the little boy.
"Why, any way you like," said the teacher.
"And any color?" asked the little boy.
"Any color," said the teacher,
"If everyone made the same picture,
And used the same colors,
How would I know who made what,
And which was which?"
"I don't know," said the little boy.
And he began to make pink and orange and blue flowers.
He liked his new school . . .
Even if it didn't have a door
Right in from the outside!

HE ALWAYS WANTED TO
EXPLAIN THINGS

Anonymous

He always wanted to explain things.
But no one cared.
So he drew.
Sometimes he would draw and it wasn't anything.
He wanted to carve it in stone or write it in the sky.
He would lie out on the grass and look up in the sky.
And it would be only him and the sky and the things inside him that needed saying.
And it was after that he drew the picture.
It was a beautiful picture.
He kept it under his pillow and would let no one see it.
And he would look at it every night and think about it.
And when it was dark, and his eyes were closed, he could still see it.
And it was all of him.
And he loved it.
When he started school he brought it with him.
Not to show anyone, but just to have with him like a friend.
It was funny about school.
He sat in a square, brown desk
Like all the other square, brown desks
And he thought it should be red.
And his room was a square brown room.
Like all the other rooms.
And it was tight and close.
And stiff.
He hated to hold the pencil and chalk,
With his arm stiff and his feet flat on the floor,
Stiff,
With the teacher watching and watching.
The teacher came and spoke to him.
She told him to wear a tie like all the other boys.
He said he didn't like them.
And she said it didn't matter!
After that they drew.
And he drew all yellow and it was the way he felt about morning.
And it was beautiful.
The teacher came and smiled at him.
"What's this?" she said. "Why don't you draw something like Ken's drawing? Isn't that beautiful?"
After that his mother bought him a tie.
And he always drew airplanes and rocket ships like everyone else.
And he threw the old picture away.
And when he lay alone looking at the sky,
It was big and blue and all of everything,
But he wasn't anymore.

He was square inside
And brown.
And his hands were stiff.
And he was like everyone else.
And the things inside him that needed saying didn't need it anymore.
It had stopped pushing.
It was crushed.
Stiff.
Like everything else.

One of the most sobering aspects of the educational process is the pressure and strain placed upon young people by the demands of the school, parents, and peers. The following selection describes the various manifestations of student distress and offers us three case studies about perhaps the most tragic of all signs of distress—suicide.

If one compares the decade 1945-54 to 1955-64, an increase of about one-third in the proportion of youthful suicides is revealed (1945-54, 2.1 percent; 1955-64, 2.8 percent). However, if we compare the present situation with the Depression years which had high (but not the highest) rates, then the current rates, although rising, would still represent a decrease in the rate of youthful suicide. The one notable exception is the suicide rate of young nonwhite males which is currently the highest it has ever been.

Still, on balance, suicide at younger ages has assumed a relative importance as a leading cause of death, simply because the general mortality trend has been dropping steadily.[1]

Be that as it may, suicide is still a special kind of guilt-provoking tragedy. While it may rank only fifth overall as a cause of youthful death, suicide is the number one *cause of* unnecessary *and* stigmatizing death.[2]

STRESS AND DISTRESS: SUICIDE OF CHILDREN, 1960-63

James Jan-Tausch

STRESS AND DISTRESS

Within the last few years there has been an unusually high interest expressed on the part of educators in the anxiety of children resulting from pressure. Most of this concern has been directed toward the secondary school student. In discussing, with a neuro-pediatrician, the time pattern of signs of anxiety among children, I was told that there appear to be certain milestones in the life of our children when school-connected anxiety seems prevalent. These are (1) the first week of school for the kindergartner when separation from his mother may be traumatic; (2) the first week in January when the novelty of school has worn off for some youngsters and a week at home with mother was so rewarding that social regression has taken place; (3) the middle of November for the first grader when the first report card or parent conference has taken place and parents are made aware that Johnny is having difficulty learning to read; (4) April and June for the first grader when retention is probable or certain; (5) various times during the fourth grade when children who do not read well are asked to use textbooks in history, science, and arithmetic which are too difficult and complex for them; (6) various times during the seventh grade when many children lose the stability of one teacher and one classroom to enter the departmental program of change in teacher, change in classes, and confusion in movement; and (7) the eleventh grade when college board examination results seem to decide the educational fate of those whose parents aspire that they attend college.

In addition, school psychologists report that at the end of every marking period, at every examination, and at the close of every school year, children give evidence of

---

1.Richard H. Seiden, *Suicide Among Youth: A Review of the Literature, 1900-1967,* Joint Commission on Mental Health of Children, Task Force III, Washington: U.S.G.P.O., 1969, pp. 21,22.

2.E. S. Shneidman, "Suicide Among Adolescents," *California School Health* 2, no. 3 (1966): 1-4.

Reprinted by permission of the author, James Jan-Tausch, from Raubinger and Rowe, *The Individual and Education* (New York: Macmillan, 1968), pp. 206-9, 222-35.

uncontainable anxiety by cheating on tests, by changing grades on report cards, and by absenting themselves from class without any reason other than inability to face what they see as a most distressing experience.

Let's take a close look at some of these pressures and see if we can separate the legitimate from the unwarranted.

As criteria for determining into which category a particular act falls, I would suggest that we agree: (1) that children need not pursue the goals of adults that conflict with those of the child when the child's goals are realistic and worthy; (2) that motivation is an *inner* predisposition to act and that it is in contrast with being pushed from without; and (3) that each child has a basic right to differ in talent, energy, and interests from his siblings, his neighbors, his classmates, and his relations, including his parents when they were children.

One of the heaviest burdens a child carries during his school years is the tag "capable of doing better." Usually this "albatross" is placed around the neck of a child after he has obtained a fairly high score on a group intelligence test. Sometimes it is a result of a child following a more successful brother or sister in school. At other times the leadership position of parents in the community tends to influence teachers to expect superior performance from the child. All of these could be misleading. I suggest that the only true evidence that a child is capable of doing better is found in his record which shows that he actually did function previously at a much higher level. When this is found to be the case, it behooves the teaching staff to determine the circumstances under which the child performed better and recreate them as closely as possible. "Capable of doing better" should then be followed by a statement of the conditions which need to apply if our expectations are warranted. The important factor here is that learning takes place only when a response is rewarded, and true rewards are based on interpersonal relationships. Good or fair responses by the child are usually not rewarded by the adult when excellent responses are expected.

Another pressure placed on children is inherent in our marking system. We have developed a system of reporting to parents which is really a comparison of the child with his classmates as evaluated by his teacher. A child in a school district where most pupils do not do well academically, who receives A's and B's who then moves into a district composed of highly articulate and competent students, may find himself receiving D's and F's. Or one teacher may give an A or B because the child makes a sincere effort to learn the curriculum but another teacher in the same school may disregard everything else except the end-of-the-marking-period test to determine the child's mark. The solution is not universal agreement as to what comprises an A, B, C, D, or F—for that would still make the mark itself the goal of the child, teaching staff, and parent, which is certainly not the true goal of education. Unrealistic goals serve as creators of anxiety which is usually relieved by neurotic action on the part of the child.

Reporting to parents might better be effected by a determination of the objectives of an educational program for a specific child and a sharing among the teaching staff, parents, and the child himself as to the manner in which the objectives might be reached. The objectives could be described in terms of concepts, skills, attitudes, and values. Success could be reported similarly, and lack of success could be described in terms of the nature and cause of the specific disability. In this way learning might be its own reward, and reporting to parents would be extended to reporting from parents and reporting to and from the child.

A third great pressure placed on children is that exerted by parents who are usually responding to the pressures of society and, to some extent, to the pressures of the educational establishment itself. This is the pressure to win scholastic honors as a ticket of admission to preferred institutions of higher learning, both as a means of earning a high income in adult life and as a sign of social prestige.

As early as the seventh grade, and in some instances earlier, children who are doing satisfactory work in school are being provided special tutors to help them become superior. Parents are assuming personal responsibility for some part of the child's homework and in some cases they are assuming full responsibility for special projects suggested by classroom teachers. Parents involved in such activities are themselves anxiety driven by a confused and complex society which seems to become more self destructive as it discovers the most deeply buried secrets of the universe. These parents act from what they consider to be a position of love and care for the well-being of their children. In at least one case that I know of, the well-intentioned urging of a father resulted in the suicide of a sensitive hard-working good student.

The peer group exerts a very real pressure on each child that it includes as well as each child that it excludes. In the former case it is the pressure of conformity that is brought to bear on the individual—a conformity which stifles creative expression. In the case where the youngster is on the outside and wants to become part of the group, recourse may be made by him to bribery and adoption of values and goals that are not his own.

Common symptoms of pressure on children are cheating, lying, excessive withdrawal, hysteria, memory lapses, unwarranted aggression and frequent absence from school without good cause. A tragic, but less common reaction to pressures may take the form of physical self-destruction. A study in depth revealed that 41 students in New Jersey public schools are known to have ended their lives by suicide during the period September 1960 to June 1963.

In addition to the actual cases of suicide reported, there is sufficient research to support the thesis that nine serious attempts at suicide are made and fail for every one that succeeds. There is also evidence that ten children make emotional threats to commit suicide for each child who attempts the act.

Failure in school, as measured by marks, was not in itself the most significant factor descriptive of the potential suicide. However, there was an almost unanimous evaluation by teachers and parents that this child was "capable of doing better."

More serious was the lack of participation of these children in extracurricular activities. With very few exceptions, the suicides in this study were not members of a chorus, a team, a cast, or a publication.

Some children need the strong support of an adult with whom they can confer and in whom they feel free to confide. This is a person upon whom they can depend to safeguard their secrets and to whom they can look for support in time of need. The most significant factor related to suicide among school children was the relationship between the child and the people with whom he socialized. In every case of suicide, the child was described as having no close friends with whom he might share confidences or from whom he received psychological support. The critical difference between the suicide attempt that failed and the one that succeeded, was the presence in the case of the one who failed of someone to whom he felt close, someone who shared his inner thoughts, someone who accepted him as he was.

The child who threatens suicide and is not taken seriously finds his frustration and despair all the more difficult to contain. He feels the need to prove the sincerity of his threats. It is important that we recognize early in the child's life the signs by which depression is manifested in children and that we employ the measures to relieve and eliminate them. These signs are excessive dependence, patterns of aggression and hostility, and frequent expressions of self-guilt and inadequacy.

Although it is tragic when a child dies by his own hand, the averting of death is not necessarily the only reason help should be offered to the child who is depressed. Depression and despondency reduce man to a miserable existence in which he is unable to contribute to society and unable to make creative efforts in his own behalf. It is in the best interests of society that these troubled youth get help and support.

Examining the records of the children who saw self-destruction as an answer to their problems, we see evidence of parents demanding more of the child than he could give, teachers expecting a level of thinking that was beyond the capacity of the pupil, and peers insisting on a code of behavior which was inappropriate to the needs of the individual. All these constitute pressures under which young people bend and sometimes break.

SUICIDE OF CHILDREN, 1960-63

PARENTAL PRESSURES

When Warren Ross was in the first grade at Lincoln School in Manhattan, he was involved in a fight with a classmate. Warren knew nothing about the art of self-defense and after receiving the first hard blow he might have quickly left the scene to hurry home, but he found escape impossible as the contestants were surrounded by a two-deep ring of onlookers who pushed Warren toward his opponent everytime he sought to end the fight voluntarily. When Warren finally reached home his face had been pummelled, and he had lost a tooth. Even more painful to Warren than the physical beating he had received was the memory of the taunts of his classmates and the stinging cry of "sissy" which continued to echo in his thoughts.

Warren's experience that day had a profound effect on Mrs. Ross. She decided right there and then that she would once again escort Warren to and from school. She would also save every cent she could so that they could buy a home in the New Jersey suburbs where "nice children would not be set upon by dirty ruffians." While Mr. Ross, Warren's father, agreed on the plan to move, he frequently expressed the thought that Warren should have been forced to face up to his tormentors until he learned how to inflict punishment upon those who challenged him and until he gained the respect of his classmates. The Ross family didn't move until Warren was in the sixth grade. During the intervening five years Warren was never outside his home to play with other children except when he was in school under the supervision of his teachers. Mrs. Ross had become convinced that Warren had to be protected, for the neighborhood children played in gangs and Warren would be "picked on."

In school the teachers reported that Warren did not mix well with his peers and was very quiet and reserved in class. He was most cooperative, however, and his scholastic achievement was rewarding. Compared to the other pupils, Warren was an A student. By the time Warren moved out of New York City, he had achieved a reputation among his parents, grandparents, and other relatives as a very good student. Mr. Ross found Warren's fine scholastic record as the only thing he could be proud of regarding his son. By the time Warren reached sixth grade, it was already decided in Mr. Ross' mind that Warren would be an engineer. He frequently expressed the thought to Warren as well as to visiting friends and relatives that Warren would surely win a scholarship to one of the fine engineering colleges. Warren would seem very pleased to hear his father say these things, for those were the only times Mr. Ross seemed to show approval of Warren.

The Ross' new home was a very modest one in suburbia, but Mrs. Ross was very pleased with it because now Warren could have "desirable" playmates and the family could live a more "normal" life. Mr. Ross was also gratified that many of his neighbors were professional men, engineers, chemists, attorneys, etc., and although Mr. Ross had not completed college, he had a very high respect for college graduates and was sure his son would be a most successful one.

Before the first year at their new home had passed, Mr. and Mrs. Ross found reasons for grave concern. Warren did not make any friends in the new school district and he didn't seem to want to try. Complaining of "cliques," he preferred to stay in his own room and study. As a matter of fact, Warren found it necessary to study very diligently, for in his new school many of the other children did as well in class as he did and some did better. Warren's report card showed B's where formerly there had been A's. Occasionally a C would appear.

Mrs. Ross decided to help Warren by becoming a den mother for the Boy Scouts but Warren was still not accepted by the other boys and even when the meetings were held within his own home, Warren shied away from the others. At other times he complained that he had so much studying to do he couldn't spare the time to go to the school and YMCA sponsored socials. At one den meeting, Warren spent the entire time locked in the bathroom.

Mr. Ross resolved to aid Warren with his studies. He purchased an encyclopedia set and almost every evening devoted at least an hour to help Warren with his homework. By the time Warren entered high school, Mr. Ross found that he was doing most of the homework himself, for when he tried to help Warren, an emotional scene resulted. Later Mr. Ross explained that he would not have done so much of Warren's homework except for the fact that he knew other parents were helping their children and he couldn't stand by and see Warren's marks slide from A to B to C.

By the time Warren entered high school, his parents had stopped urging him to find friends, but their anxiety over his marks was painfully apparent. Although the high school guidance counselor suggested that Warren not take the college preparatory course, the parents insisted that he enroll in it. They were determined that the investment in their home in suburbia be justified at least in terms of the educational opportunities it offered Warren. More than eighty per cent of the students enrolled at Suburbia High went to college. About fifteen per cent, almost all girls, took the business course and the rest of the students followed a program called by everyone the "gut" course. Those enrolled in this program were referred to as the high school "rejects." No, Warren would take the college prep program and, what is more, he would take Latin as a foreign language.

After the first marking period in Warren's freshman year, Mr. Ross hired a high school teacher to tutor Warren, for Mr. Ross felt inadequate to meet the scholastic demands of the secondary school, and he was more determined than ever that Warren win a scholarship to college. In addition, the first report card had showed Warren with no mark above a C.

For the rest of Warren's first year in high school, he was compelled to work four to six hours every day on his homework. When left to himself, however, Warren was often found to have accomplished little or nothing. It also seemed that the only time his father spoke to him was to ask him about his school achievement or to tell him about the success of the children of his fellow workers.

During examination time toward the end of that school year, Warren's behavior in school became so bizarre that he was referred to a guidance counselor, who called in the parents for a discussion of the situation. Acknowledging an inability to communicate effectively with Warren, the guidance counselor suggested that Warren be taken to a psychiatrist. Mr. Ross promised to consider the suggestion. That evening Mr. Ross figuratively "took the boy apart" and threatened that Warren would have to attend summer school if he didn't pass all his subjects with a mark of C. There would be no psychiatrist!

Warren received a failing mark in Latin and a D in algebra. He spent part of that summer in school where the Latin mark was changed to a D and the algebra mark was raised to a C.

Mr. and Mrs. Ross were aware of the day the report cards were to be given to the students at the end of the first marking period in Warren's sophomore year at Suburbia High, and, as the day drew near, they frequently asked Warren how he thought he was doing. To their relief, Warren gave no sign of the tenseness he had shown the previous year at report card time, and they were happy to know that he thought that he would do well. They were very pleased when Warren showed them that first report card. There was no mark less than a C and both Latin and geometry marks were B's. The geometry mark looked as if it might have been a D which was changed to a B, but Warren assured his parents that he had received an A on his last test and his classroom responses had been well received. Mr. and Mrs. Ross who wanted to believe this accepted his explanation without further question.

Warren did not return that report card to his homeroom teacher the next day, but reported that he had lost it and paid the twenty-five cents for a new card. A close examination of the new report card would have revealed a D mark was given Warren in both geometry and Latin. In the privacy of his room that evening Warren copied his father's signature on the new card and hid the original card with the changed marks in his geometry textbook. Warren's sophomore year was a pleasant one for Mr. and Mrs. Ross, for not only did Warren not need a special tutor but his report card showed B's and A's in all subjects. The one thing that did bother them was the growing realization that Warren was spending almost all of his time at home locked in his room and, except for an occasional monosyllable answer to a question at the dinner table, he never spoke to his parents nor to anyone else for that matter.

In school, Warren did everything he could to avoid notice and although he did poorly on his tests, the guidance counselor "knew" that Warren's parents observed him carefully at home and made sure he studied. His failing reports evidently were being received by the parents as unavoidable. Not hearing from the parents regarding them seemed proof to the counselor that the parents accepted Warren's apparent failure.

Examination week for sophomores at Suburbia High started on June 18th. Warren's first examination, geometry, was to be on the Monday following Father's Day.

Mr. Ross was hopefully concerned about the geometry examination. If Warren obtained an A in the exam, it would make up for the B Warren had received for the first marking period and make it possible for him to get an A for the year. With this in mind, Mr. Ross said to his son that Sunday afternoon, "Warren, why don't you study your geometry this afternoon while your mother and I take a drive out to your grandmother's, and then in the evening when we come back we will have some cake and ice cream and watch television to celebrate Father's Day." Without even waiting for a response Mr. Ross started for the door.

Four hours later the parents returned. Noticing a light on in the attic, Mr. Ross ascended the stairs to check. When he reached the top step he suddenly cried out "Oh, my God!" and slumped involuntarily to a sitting position. Lying on the floor in a precise circle were school papers. More careful scrutiny would reveal them to be geometry test papers, each marked with a red F. On a tool bench was a geometry textbook, and hanging from a ceiling rafter with a clothes line around his neck was the stiffened corpse of Warren Ross, aged fifteen.

THE ATTEMPTORS: A PACT

I, Alice Hurley, was born in Canada during World War II. My parents had married after a three-week courtship. Father had been on the staff of the nearby university and was an officer in the army when he met my mother at a social. Just before I was born, my father was transferred to a base in Mississippi where he stayed for the duration of the war. After not hearing from my father for three months, my mother sold the furniture in our flat and with me in her arms went to Mississippi where she forced my father to obtain accommodations for us.

My mother later told me that the first two years of my life were among the most miserable of hers. By the time my father received his service discharge, the family situation had become so intolerable that my parents agreed to a legal separation. My father returned to his position at the university in Canada and my mother and I remained in Mississippi.

My mother received financial aid from my father for about three years. When the money stopped coming, she made arrangements for me to stay with a neighbor while she went to work. This arrangement lasted for about four years. Uncle Frank then came to live with us. I was told that Uncle Frank was mother's cousin. After about six months of violent argument and frequent staying out late, Uncle Frank left us. The next year I remember only as one in which my mother was very depressed and I was sad. Then Uncle Phil moved in.

Uncle Phil was a gentle person and my mother seemed to be very happy. After Uncle Phil was with us about a year and I was about ten years of age, my mother told me that Uncle Phil was really not my uncle at all, but just a good friend she was going to marry as soon as she got a divorce from my father. I remember crying myself to sleep the night my mother told me about Uncle Phil. I prayed that my father would come back. That night I dreamed that my father had returned to our house. I remember talking to my father every night for quite a spell. Sometimes he would appear in the room with me and I was very happy—despite the fact that he never talked to me but just stood there.

When my mother told me she was going to have a baby, I remember being very happy. It never occurred to me that anyone but my father could be the father of the new baby, and I expected my father to come home when the baby was born. My mother seemed to be quarreling with Uncle Phil more and more and my name would come up frequently in the argument. Then one day my mother came home when Uncle Phil was giving me a bath and a big fight started. Uncle Phil left the house that very night and never returned. For two days mother didn't leave the house. She just talked to herself and drank whiskey.

Within a month, Mother and I were on our way to New Jersey. I was very upset about this and pleaded with my mother not to move. I thought my father would never be able to find us if we left Mississippi and didn't return to Canada. It was then my mother told me that I was the reason my father had left home. She said he couldn't stand children and especially disliked little girls. From that moment on I think I despised my father and lost all feeling for my mother, yet there were times after that I was sure my mother was wrong about my father.

My little sister was born in New Jersey and I spent almost all of my time helping my mother take care of her.

I had started school in the district near the army base in Mississippi and liked it from the first day. It was very difficult to form friendships with the other children because most of them were the sons and daughters of servicemen who were rarely stationed for more than six months at this base. I remember being told that I was the only child in first grade in June who had been there the previous September. I had no difficulty learning to read and enjoyed reading so much that I read just about every book I could find. Reading books made it possible for me to get along without any friends.

I had just finished the fifth grade when I came to New Jersey. The only difference between the New Jersey school and the Mississippi school that I noticed, was the increased amount of reading material available. I loved to read the encyclopedias and the geography and history books. I remember finding the city in Canada in which I was born, mentioned in the encyclopedia. I frequently read about it as well as the university at which my father was a professor. The children in my classes were not very friendly but I was busy reading so I didn't seem to mind not having friends. It wasn't until I was in high school that having friends became important, having the right friends that is.

It was while I was a sophomore in high school that something happened that changed my world for me. Up until that day I was doing well in school receiving A's and B's in all my subjects and starting really to enjoy going to class. I remember a trick I used to play on the teachers. I would only raise my hand in class when a very difficult question was asked. If the teacher didn't call on me immediately or if any other pupil raised his hand I would lower mine and if called upon I would not answer. One teacher was especially nice to me and I thought my father must be like him in class at college. One day after school I returned to his class and told him I loved him and I wanted to kiss him but he became very angry and told me I was a bad girl. It was that very afternoon when it happened.

Mother had gotten a job in a factory and didn't get home until six o'clock. Aunt Martha left the house just as I reached the door. She was in a hurry to get to her job as a waitress and she wouldn't be back until midnight. It was my job to take care of Mary, my sister, and Bobby, my little cousin. About five o'clock the door bell rang. I had been cautioned against opening the door to strangers so with the chain on I opened the door slightly and inquired "Who is it?" Standing in the doorway was a well-dressed man in his late thirties.

"Are you Alice Hurley?" he inquired.

"Yes," I answered. "What do you want?" The man replied that he was a friend of my father's and he would like to talk to my mother. Without fully realizing what I had done I removed the chain and told him to come in. He started to question me about my mother and about me. Every attempt I made to ask him about my father was met with evasion. Slowly my temper rose and I started to feel angry at this man and at myself for having permitted him to enter the apartment. Then he asked me a direct question. "Do you love your father?" and for some reason I don't understand I screamed "I hate him! I hate him!" Quickly and strongly he slapped my face and at the same time shouted "I hate you too—you ugly brat." He would have hit me again except for the fact that mother entered the room at that instant and threw herself at him. I really don't know what happened the rest of that evening though my mother told me that I had fainted and then fallen into a deep sleep until the next morning. Both my mother and I stayed home the next day. She explained that the man was my father and that he was seeking a divorce. He would not return, she promised me. Somehow I was disappointed that he wouldn't return and berated myself for having talked to him that way and yet at the same time I could not admit to having any strong feelings about him. For days I had the feeling that my experience was a nightmare and everything afterward seemed unreal. I became very depressed and lost interest in everything. I didn't study, I didn't read, I didn't even think; I was in a daze. I came out of this mental confusion shortly after the beginning of the next school semester and immediately felt the need to do something desperate. I didn't care if I died in the attempt. It was during this period that my mother found me in the bathroom bleeding from wrist cuts. I felt no pain and uttered no sound. My mother stopped the bleeding and took me to the local hospital where I was further attended to and interviewed at length by a doctor. I was allowed to go home the same day when my mother promised to bring me to a doctor, a psychiatrist, the next day. I was still in a daze the following day when I went to see the psychiatrist. I really don't remember much of my conference with the doctor except that he made me promise that I would come to see him every week. I never went back. My mother explained that she just could not afford to pay for the visits, and she had no money saved for such emergencies.

My attendance at school was poor that fall. I was absent at least twice each week. My mother would always write excuses saying I was sick. My marks tumbled to D's and F's. I found myself not studying but somehow wanting to hand in written work. I wrote many poems and essays. I wrote reports. Somehow I found it easy to write about myself and how I felt about the world. I grew bitter and cynical. It seemed strange to me that my written work would always have a mark on it but no comment by the teacher. The teachers never seemed to see me in the writing.* They graded the form, the style or the grammar but they never communicated their thoughts in response to mine. I felt as if I were revealing my innermost thoughts but no one could hear me.

I was in one of my depressed moods when I got the urge to take in one dose, the entire bottle of medicine given to me by the doctor when I cut my wrists. The bottle was almost half full. I had the empty bottle in my hand and was falling asleep when my Aunt Martha found me and called an ambulance. The hospital used a stomach pump on me and again advised that I see a psychiatrist. My mother promised to send me to one. This time I asked my mother not to. I promised her that I would behave better. However, a week later I was up on the roof of our apartment house looking out over the city and not sure of why I was there when I was startled to hear a voice behind me. "You're Alice Hurley, aren't you?" I turned to see a boy about fifteen sitting with his back against the chimney facing me.

"Who are you?" I asked.

"I'm Peter Curden" replied the boy. "I'm in your history class at school—were you going to jump?" The last question somehow startled me.

"No," I denied. "I was just trying to get away from people. I wanted to be alone. What are you doing here?"

I found Peter to be a very nice boy, the only boy I ever talked to that made me feel unafraid. We met on the roof many times and discussed life. He never once touched me or appeared aware of the fact that I was a girl. I soon got to feel that I was talking to another girl when I talked to Peter.

Peter lived with his mother and his younger sister. His father had also left his mother. His older brother was in the Navy. Peter's father left the home when Peter's brother

---

*Samples attached to this report p. 74.

went into the Navy because Mr. Curden readily admitted to have nothing but disgust for Peter whom he accused of being a "sissy." He had no use for women.

Peter avoided boys and men because they usually molested him. His only satisfaction was his reading, especially reading concerned with philosophy.

We talked at great length about our reading and about life. We were in complete agreement that the world was entirely materialistic and the present goals of man were economic. There seemed to be no time for true expression of self and enjoyment of nature. We usually concluded that life as we are forced to live it is purposeless and that we must either awaken the world to its true purpose or seek self-destruction.

School seemed so useless that both Peter and I would be absent almost every other day and sometimes for two days in a row but never three consecutively for that, we knew, was the signal for an attendance officer to look for us. One day Peter dyed his almost white blonde hair to a deep purplish red and went to school that day. Except for the other children joking about the hair nothing was said or done to Peter about it. I guess the faculty was trying to prove it wasn't going to get upset by the foolishness of one boy.

Peter and I found ourselves daring each other to do unusual things in school to see how the teachers or the principal would react. I think he wanted to be either punished or accepted. We were neither.

With Peter, I went in the evening to the home of a teacher, to whom I thought we might talk about life as we saw it. The teacher seemed frightened by us and by what we were saying. In a fit of temper he ordered us out of his home and threatened to report our behavior to the school principal.

To both Peter and me it seemed as though the last possible person with whom we might communicate had refused to accept us as human beings with feelings.

It was late in the evening when we reached my house. We were too disturbed to want to go to our respective homes so we went to the roof to talk. There seemed to be no way of reaching anyone. Communications in this world are limited to the bare necessities to maintain life and continue on course.

We stayed up very late that night. The more we talked the more hopeless everything seemed to be. We decided we were going to communicate in such a way that people couldn't help but respond. We would commit suicide but, to make sure it would not be in vain we would do it in a dramatic way. We would jump from a high building after we had set the building on fire and attracted a lot of attention.

The next day we met in the cellar of my house where we knew kerosene was stored. Each of us filled a milk bottle with kerosene and placed it in a paper bag. Twenty minutes later we entered the lobby of the largest building in town. Walking past the elevators we entered the stairway and quickly poured the kerosene on the walls and the floor. Then with the bottle still in our hands we ran up the stairway a few steps and put a match to the paper bags. Throwing the burning bags to the floor we raced up the stairway as we heard the fire start. Still clinging to the bottles we mounted the steps to the second, the third, and the fourth floors. By the time we reached the fourth floor the fire had been discovered and we could hear people calling out in alarm. Quickly we mounted the last steps which led to the roof trap door. Our plan seemed perfect and I had a feeling of high exhilaration. Then came catastrophe. The trap door was locked! We looked at each other and without a word we broke the bottles and slashed at our wrists with the sharp glass edges. I watched the blood fall on my dress and on the steps. I was watching the blood flow, completely unconscious of everything about me, when I was seized and carried down the steps. I can't remember anything after that until I awakened in a hospital. I don't know why but when I regained consciousness and saw the nurse sitting next to me I asked one question, "How is Peter?" The nurse's answer sounded so satisfying. "Just five minutes ago, he awoke and asked 'How's Alice?' "

Both Alice Hurley and Peter Curden spent a month in the hospital after which Alice and her mother moved to another city in New Jersey. Peter went to live with his Aunt and Uncle in still another city. Both Alice and Peter completed their high school programs successfully. Alice now attends a state college where she is a commuting student and Peter is employed in a large manufacturing plant where he also attends a special training school in the evening.

In the new high schools both Alice and Peter had help from the school psychologists and the consultant psychiatrists. In addition, both Alice and Peter regularly received help from the county medical health clinic.

(The following are compositions by Alice Hurley.)
Fear, my constant companion

I want to move to Canada. God, I know I can't live here anymore. No not in this horrible city. It is wicked, it is cruel. I can't escape it. No, not even in my dreams. What is a dream? Which is the nightmare? Sleep promises escape from this misery—only sleep too is deceitful. Who will end it all for me? I try, but I cannot. I don't even have strength to end this pain. This ceaseless, unrelenting pain. Why was I ever born? What a cruel trick my mother played on me. Is there no limit? I will seek my relief in the grave. God why, why do you do this to me? Are you God or are you the Devil? God must be a Devil! Yes it is the Devil I have been speaking to. If there is a God, please let him hear me and end my agony. Who is my father? Is he the Devil? No, I am the Devil and there is no death, there is no end. Please God release me in death.

Father

> *I love my father as I love a cloud*
> *He is always with me yet never within reach*
> *I see him smile and frown and cry*
> *And I sing and fear and despair*

> *My father does not visit me anymore*
> *He never did it is true*
> *He is so stern and solemn when I see him*
> *But he loves me I am sure*

JUST ANOTHER SCHOOL DAY

Mrs. Joan Smith, eighth grade teacher at Madison Junior High School, was late getting to school on January 25, 1961. A bus had broken down on the highway and traffic had been stalled for more than a half hour. Meanwhile, Mr. Gregory, the school principal, had taken over Mrs. Smith's homeroom class and was anything but happy about it. That, at least, was Mrs. Smith's impression when she arrived at her class and relieved him of the responsibility of taking attendance.

"These children should be taught some discipline," Mr. Gregory snapped. "Especially that Jones kid."

Mrs. Smith, already pressed by clerical details, was conscious of irritation and frustration. Within a few minutes the bell rang, and the regular instructional school day began.

"Today is Wednesday," remembered Mrs. Smith, "and that means no free period." Continuing thoughts reminded her that this was also the day of her course at State College and that she had better not tire herself needlessly.

Mrs. Smith's plan to slow down her pace, however, met with no cooperation from either her pupils or the front office. The first period was disrupted by three of the pupils who had forgotten to bring their books. It was with relief that Mrs. Smith heard the bell announcing the end of the class. During the second period, the film projector broke down and most of the period was devoted to getting someone to fix it. The projector was an old one and on other occasions it had been fixed promptly, but not this day. The third period was ruined when Mrs. Smith was called from class to attend a conference with the principal and an irate parent who had accused her of not being fair in grading Tim Dunn's test paper. The accusation seemed unfair to Mrs. Smith who thought she had been especially generous in her marking, but Mr. Gregory seemed anxious to placate the parent. The meeting ended with the parent being assured that Mrs. Smith would review the paper.

Nothing disturbing happened in the fourth period except for a message from Miss Johnson, the school clerk, directing Mrs. Smith to take lunch room duty during the fifth period because Mrs. Miller was absent and a replacement was needed. This was usually Mrs. Smith's library period.

Lunch period was chaotic. There was a fist fight. One child accused another of stealing some money and still another child became ill and needed immediate care and attention.

The plans for the sixth period called for Mrs. Smith to move about the room the entire fifty minutes working in an individualized teaching situation with a slow learning class. This she did. When the seventh and last period of the day began, Mrs. Smith was tired—very tired. After the children in her seventh period class were all seated she decided to change her original plan and instead have them read ten pages of the text and answer the questions at the end of the chapter.

Mrs. Smith purposely ignored the whispering and passing of notes as she looked through her notes in preparation for her course at the college. But she couldn't ignore a loud cry of anguish that went up from one boy who immediately put his hand to the back of his head and acted as though he were in pain.

"Willie Jones, bring your work to my desk. I want to see what you have done in the last forty minutes," ordered Mrs. Smith.

"But somebody hit me," retorted Willie.

"Just bring up your paper" continued Mrs. Smith, who at this point was in no mood for arguing. Instead of waiting for Willie, however, Mrs. Smith went to Willie's desk, picked up the paper that was on his desk and said, "I thought so. Well, young man, you may do the assignment at home, and in addition, you are to have your mother sign it with a little note saying no one at home helped you do the work. And you can tell your mother you received a zero for today's work." With these words Mrs. Smith tore up the paper that Willie had on his desk. The paper had a picture of a woman drawn on it but the face was embellished with a large mustache and a beard. The features and the dress, however, were unmistakably intended to be those of Mrs. Smith.

The bell rang and after a few minutes another bell rang indicating the end of the school day for the children.

That evening it was a very fatigued Mrs. Smith who went to bed and slept soundly through the night.

Willie Jones was also late getting to school on January 25, 1961. He was awakened at an early hour by his younger brother who shared the bedroom with him. Little Freddy was just four years old and didn't know enough to sleep late in the morning. He usually awakened the whole family at the dawn of each day. Willie resented sharing his room with Freddy for he thought that when a boy gets to be fifteen years of age he deserves a room of his own. Mrs. Jones, however, didn't want to put Freddy in the upstairs spare room because it was the coldest room in the house and also because she didn't think a four year old child should have to go up and down the stairs when it was possible to have him on the first floor. Sometimes, however, when Willie wanted to be by himself, he went to the upstairs room where he stayed silently for hours on end. Occasionally he would even sleep through the night on the cot in the room.

The night before January 25th, however, Willie had slept in the bed in the first floor room. After dressing, he quickly ate breakfast and left the house with his books.

Mrs. Jones had sensed something wrong with Willie ever since Freddy was born. Try as she might, she could not get Willie to accept the idea that Freddy was a baby, and that babies needed a lot of attention and that Freddy should not be punished when he did the same things for which Willie would be chastised.

Mr. Jones, also, thought there was something troubling Willie, but he wasn't sure what it was. Even before Freddy was born Willie resented his older brother, Bobby, who was an ideal son if there ever was one. Bobby had taken to going to his father's auto repair shop almost from the time he could walk, and now he spent almost all of his free time there. He was a real help too—he knew almost as much as his father about automobiles.He was taking the auto shop course in the high school and he had been promised by Mr. Jones that after he graduated he could work full time with his father in the shop and get a regular salary. Just the week before Mr. Jones had proudly pointed to the sign above the garage entrance which read, "Robert Jones, Auto Repairs" and said to his oldest boy, "When you are twenty-one, I'm going to have the painter add the words, 'and Son.' When I retire you can just paint over the words 'and Son' and put on the letters 'Jr.' "

Mr. Jones couldn't understand why Willie didn't come to the shop more often to lend a hand. On the very few occasions that Willie did come, he did more damage than he provided help. "I guess you're not cut out to be an auto repairman, son" the father would say as he set about repairing the mistakes Willie had made.

On this twenty-fifth day of January, Willie wasn't eager to get to school—he just wanted to escape from the house. He walked down to the river, across the lumber yard and through the park before he was reminded by hearing the bell that it was time for school. Willie didn't want to be late. Even though he knew the second bell had already rung when he entered his classroom, he thought Mrs. Smith wouldn't say anything. He was uncomfortably surprised to find Mr. Gregory, the principal, at Mrs. Smith's desk.

"What is your excuse for this tardiness, young man?" demanded Mr. Gregory, who probably was more annoyed at Mrs. Smith's failure to arrive on time than he was at Willie.

The question "Why are you late?" went unanswered. Raising his voice in exasperation, Mr. Gregory ordered "Come to my office at 3 o'clock. Maybe you'll have an answer then."

A few minutes later, Mrs. Smith hurried into the classroom, and Mr. Gregory returned to his administrative duties.

To Willie Jones, that school day did not seem much different from many other frustrating days he had experienced.

In the first period, the math teacher introduced a new concept which Willie just didn't understand. He asked no questions because he didn't want to call attention to what seemed to him to be his own failure in comprehension.

The second period was more rewarding in that Willie responded successfully to a question the history teacher asked. Willie was able to give the correct answer because he had watched a television program the previous evening which dealt with the subject. The teacher acted surprised at the correct answer and quipped "Don't tell me you've taken up studying, Willie?" The class laughed and Willie found it impossible to make any further contribution to the discussion.

Science followed history. Miss Dolan was both Willie's science teacher and his guidance counselor. Willie liked Miss Dolan and felt at ease in her class. Occasionally Miss Dolan would invite Willie to drop in to see her on her counseling periods, but Willie never would ask his teacher's permission to leave class to go to the guidance office. On the one visit he made when Miss Dolan called him out of his English class he didn't know what to talk about. In addition, he had missed a homework assignment in English for which he got into trouble and had to do a punish lesson.

Today Miss Dolan had Willie's cumulative record folder on her desk. Mr. Gregory had requested it and before she gave it to him she reviewed it herself.

I.Q. 95 Reading Grades:Vocabulary   *3.4*
                 Comprehension   *4.5*

Retained in grade four
No close friends
All teachers say Willie is "capable of doing better." Some teachers note that
    Willie "cannot be reached."
A letter from Willie's mother to his fourth grade teacher asking her to
    please help him with his reading.
Willie's absence record was above average and his tardiness record in-
    creased in each grade.

Willie's assignment in science class that day was to draw a diagram of the digestive system. Except for errors in spelling, the drawing was good.

The fourth period was a total loss for Willie. He went to the gym but received a zero for the day and was not permitted to participate in an intra-class basketball game because he had forgotten his sneakers.

Lunch period was uneventful. Willie sat at a table with his brother and some of his brother's friends but did not enter into the table talk. Willie's brother brought lunch from home each day and that gave Willie an excuse to eat at Bobby's table, for Willie would have found it difficult to sit with any other group.

Music period followed lunch and Willie, for the first time that day, felt happy. Mr. Dearborn, the music teacher, thought Willie had a good voice and Willie liked to sing. Mr. Dearborn announced that there would be tryouts after school for the boys' chorus. The boys' chorus sang at the elementary school assembly, at the high school concert and at the graduation exercises. Sometimes they also sang at civic affairs. Although Willie's voice was good enough for him to be a soloist, Willie derived greater pleasure from singing as part of a group.

Willie almost forgot his appointment with Mr. Gregory at 3:00 P.M. when he heard the announcement about chorus tryouts.

In Mrs. Smith's seventh period English class, Willie was supposed to read ten pages of his textbook but the book was too difficult for him. After making a futile attempt to do the assignment, Willie busied himself drawing pictures of how he thought Mrs. Smith would look if she were a man. Suddenly he felt a sharp sting on the back of his neck. Without thinking, he let out a cry of pain. Mrs. Smith was not interested in Willie's claim of being hit and took away his drawings. He received a zero for the day and was asked to do the assigned reading at home and also get a letter from his mother attesting to the fact that he did the work without help. Willie accepted the punishment without emotion. He was eagerly anticipating the chorus tryouts.

The period finally ended and Willie took himself to Mr. Gregory's office. Sitting on the detention bench in Mr. Gregory's office was not a new experience for Willie, but today he was hoping he could get in to see Mr. Gregory and get the tongue lashing over with quickly so he could go to the auditorium for the chorus tryouts. It was almost with a sigh of relief that Willie responded to Mr. Gregory's call to enter his office. It wasn't until he heard Mr. Gregory ask "Well, are you prepared to tell me now, why you were late?" that Willie realized he had no acceptable response to make to that question.

"My mother was sick this morning and I had to help dress and feed my little brother and I didn't watch the time," blurted out Willie in a desperate attempt to win the sympathetic approval of Mr. Gregory.

"That can easily be checked and here comes your brother who will tell us what happened," replied Mr. Gregory as Bobby Jones entered the office. Unfortunately for Willie, his brother revealed the truth and Mr. Gregory became even more angry.

For fifteen minutes, Mr. Gregory lectured Willie on being prompt, on being truthful, and on trying harder to be a good student. The last five minutes of the talk were completely wasted on Willie who was starting to panic at the thought that he would miss the tryouts. Finally, he could contain himself no longer and said, "Can I leave now, Mr. Gregory? I have to go to the chorus tryouts."

Maybe it was a reaction to his being interrupted or perhaps Mr. Gregory would have made the same decision in any case, but his response was crushing. "Willie, I couldn't possibly allow a boy who tells lies to represent our school in the chorus." Willie really didn't hear what followed. As a matter of fact, Willie was back at home and upstairs on the cot before he was aroused out of a dazed state by his mother demanding that he go to the store for some needed groceries.

An early dinner at which Bobby informed the family of Willie's trouble with Mr. Gregory and at which Mr. Jones berated Willie for his misdeeds and warned him against such future actions was followed by Willie's attempt to forget his troubles in a television program.

Although it was his favorite program, it took Willie a while to develop interest in it; just as he did, Freddy turned the dial to another channel. Willie immediately returned the dial to its original setting where it stayed only a moment before Freddy once again turned it to the channel he preferred. For the next minute or two the dial was repeatedly switched back and forth between the two channels. The duel ended with Freddy bursting into tears and running to report his troubles to his mother. In less than a minute, Mrs. Jones came out of the kitchen, walked over to the television set, turned the dial to the channel Freddy wanted and informed Willie, "After your disgraceful behavior today in school, I don't think you should be allowed to watch television tonight. Go to your room, do your homework, and then go to bed."

Unlike other times Willie did not protest, but meekly walked out of the living room and headed for the room upstairs. Mrs. Jones was surprised at his sudden obedience, but muttering, "That boy—I don't know what I can do with him," she returned to her duties in the kitchen.

Nothing was heard from Willie that evening nor even the next morning. Impatiently Mrs. Jones finally went upstairs to wake him. Willie wasn't to be awakened, however, for the previous evening he found a final answer to his world of problems.

Suspended by the trouser belt he had fastened around his neck, Willie was hanging from the ceiling light fixture.

UNLIKELY TO SUCCEED

The twelve members of the admissions committee at St. Paul's School in Concord, New Hampshire, dutifully poured over the boy's record. One, Spencer C. Thompson, 13, wanted to enter the third form (first-year high) next fall from St. James School in Maryland. His grades: English 94; history 85; mathematics 50; Latin 30. In a class of 14, the record showed, he ranked 12th.

"Spencer is rather delicate," wrote his headmaster, "owing to a severe pulmonary illness two years ago, but he seems to have recovered satisfactorily. He is too small to be effective in contact sports, but he greatly enjoys riding and swimming. The boy is certainly no scholar and has repeated his form twice. He does well in English, however, and possesses an excellent memory. In fact, he won the school prize for reciting poetry last year. He has also, I regret to say, a stubborn streak, and is sometimes rebellious in minor matters, although he usually conforms. He is at once backward and precocious, reading books beyond his years, and yet ranking at the bottom of his form. He has, I believe, a native shrewdness and is a manly little fellow, high-spirited and well-liked, who unfortunately has not made the most of his opportunities here. I can recommend him to you on the grounds of general ability."

Spencer's other mentors were less kind. A special English teacher thought him "rather stubborn". His Latin teacher found him "most difficult to teach. He seems to have little or no understanding of the subject except in the most mechanical way. At times he seems almost perverse in his ability to learn. I suspect that he has received help from other boys in his prepared work."

All twelve on the St. Paul's committee voted not to admit Spencer Thompson. Only then did William A. Oates, director of admissions, reveal the truth: Spencer C. Thompson was really Winston Spencer Churchill. The record which the St. Paul's admissions committee had read consisted largely of verbatim transcripts of Churchill's first years at Harrow.

"We do this once in a while," said Oates. "Inescapably, we must deal with the record. After some time you think that you know what you are doing. But we do get caught."

In keeping with the established policy of the school, Mike Gallion's first unit of work in his senior class had been a project designed to strengthen the ability of his students in the use of the research tools—the card catalogue, the vertical file, the Reader's Guide, and the standard reference works. In order to make this meaningful to the youngsters, each had been permitted to select his own problem for research; and they had gone about their work with varying degrees of enthusiasm and with varying amounts of self-direction. After a few briefing sessions on the use of the standard reference works, instruction had become largely individualized. Monday, Wednesday, and Friday had served as clearing houses for information on common problems which the students had encountered in using the reference tools. At the beginning of the unit, Mike had indicated to the group that the end product—their final report—would be used as the evaluating instrument for judging how well they had learned to use the different reference tools.

And now Mike could see his own problems beginning to develop. Fred Smith failed to turn in his report. Mike had learned from other teachers that this was very typical of Fred. This was the culmination of Fred's rather indifferent approach to the unit: a number of times during their library research hours Mike had had to pull Fred away from the current sports magazines in order to get him back to the problem he was supposedly investigating; and now on top of this general matter of failing to get down to work, Fred had turned in no report whatsoever. Mike hated this business of "grading" people at best, but here was a clear-cut case in his judgment where the individual was not doing satisfactory work. The grade of "F" had caused little hesitation in his mind.

It had only been three hours, however, after he had turned in the grades when Bill Evans, the coach, had stopped by his office to see if the matter could be overlooked this time. Eligibility lists had to be sent out that afternoon; and if Smith were listed as failing, the football team would have to go into the field without its only good end. "The team really needs Smith," Evans had assured him. And now that the day was drawing to a close, he was sure that Evans would be up expecting an answer. Judging people, Mike reflected, was even more unpleasant than he liked to think.

CASE STUDY:
CITIZENS FOR IMPROVEMENT OF
OUR PUBLIC SCHOOLS

The high school library committee had been called into emergency session and Mike Gallion was actually relishing a committee meeting for a change. Rumor had indicated that the meeting had to do with the recent "investigation" of the high school library —the one that had sent the librarian, Miss Jones, home with a sick headache. Apparently the investigating committee of the Evansville Citizens for Improvement of our Public Schools had acted quickly, for Mike could see that the "Bill of Particulars" which lay before the principal was not short. And when the principal began his reading, interesting it proved to be:

> "Inasmuch as the minds of high school youngsters are immature and susceptible to the influence of radical and immoral ideas, we demand that the following materials—subversive to the morality and patriotism of youngsters—be removed from the shelves of the high school library. Each of these works has been carefully examined by our high school committee and found to be the type of book from whose contaminating influence we wish to protect our youngsters:
>
> 1. Miller, H. *Tropic of Cancer*. Lewd and immoral, certainly tending to create an irreligious and delinquent attitude toward life.
>
> 2. *Candy* and *Fanny Hill*. Tending to promote sexual immorality in youngsters.
>
> 3. Puzo, Mario. *The Godfather*. Gives an unflattering and prejudicial view of one particular group in our society.
>
> 4. Stearns, Raymond. *Pageant of Europe*. This readings book contains selections from Communist leaders, including Marx's *Communist Manifesto*. Descriptions of mine conditions and factory conditions in England are critical of the free enterprise system.
>
> 5. Benedict, Agnes. *Races of Mankind*. This attempt to minimize racial differences and imply that all humans possess similar qualities might easily be interpreted by youngsters as an argument in favor of racial intermixture and intermingling.
>
> 6. Darwin, Charles. *Origin of the Species*. This book presents as historical fact many ideas which are contrary to the basic religious tenets of many of our members. It does not even present the contrary side of the argument. Inclusion of this book on school shelves is in direct violation of the religious freedom and safety of many of our members.
>
> 7. *Debater's Handbook*. Although purporting to present both points of view on many controversial issues, this debater's handbook can provide no assurance that the students using the volume will either read both sides or come out with the correct answer to the problems dealt with.
>
> "Our high school committee would like to call your attention to the following additional practices which we consider inexcusable:
>
> 1. Our committee noted that your school library subscribed to the publication *Commonweal*, which we wish to call to your attention as published by a

particular religious group, the ideas of which are inimical to those of many members of our committee who have children in the public schools.

2. We further noted that your library subscribed to the consistently left-wing publication *Ramparts,* a radical publication addicted to carrying articles by persons of subversive tendencies.

3. The bulletin board in the first floor hall was devoted exclusively to a display on UNESCO, an organization specifically dedicated to carrying articles by persons of known subversive tendencies.

4. Our committee further noted the following two public performances by the high school as violating the canons of good public education in American schools:
   a. In November, your school performance by the dramatic and dancing groups was *Hair.* Although this piece is sometimes considered high art, the moral overtones of the work are completely unsuitable for immature minds, and an immoral and decadent view of contemporary society.
   b. In December, the annual Christmas performance was notable in terms of the number of Christmas carols which were of foreign origin. Only *one* of the numbers performed was specifically American in origin. It is abundantly clear that there is no dearth of American Christmas carols which might have been sung.

We are awaiting anxiously your assurance that these matters will be seriously investigated and the appropriate action implied by our report taken at once.

This was the kind of a problem that Mike Gallion liked to face.

CASE STUDY:
DOUG

Friday was the first day that Mike Gallion had sent Doug Lee from the class. He couldn't have timed it better, he reflected caustically, with Doug's father coming for a conference with all his teachers after school on Monday. Mike supposed it was just end-of-the-week irritation that had gotten into him and one paper airplane in one classroom had been just one paper airplane too many. Now that he had "exiled" Doug and told him to report after school, he supposed that he wouldn't keep Doug more than a minute or two after school while he talked to him about it—just for form's sake. He was already out of the mood he had been in during third hour, and now he wished sincerely that he had allowed the incident to pass by unnoticed.

The talk with Doug went as he had anticipated it would. Doug arrived in the office —a little late to be sure—with his half smile and somewhat uncertain eyes. He was "sorry" and "it wouldn't happen again" . . . and Mike guessed it wouldn't be the same identical thing next time, but something not too unlike it. Doug was an unpredictable boy to have in class—usually shy and retiring, never having anything to say when you called on him and generally blushing at his own inability or the pain of having his name called, and then sometimes boisterous and noisy and uncontrolled. The only things you could really predict about Doug were that he wasn't going to add anything to class discussion and the papers he turned in weren't going to be very much.

Mike went over in his mind the fall briefing session the new teachers had had on "problem students" in their classes. Doug had been one of the "problem students" on whom the teachers had been pretty well agreed. Doug was doing very little in school —anywhere, except possibly in art. He was quite a skilled craftsman in art—no one could deny—and Mr. Blake, the art teacher, had been pleased to display the enameled cufflinks Doug had made in the art display in the first floor corridor. One of the teachers had later purchased them for a gift. And at the moment, Mike knew, Doug was working on a broad, tooled belt of the kind in which adolescents seemed to take particular pride. Mike had taken the time to stop by at the art room on more than one occasion to compliment him on this belt. And through his work in art, Mr. Blake had learned a little more about Doug. But such knowledge as the fact that Doug had long been interested in archery had led to a blank wall when Doug consistently ignored the coach's suggestion that he bring his bow to school some day.

It was not that Doug's parents were unconcerned about his consistent pattern of D's and F's in school. The Monday meeting on Doug, he was sure, had been called at the request of Doug's father and as a result of the Lee's recent visit with Mr. Church, the principal. Mr. Lee, it had developed, was a traveling salesman for a large distillery and was on the road much of the time. He was generally home weekends, but his schedule was irregular and he was gone many days of the week. Since Doug had entered high school, his mother had started clerking in the drapery department at Charm's Home Furnishings. They had recently bought a house in a "nice" section of town, but their conference with the principal had suggested that they had not gotten to know their neighbors very well. "Probably because my husband is on the road so much," Mrs. Lee had speculated. It was at this point that Mr. Lee had probably requested to meet with Doug's teachers to see if there was anything which could be done to improve Doug's work in school. As far as Mr. Lee could see, Doug was getting nothing out of school. "It might be better," he had commented to Mr. Church, "if Doug dropped out of school and took a job. He'd probably be doing himself more good that way than merely loafing in school, and then maybe after they held him to that for a while, he'd be more than glad to come back to school." The Monday conference, Mike understood, was partly to face up to that problem.

Mike could afford to smile at the possibilities which this conference seemed to suggest. His fellow teachers loved to air their views on kids and parents in private, but he wondered how they'd go about getting them out in the open with Mr. and Mrs. Lee there. There was Jane Potter, for example, who felt that Doug was really "a good boy" —and his non-verbal intelligence tests did reveal he had a *lot* of ability—and that the real job of the school was to convince Doug to make more of himself than his father had. After all, people with ability can always make something of themselves. Mike wondered how she would express this idea with Mr. Lee sitting at the conference table. And then there was Miss Leslie who had been so shocked at the idea of permitting Doug to withdraw from school in order to work. Mike wondered how she would express her beliefs that the main job of the school was to counteract any such influences which Doug got from his father. *That* wouldn't be an easy idea to express at the conference. And then there was Mike himself; he wondered what he *did* believe ought to be done, and how he'd go about proposing to do it.

The class was of average size, with about thirty pupils, including two girls, in a senior high school with an enrollment of eight hundred and fifty students. The students were to study American literature as a "12 General" class. This meant that they were seniors in a "general" course in American literature, that is, in a course specially designed for students who were not considered capable of the work required in the more advanced and comprehensive history courses for seniors. Besides the low-ability students, this class was filled with pupils who had caused disciplinary problems in the more advanced classes.

The "general" classes were catchalls for unclassified students. "They don't want to be in school, and none of the other teachers want them in their classes, so they just get dumped in one class," said one teacher in describing the class. In a homogeneously grouped school, the only homogeneity in this class was the pupils' desire to get out of school and their lack of interest in any kind of schoolwork.

Most of the pupils in the class had made it plain that they were not interested in school. They refused to do any assignments, or they copied work from another student if they did anything. One teacher having this class in English explained, ". . . if you just keep them busy, . . . anything to keep their interest. . . ." Their general mathematics teacher explained, "You can't teach them much; if you can get across one principle to one student, consider yourself accomplishing something." Two students left school in the middle of the term when they reached the enlistment age of the Armed Services.

It was a difficult task to keep these students after school, because then they usually had after-school appointments with other teachers or they were signed up for detention for from three to ten days. When the students were kept after school, it interfered with their jobs, as ninety percent of them had part-time work after school. One teacher's statement was, ". . . you hit them where it hurts when you keep them after school and they can't work. Money is the only thing that makes something important to them."

The students were from low-income families—some from broken homes and others with many younger brothers and sisters. Their jobs were important to them and, as one student explained, "You're doing something at work; you don't accomplish anything at school." When asked why they did stay in school, the students replied, "My father wants me to," "I need a diploma to make more money," "I want my diploma before I join the army."

Several of the pupils were interested in school, however. Gene raised his hand whenever he dared be ridiculed by the rest of the class. His answers, however, showed a lack of understanding, and it was found later that the boy had a sixth-grade reading level. Tanya wanted to go to art school. She took an interest in class when she wasn't speaking to her friend, Lisa, or letting one of the boys copy her homework. Lisa worked hard; she handed in every assignment written out carefully, but often she did the wrong assignment or just copied what she could out of the book. Her weekly quiz papers were almost always failures. Edith worked as a waitress after school.

Mr. Joy, the high school principal, was well aware of the class that had developed in "12 General." "Once that class graduates, we'll be rid of the general classes," he explained. His solution to the problem was not to label any class as a general class; each class would be given a number: 1, 2, or 3, according to ability in either the college-preparatory or business program.

When four of the senior boys in the general group appeared before the principal asking permission to leave school to join the army (having reached enlistment age), Mr. Joy was faced with a difficult situation. None of the teachers would object to the boys' leaving, but the school board had protested at the dropout rate of the school, and particularly of this general class. When the principal explained that the high school had a large number of pupils uninterested in going to school and that perhaps both the pupils and the school would gain from the dismissal, the school board replied: "If the pupils are uninterested and unable to do their work in high school, it is a bad reflection on the competency of the high school teaching and administrative staff. There is a compulsory age set in our state, and it is the duty of every teacher and administrator of the high school to see that the students graduate with a program designed for their individual need, adaptability, and capacity." One member of the school board felt that the high school could operate on a flexible principle in regard to compulsory age: "The school should determine with the individual students their educability, school attitude, and health to see whether they should stay in school."

Mr. Joy knew that the teachers felt that "the students who are preventing others from getting an education should be sorted out." He also knew that the students in question had no desire to be in school and were learning nothing. However, the school board and the superintendent wanted the dropout rate to go down, and they were Joy's superiors. But Joy also felt an obligation to the teachers in his school, and he knew that education would improve if the boys were allowed to leave. They had reached enlistment age but were under the age the state had determined for leaving school. Joy had the right to allow the boys to leave school, but did he want to use it?

SEX AND
THE HIGH SCHOOL GIRL

Mary, a pleasant but not particularly attractive youngster, has started dating a boy from the lower class. You often notice the two together in the halls, and while their conduct cannot be classified as seriously "immoral," it often does not meet up with middle-class standards of desirable behavior. You are certain that Mary's parents would disapprove highly of her dating this boy if they knew about it and, because they are of a very conservative religious background, you believe would be apt to punish her through rigorous curtailment of her social life if they knew she was associating with this boy. If you were Mary's adviser in this situation, what would you do? On what grounds would you do this?

It was great to be hired for that first teaching job, thought Carol Brown. The search for a position after her graduation from the state university had been more difficult and time consuming than she had imagined. Finally, a position opened up at Sun Valley elementary school in the Southwestern city that was her first choice. She accepted the job immediately when the principal called her.

After she arrived in the city, she began to find out more about it. She knew that the area was famous for "sun and fun," but she had not realized that ten percent of the city's population was Mexican-American (Chicano). She was also surprised to find that Sun Valley was located in the lowest socioeconomic area in town. The principal told her nearly half of the students enrolled in Sun Valley were Chicanos.

The principal was reluctant to generalize about the Chicano students. Some were bright and ambitious; others appeared alienated and withdrawn. Many of the students were bilingual and some of the youngsters spoke only Spanish when they arrived at school.

The whites (Anglos) and Chicanos usually stayed with their respective groups, but particularly the boys did intermingle when engaged in sports and games.

The first day of school arrived. Sun Valley was filled to overflowing with active and sometimes noisy boys and girls. Miss Brown had been assigned to a fifth grade class of 35 pupils.

After all the children had been assigned to their seats, Connie raised her hand.

"Yes, Connie?" said Miss Brown. "What is it?"

"May I speak to you, Miss Brown?" The voice was full of portent and the tone asked for privacy, and Miss Brown smiled to herself at the Southwestern mixture of drawl and twang in the girl's voice.

"Yes, of course." Miss Brown beckoned the child to her desk. "Now," she lowered her voice, "what's the trouble?"

Connie leaned closer. "My mother doesn't want me to sit in that seat," she confided.

Miss Brown was puzzled. She hated the rows of double seats bolted to the floor. It left so little opportunity for flexible grouping and cooperative learning. But this was the first day of the new school year, and the children had hardly been in their seats five minutes. What *did* the child mean?

"Why not, Connie? What's the matter with the seat?"

"Well. . . . My mother says they're dirty and I'm not supposed to get too close to them."

Miss Brown looked at Consuelo Lopez, who shared the double seat with Connie. Consuelo looked at the teacher with wonder and a touch of apprehension. She looked around the class. It was clear that many of the students had heard Connie's request and were waiting for the teacher's answer. Miss Brown looked at Connie and asked her to please take her assigned seat for a minute. She had something to say to the class.

1. What would you say to the class?
2. What curricular plans would you try to implement?
3. What seating arrangements might you suggest given the present arrangement?
4. Are there human relations activities which might improve the understanding between the two groups of students? If so, what are they?

TRANSITIONAL PERSPECTIVES

This section of the book focuses on those authors who are concerned with the failure of American education to keep pace with a rapidly changing society. Coppedge documents aspects of our changing value structure and its impact upon education. Jean Grambs deftly describes the enormous forces influencing public education and concludes that the school is not yet ready to build a new social order. Then Ian Wilson offers us the salient features of "The New Reformation," while Gail Inlow boldly sketches a new "Value Synthesis."

Next, our authors delineate many of the contemporary educational practices which are often criticized and also offer some suggestions for change: Peter Wagschal on *relevance,* and James Conway on our *reward system.*

Sidney Simon, *et al.,* discuss our grading and evaluation assumptions and procedures.

Educational change—the possibilities and the probabilities—is featured in the selections by Arthur Pearl and the Shanes. Jack Frymier points out one of the main barriers to change and "Curriculum and Change" provides the impetus for an analysis of the assumptions underlying curriculum.

Finally, attention turns to several of the present issues in the teaching profession such as accountability, teacher supply and demand, and how to teach. Our authors are M. M. Chambers, and Elaine Denholtz.

Dr. Grambs provides us with a compelling analysis of our present society and the inhibiting forces—both within the school and outside the school—which make truly significant educational change very difficult to accomplish. What is the message for you as future educators? Are you capable of becoming a "significant elder"?

FORCES AFFECTING
AMERICAN EDUCATION

Jean Dresden Grambs

The world is too much with us; late and soon,
Getting and spending, we lay waste our powers:
Little we see in Nature that is ours.
                    —William Wordsworth

Wordsworth's description of his world in 1806 is more appropriate to our times than to his, and in ways that are overwhelming, confusing, frightening, and exhiliarating.

The educational enterprise, however perceived, in whatever era or culture, is a process inextricably bound to the past, present, and future of the people who see to it that children are "educated." The child is "educated" by his society as well as by the school.[1] The "brand" of his society is upon him the instant he appears, in the sterile world of the delivery room or in the squalor of a backwoods shack.

The concern about the kind of human being this child will become is the pervasive theme of this yearbook. It would appear, on reading other chapters, that the world, that is indeed too much with us, is not a welcoming, encouraging, or supporting world. It is a world which makes the future of the infant, however or wherever born, one which aware adults view with far more alarm than they view the antics of the current younger generation.

Many observers find in the wave of student protests and the varieties of community confrontations, even those resulting in violence and destruction, some elements of strength.[2] Only when a person can perceive the difference between the ideal and the real, and can know that the ideal is accessible, will he make vigorous efforts to reach the goal. The revolt by students, and the rising militance of teachers and blacks, indicate that persons traditionally perceived as, and perceiving themselves to be, powerless are in fact learning the intoxicating uses of power. Much of the rhetoric of the revolt by students, teachers, and blacks has to do with ideals sought, with sudden awareness of the gap between political and pulpit oratory, and with the mean streets down which one walks.

Yet beyond the positive elements that have produced such interesting phenomena, one may look ahead and see the ominous potential of the counterrevolution. Sowing a few wild oats is permitted each generation; to sow a whole acreage is blasphemy. And

---

Reprinted by permission from Mary-Margaret Scobey and Grace Graham, eds., *To Nurture Humaneness: Commitment for the '70's.* 1970 Yearbook (Washington, D.C.: Assoc. for Supervision and Curriculum Development, 1970), pp. 111-19.
[1]Jean D. Grambs. *Schools, Scholars, and Society.* Englewood Cliffs, New Jersey: Prentice-Hall, Inc., 1965. Chapter 3, "Society as Education."
[2]"Stirrings out of Apathy: Student Activism and the Decade of Protest." Whole issue, *Journal of Social Issues* 23: 1-137; July 1967.

blasphemy, like witchcraft, must be hunted out and destroyed by any and every means.

The major force impeding the realization of the humane person in tomorrow's world is that the humanity called for has never been very popular. In fact, the person with true charity, guided by deep regard for his fellow man, creative in using his abilities, is, at most, crucified, at least looked upon as immoral, insane, or stupid.

There is, indeed, a very old-fashioned flavor about the kind of humane person described in previous chapters of this yearbook. Thoreau would find him companionable. So would Bronson Alcott, and even Jesus Christ. The difficulty is that such humanity—old-fashioned or not—is on the defensive for even minimal survival.

Item: the more we find out about the hidden springs of human motivation, the more insistent are groups that this knowledge is subversive or subverting. Recently I received an urgent message to get in touch with a curriculum coordinator in a nearby suburban county. She was in a meeting when I returned her call, but evidently the problem was sufficiently crucial that she left her meeting to talk with me.

"We are introducing a new family life-sex education program in our county," she said. "Part of the training program for the teachers and others includes some use of sensitivity training." Now that the training program was completed and the program about to be instituted in the schools, the county was being swept by rumors of subversive activities. It seems that sensitivity training had been labeled as a dangerous and probably communist-inspired procedure. This kind of sensitivity training, according to an ominous rumor, involved the participants in licentious interaction. Her problem: how does one counter such rumors? Where is a good source for a professional description of sensitivity training as used in family life-sex education programs?

Although this particular version of the attacks on sex education was new to me, I had seen several news items over the past months indicating that the John Birch Society had publicly labeled sex education as subversive. The latest *NEA Reporter* at hand stated that:

> Attacks by extremist organizations on family life and sex education courses are disrupting the schools and educational climate today in at least two dozen states. The usual extremist tactics of abusive phone calls to school boards and school personnel and of factually inaccurate and sensational material flooding the community are being employed to condemn family life and sex education courses.
>
> The John Birch Society and the Christian Crusade are cooperating in this attack by distributing anti-family life material through front groups, supporting ill-conceived court cases against school boards, and lobbying to influence state legislatures to pass laws prohibiting sex education in the schools.[3]

After talking with my friend, I called the National Training Laboratory office at the NEA and talked with a director. He was not surprised by my report, but told me that in response to similar requests NTL at that moment was preparing several statements to clarify the professional training which they, and similar groups, sponsor.

The preceding account is given in detail because it exemplifies the quandary of American education. The observer of the educational scene will, however, find little that is new. The quandary itself is as old as education: remember Socrates? Education designed as a liberating and humanizing force is, in nearly all cultures in nearly all eras, always a threat to the status quo.

The dilemma today can hardly be considered much different from previous crises (Who remembers Zoll? the Pasadena Story?[4] the Levittown uproar over "The Lone-

---

[3] *NEA Reporter,* No. 8, April 25, 1969.
[4] David Hulburd. *This Happened in Pasadena.* New York: The Macmillan Company, 1951.

some Train"?[5]   What happened to the Progressive Education Association?[6]).   The difference is that the reach of educational revolution, and the impact of the counterrevolution, are being felt in more areas, in more school systems, and by as wide a public as tunes in on the late news on TV. In reviewing a well named book, *Teaching as a Subversive Activity,*[7]   Peter Schrag says, "Good teaching should, needless to say, always be subversive. But can any society really honor, or even tolerate it?"[8]

STRUGGLE OF THE TWO CULTURES

The major pressure on education today, as always, is the omnipresent one of tradition, reaction, conservatism, and established interests. The struggle is one between the unchanging folk society and the rush of change precipitated by a technological society. All of us are schizoid in this regard. We are, perhaps, not sufficiently used to the culture of civilization to be completely at ease with the constancy of change. All of us are ambivalent when we see old mansions torn down for new freeways, rolling hills turned into suburban bedroom communities.[9]

At the same time we are revolted by the disintegration of the inner city and the destruction of humane values by a calculator system that appears to trap millions into a generational cycle of poverty, despair, and destruction. Is it worth preserving the old mansion if the new freeway will provide access to jobs in suburbia for the inner-city resident who cannot get out now? Is it worth millions to capture a Rembrandt for the local art gallery when inner-city library hours are curtailed for lack of funds?[10]

The response to education as dangerous runs the gamut from Birch Society protests about sex education to allocation of funds which effectually perpetuate inequality in educational services.[11]   Against these external threats to the kind of education conceptualized in other chapters of this book, the educator finds no simple answer.

Educators unfortunately are products of the same system; in fact, if they have become supervisors or curriculum coordinators, it is because they have not been too aggressively at war with the system and therefore are "safe enough" to be promoted within the system. I would strongly suspect that secretly many of the educators in that county with the problem of "subversive" sensitivity training would agree that these modern techniques are probably suspect. Educators have always been suspicious of psychology,[12]   and the story of education is a story of the warring of generations.[13]   So the enemy is not necessarily outside education; the external forces which pressure education often find a warm welcome within the classrooms and offices of the "establishment."

When the pressure upon education from outside is met by capitulation within, one should not be surprised. Typical response to attack, threat, pressure, is to become

[5]Joseph E. Maloney. *"The Lonesome Train" in Levittown.* Inter-University Case Program #39. University: University of Alabama Press, 1958.

[6]Lawrence A. Cremin. *The Transformation of the School: Progressivism in American Education, 1876-1957.* New York: Alfred A. Knopf, Inc., 1961.

[7]Neil Postman and Charles Weingartner. *Teaching as a Subversive Activity.* New York: Delacorte Press, 1969.

[8]Peter Schrag. "Can the Traditional Classroom Survive in Today's School System? A review of *Teaching as a Subversive Activity." New York Times Book Review,* May 11, 1969. p. 22.

[9]Gene Marine. *America the Raped.* New York: Simon & Schuster, Inc., 1969.

[10]Mary Beasterd. "It's Your Library and Its in Trouble." *The Village Voice,* May 8, 1969. p. 12.

[11]Donald W. Whisenhunt. "No Easy Course to Equality." *Civil Rights Digest* 2: 44-47; Winter 1969.

[12]Roger G. Barker. "Difficulties of Communication Between Educators and Psychologists: Some Speculations." *Journal of Educational Psychology* 33: 416-26; September 1942.

[13]Willard Waller. *The Sociology of Education.* New York: John Wiley & Sons, Inc., 1932.

defensive and even more protective of the status quo than before, or to join the attackers. Since educators are made from the same mold as those they educate, the charge of their being "gutless" educators is often founded in fact. Many educators on the whole want "law 'n' order," just as much as do the Friends of the FBI. Educators are just as driven to rage by four letters words, by miniskirts, and by long hair as any man in blue. One principal, who is well respected for supporting teachers who experiment with the curriculum or indulge in minor intellectual eccentricities, begged his faculty: "I'll give you almost anything you want in supporting educational change, if you in return will just give me support for our dress code which prescribes decent skirts and proper haircuts." A junior high school administrator capitulated to student demands for changes in dress to the point of allowing boys to wear tennis shoes "if the shoe strings were of matching color."

The question is not so much, then, what external forces impinge upon the realization of humane education, but why is there so little dissonance between those "outside" and those "inside" the system.

In surveying the proliferation of materials analyzing the current educational ferment, one may ponder a recent article by Edgar Z. Friedenberg.[14] He states:

What seems to be the hardest today for young radicals to face, in their conviction that authority has become illegitimate, is the implication that the source of the illegitimacy is the American democratic process itself. It is one thing to assert that "the system" is corrupt . . . It is another, and more difficult for a radical American, to grant that what is wrong with America may be characteristic of mass democracy itself.

Democracy legitimizes the will of the people, and finally, after decades of evolution, "the people" are being heard. The people are conservative, suspicious, half-educated, provincial, scared, and insecure. They teeter on the economic edge of the upper lower class or lower middle class, dimly aware that whatever economic security they do have rests on the fantastic pursuit of an indefensible war and an arms race against a faceless but clever communist conspiracy.

As Friedenberg points out:

In a society as open, invidious and competitive as ours, the kinds of people who succeed are usually incapable of responding to human demands; and the political power of the masses is used merely to express the hatreds and the envy, and to destroy anything that looks like genuine human satisfaction, especially among the more vulnerable members of higher social classes. Higher status youth . . . have become the chief target of the working-class sense of outrage and defeat. It is difficult for white, middle-class parents to imagine . . . the degree of harassment to which their adolescent children are subjected by hostile and vigilant school authorities, and by police. . . .[15]

In the words of a *New York Times* editorial, commenting on the latest reaction to student violence:

The reform of the campus requires not mindless cheering squads for real or alleged reforms in the wake of disruption, but a reaffirmation by the great mass of moderate faculty and students of the rule of reason and law. Blind attacks on the administrations can only have one effect—to make the radicals' caricature of the establishment self-fulfilling prophecy.[16]

---

[14]Edgar Z. Friedenberg. "The Revolt Against Democracy." *Change* 1:11-17; May-June 1969.
[15]*Ibid.*
[16]*New York Times* editorial, "Crisis Management on Campus." May 11, 1969.

The convergence upon old and young alike of unprecedented affluence and the continued and corrosive insecurity about the future bring out the latent paranoia in all of us. It is this mindless force which makes it possible for the true paranoid to turn a country, or a campus, upside down. Bettelheim sounds a warning:

The proportion of paranoids among students is no greater than in any comparable group of the population. But they are more dangerous because of their high intelligence, which permits them to conceal more successfully the degree of their disturbance. And student revolt permits them to act out their paranoia to a degree that no other position in society permits. How understandable, then, that all paranoids who can, do flock into the ranks of the militants. Unfortunately, most non-experts do not know how persuasive paranoids can be, at least until they are recognized. The persuasiveness of a Hitler or a Stalin is now regarded as the consequence of his own paranoia and his unconscious appeal to the vague paranoid tendencies among the immature and disgruntled. I have no doubt that the ranks of today's militants contain some would-be Hitlers and Stalins.[17]

It is this same mindless force of hatred and mistrust which permits policemen to become senselessly brutal in their response to middle and upper class student activists, and to become incensed by black militants to the point of murder.

The paradox, however, must again be stated: all of these forces which impel riots and disorders, which provide a backdrop of support of repressive measures for protesters, or even entrap otherwise rational citizens into believing that sensitivity training is subversive; all of these elements are echoed by school personnel in one guise or another. The external forces, if there be any, are mirror images of what is, in fact, the pervasive message of the typical school. Russian schools, we are told, produce conforming communist citizens because the out-of-school world is consistent with what the school teaches.

The situation in the United States is not as different as idealistic educators would like to think. Within the classrooms of our schools, cheating is rewarded, material gains (grades) are superior to spiritual ones (learning); lack of conformity is persecuted if found among teachers, students, or even administrators; and those who have the least, get the least—just as in the world outside, or the world of TV. The difference is hardly as great as we would wish. And the phoniness and superficiality in the world of the school are just as apparent as in the fantasy world of the television drama.

In school, children are taught about equality; they repeat daily a pledge which states without ambiguity that this is a nation dedicated to equality. Then in everyday rituals in every class session they observe how inequality is in fact the basis of school operation. The obedient bright get the best grades; the rich get the school offices; the blacks are expected to fail and do[18]; passive girls do better than boys with initiative and inventiveness.

On TV they constantly see violence in every form; they are told that if they use a special lotion, deodorant, toothpaste, or cigarette, the world of youth, loveliness, and, by implication, satisfying sexual orgasms may be theirs. Children, youth, and adults thus learn over and over again that school is no more real than television, that no one is worthy of their trust, that no one is really lovable, that there is no future, and that they are powerless.

---

[17]Bruno Bettelheim. "The Anatomy of Academic Discontent." *Change* 1: 18-26, May-June 1969.
[18]William H. Grier and Price M. Cobbs. *Black Rage.* New York: Basic Books, Inc., 1968. Chapter 7, "The 'Promise' of Education."

The alienation of bright youth described by Keniston[19] is one symptom. Then one turns to the picture painted by Liebow in *Tally's Corner.*[20] If these seemingly drifting and rootless men appear to be present-oriented, it is, as Liebow states, that they are "'present-time oriented' ... precisely because [they are] aware of the future and the hopelessness of it all." And finally we come to the kind of response to the exercise of power which is expressed in a vote against fluoridation. Reviewing the study by Robert L. Crain *et al., The Politics of Community Conflict: The Fluoridation Decision,*[21] Seeman states that what appears to be a rather mindless response to "alienation" may in fact be a response to a particular kind of political climate relative to our concept of participatory democracy[22] —the same kind of response which tends to bring out "no" votes in school bond campaigns when there is a real effort to get out the vote.[23] The sum of these varying views of our society reveals more about the problem than we perhaps can afford to know.

The child can only become what his society will encourage and reward him for becoming. As Jacobs so well states in anthropological perspective:

... a child must and can internalize only what its significant elders possess. ... A culture perpetuates much of its adults' immaturity from generation to generation. Only those youngsters break the net of significant elders when new and equally significant elders appear. Here is the unique opportunity of a mature and sophisticated teacher. He has at least a chance of taking 20 or 30 partially developed little personalities and bringing them forward in spite of built-in limitations in their parents and other close kin. ...

Again, when teachers' personalities are hardly richer or more mature than the kin, youngsters are trapped. There are now no distinctive elders with whom they may identify: teachers only reinforce the internalization of views and values which commenced with kin. Much of the population of western civilization is caught in such a web.[24]

School—education—in the context of today appears at the worst to be a production line for violent or alienated persons, or, at the least, an irrelevant factor in the processing of the coming generations.

The humane person so ardently espoused by other authors of this yearbook would find no haven in the typical school, were he bold enough to try to be a teacher, supervisor, curriculum coordinator, or administrator.[25] He would have a tenuous place in a college or university if he had the wherewithal to survive the gamut of graduate degrees. What is outside the school is within the school; what is phony, degrading, disorganizing, and dishonest in the outside world is reinforced, with punishment, within the school. The answer to the question George S. Counts asked in 1932, *Dare the School Build a New Social Order?* is still, "no."

---

[19]Kenneth Keniston. *The Uncommitted: Alienated Youth in American Society.* New York: Harcourt, Brace & World, Inc., 1965.
[20]Elliott Liebow. *Tally's Corner: A Study of Negro Streetcorner Men.* Boston: Little, Brown and Company, 1967.
[21]Robert L. Crain *et al. The Politics of Community Conflict.* Indianapolis, Indiana: Bobbs-Merrill Company, Inc., 1969.
[22]Melvin Seeman. "The Alienation Hypothesis." *Psychiatry and Social Science Review* 3: 2-6; April 1969.
[23]Richard F. Carter and William C. Savard. *Influence of Voter Turnout on School Bond and Tax Elections.* Cooperative Research Monograph #5, U.S. Department of Health, Education, and Welfare. Washington, D.C.: Superintendent of Documents, Government Printing Office, 1961.
[24]Melville Jacobs. *Pattern in Cultural Anthropology.* Homewood, Illinois: Dorsey Press, Inc., 1964. p. 146. See also: Richard Hofstadter. *Anti-Intellectualism in American Life.* New York: Alfred A. Knopf, Inc., 1963.
[25]Neal Gross and Robert E. Herriott, *Staff Leadership in Public Schools: A Sociological Inquiry.* New York: John Wiley & Sons, Inc., 1965.

In this selection, the author views today's militant young people as the revolutionaries who are promoting sweeping value changes in the next few years. Do you see yourself as a revolutionary? Do you agree with the author's characterization of the values that are emerging? If so, what do these values imply for education? Do you agree with the author's two major implications, relevance and the importance of the affective, noncognitive domains?

WHAT THE WORLD IS COMING TO

Walter R. Coppedge

In the lifetime of the middle-aged and older, the ability to remember Pearl Harbor has provided a continental divide for the twentieth century. Those too young or unborn then were casualties of history, without the peculiar historical consciousness of my age group. "Over 30" really means that one remembers Pearl Harbor; under 30, one doesn't and one refuses to make many of the quarrels of parents the cause of youth.

Last year a very significant thing happened. The Apollo 11 moon-shot voyage made 1969 a major reference point in history, like 44 B.C., 1066, 1492, and 1776. The voyage of Columbus divided the Middle Ages from modern times; 1969 will separate terrestrial man from space man, earth history from cosmic history.

This extraordinary feat symbolizes aptly and dramatically what is now commonly acknowledged to be a revolutionary age, for the change this century has experienced and is yet to witness must be considered exponential. The foundations of Western culture were severely shaken by two world wars; the Scopes trial and the diffusion of Freudian investigation destroyed for modern man the authority of the past. The seamless cloak of Western culture is now a crazy patchwork quilt which existential man gathers about his nakedness.

In our time there have been the political revolutions of the Soviet Union, Southeast Asia, Latin America, and China. But in a very real sense today in Western Europe and the United States, the most dramatic revolutionaries are not necessarily political, they are cultural. They are in our colleges and high schools.

"Revolution" in this sense means a profound shift in the values of a society as it undergoes basic economic and cultural changes. The militant young, perhaps a statistically inaccessible minority, have been an advance guard; they have signaled in the fashions, styles, and politics the radicalness of the change. As in most revolutions, the authorities are confused as to the meaning of events around them and are unsure of their own values. These uncertain attitudes have created permissive concessionism and ambiguities in ruling or administering, thus enabling the exploitation of a revolutionary situation.

About this revolution—in which only a tiny fraction are political revolutionaries—there are some interesting generalizations I will audaciously offer:

Today, as in no other time, the young are their own model. The rites of passage with which we are most familiar—the donning of togas, ordeals of pain, presentation at deb parties—have no modern symbolic equivalent, since the young do not aspire to (and perhaps even condemn) the sense of experience of the older generation.

Reprinted by permission from Walter R. Coppedge, "What the World Is Coming to," *Phi Delta Kappan* 52 (October 1970): 75-78.

Manifesting such sincere and remarkable indifference and equipped with a brash and unreflecting confidence, the young are now in a position (particularly since the Sixties) to impose their own styles on the older generation so that the pattern is reversed: The old aspire to be like the young and the ambivalence of older generation values is heightened.

A few examples will instance this obvious truth. Mini-skirts, sideburns, and mod clothes are directly the result of the Beatles phenomenon—all fashions introduced by the young and now adopted by the middle-aged (or "wrinklies," as over-thirties are sometimes known). Popular music is now largely dominated by the beat Elvis and the Beatles introduced to a very unappreciative older generation just a few years ago. The dance form now dominant is the tribal gyration which "wrinklies" watched uncomprehendingly in 1960; tangoes, waltzes, rhumbas, and the sedate fox-trot are relegated to the discarded heap of minuets, lavoltas, and fandangoes. Our language has been similarly affected by the laconic simplicities of the younger style, whose idiom has derived from music ("groovy") and drugs ("hippy").

Given the lack of aspiration for such middle-class American staples as a mortgage on a home in Meadowfarm Estates, 36-month payments on a Buick, and a membership in Kiwanis, it is no wonder that there is increasing dissatisfaction with more substantial symbols of bourgeois America: capitalism or "plastics!" (the advice encapsulating the system which Benjamin rejects in the 1968 film *The Graduate*). The flag now becomes a symbol of conscription as well as "imperialist aggression"; conventional manners are thought to mask insincerely the real indifference we feel toward one another as well as to camouflage racial hostility; traditional institutions like the church have seemed increasingly irrelevant and irritatingly hypocritical. (Benjamin, again in *The Graduate,* rescues his girl from a meaningless marriage and bars the narthex door with a cross to lock up the enraged congregation.) At the university, the assault on American and Western culture has been frontal. Perpetuating both the technocracy which enables capitalism to flourish and the traditional liberal and humanitarian values, the university is our most revered American institution, our most sacred intellectual refuge. To defecate in Grayson Kirk's wastebasket is to commit the ultimate secular blasphemy. That action summarizes all the gross-outs, obscenities, and contempt for the establishment which student radicalism has displayed from the days of the Free Speech Movement at Berkeley in 1964 to the takeover at Cornell in April of 1969.

The sense of past—never truly apprehended by a generation which has learned far more from television than from books—is superseded by the urgency of the present. Whether the problem is black separatism or Vietnamese withdrawal, the young are involved *now* in problems for which they want immediate answers. Involvement is the issue in two recent movies which portray the ethos of the young. The city discovered by the "Midnight Cowboy" in the film of that name is a viciously competitive sexual and economic jungle which produces such symbolic cripples as Ratso. In *Medium Cool* (a richly ironic title), the message is even clearer: We live in a land of violence, and we who ignore the confrontations we must daily encounter—the simple ones of human need and suffering as well as the more complex issues of politics and race—we who ignore these problems do so by a slow hardening of the heart, by the atrophying of concern, by purchasing detachment with the coin of indifference.

History appears to have little relevance for so romantic and visceral a generation. What is real and immediate is sensation and its quest, as evidenced in underground movies, drugs, op art, and rock music. Blowing one's mind—i.e., experiencing a nonrational emotional high—is desirable. Fueled by adrenalin, militants from Paris to Tokyo, Stockholm to Mexico, have stormed the university, saying that they want to make life new, that they want Revolution. (There was an extraordinary appositeness in a wall slogan during the May riots in Paris: "The more I make revolution, the more I want to make love; the more I want to make love, the more I want to make revolution." Such a graffito epitomizes the emotional intoxication of making common cause in revolt.)

Perhaps the most salient phenomenon of the youth is the uniqueness of their communication. Although the underground press in the United States claims a readership of over 600,000, the written word is not the primary vehicle by which the young express themselves to one another. Mammoth youth assemblies are something history has not seen since the Children's Crusade. The Washington moratorium drew 250,000, but the Woodstock music festival attracted 300,000 young people who, in the midst of squalor and rain, generously shared their food and drink and displayed a kindly affection to outsiders which amazed the local constabulary. Rock music is indeed a prime vehicle for wordless but powerful transmission of feeling and attitude. This most interesting form of music in 50 years has been virtually ignored by the university.

Perhaps because in the past a sensitive exchange of viewpoints between the young and the establishment has not been possible, the violent communication of the platform take-over has become almost a pattern on the national scene; let us only cite radical action in the last two years among such diverse but august groups as the American Medical Association, the American Bar Association, the National Conference on Social Welfare, the American Political Science Association, and even the Modern Language Association. The young who seize the microphone may not have all the ideas, but they do have ideas—fresh, inventive, fertile, challenging ideas which are energizing and often redirecting the social purposes of these professional groups. If the group is not responsive, a splinter group of the young is formed; thus the Free University became for a while a free-wheeling splinter institution whose existence radically criticized what went on in the halls of academe.

Nowhere is the impact of the young on American society more serious than in advertising, where the old "reason why" ad has been replaced by an unconventional, whimsical, or shocking presentation. One observer of the trade noted that at the age of 33 a man may be getting a little senior, and employers favor a man in his early twenties to one nearing the magical dividing line. If advertising is a direct agent of change in society, then we would do well to contemplate the awesome power for changing our lives possessed by the under-thirties. A glance at the language of the young will also show the difference: It is desirable to be "loose," because the loose are not rigid or "hung-up" like the old. "It" means action of all kinds, commercial or artistic, although the word "action" originally described easy but interesting sexual activity; hence in recent slang it was very important to be "where it's at" or to be "with it."

These changes have two principal implications for education. The first is a word so familiar as to have become cant in educationese: relevance.

Too often in the past we have insisted on *instruction* rather than *education,* on that mode of teaching which piles up facts (the root meaning of the Latin *in + struere*) instead of that which educes or draws forth, brings out, develops from a latent condition. We have expected the student to extract from a mass of unrelated materials, called a curriculum, something which he will find pertinent to the pursuit of life or a livelihood. In college the student must reach the level of the instructor or fail, fall in that race course, originally called the Circus Maximus, from which the word *curriculum* derives. In the future, it will be increasingly the business of the educator to begin with the experience of the student, to reach down to his level so that curiosity is teased, provoked, stimulated, engaged to build and proliferate.

No one of course has ever proposed an irrelevant education, relevance being entirely subjective. But we teach ancient history as if it *were* irrelevant, Latin as if it were dead. The fact is that a study of Periclean Athens has quite a lot to say about the urban crisis in the second half of the twentieth century, and some knowledge of Latin is of immense value in equipping the student with the ability to manipulate symbols which we call verbal skill. If we really knew Thucydides, as Henry Steele Commager observed last November, we would never have engaged in the Peloponnesian War we call Vietnam. For the educator, the principle should be clear: begin with what *interests* the student, moving from the specific to the general. Sylvia Ashton Warner found that she could not teach Maori children about life in an English village, but she could open their minds to reading by building on such emotive words as *knife, kiss, cold, volcano, blood.* Similarly every student wants to know about love, sex, war, and so on—for these forces touch his life.

A student unable to master the intricacies of Galbraith or Adam Smith might nevertheless come to an understanding of the complexity of the marketplace if he can observe what happens in the department store or filling station where he works. I have found my own imagination taxed in attempting to answer my six-year-old's extraordinarily interesting questions: What is fire? Why are there burglars? The able teacher could develop mini-courses, for questions such as these, intelligently and sensitively answered, produce precisely that multiplier effect which Rousseau noted in his *Émile* 200 years ago.

We don't acquire our really important learning in packages. As interested explorers we are not concerned about boundaries which mark those august empire states called disciplines—separating literature from history, sociology from psychology, chemistry from biology and so on. But as educators we begin to be concerned about passports, visas, and entry and exit permits, failing to realize that the student wants to explore life in its mysterious wholeness, rather than in the exclusive little principalities of subject areas.

The second quality we must recover in education is the sense of mystery: of selves and worlds not palpable to the cognitive mode. We are concerned with life, we say. Therefore we organize the study of biology, but somehow we never apprehend the miracle of motion when we dissect a frog, or the truth of a flower when we count stamens and pistils. We talk about the spiral nebulae but how seldom do we, as Whitman suggested, look up "in perfect silence at the stars."

We teach as if the only realities were those captured at two removes in those rivers of ink which are words. We ignore the psycho-physical relationship of mind and body, feeling and language.

We teach children to add, but we are indifferent to whether or not they can smell. We are concerned that they discriminate between red and green but we are oblivious to their sense of the tactile differences in stones, woods, fabrics, and metals. We care about their distinction of some kinds of sound, but we care nothing about whether they know by taste a kumquat from a cantaloupe. These immemorial modes of knowing are atrophying under our overwhelmingly verbal educational system. The off-Broadway youth musical *Salvation* is fascinatingly corroborative of this indictment: Two song titles, "Let's Get Lost in Now" and "Tomorrow Is the First Day of the Rest of My Life," reveal the sensory significance of the present.

Our system is also overwhelmingly rational and cognitive, and in the last few decades it has either ignored or sacrificed the intuitive or affective. That kind of teaching which advocates dispassion, disinterest, and detachment is disastrous to a generation calling for commitment. The analytical professor will not speak to this generation who are crying for professors who profess.

Disenchantment with siccative rationalism, with that settled lowest common denominator of experience called common sense, manifests itself in the pursuit of the occult. Free Universities across the nation sponsor classes in Eastern thought; the ancient Chinese book of fortune-telling, the *I-Ching,* has become a best seller on progressive college campuses. Psychedelic paraphernalia —black light posters, incense, Oriental art—are obvious household equipment throughout student apartments. The intense interest in astrology epitomizes the fascination with the occult.

It is pertinent to remark here the enthusiasm for nature observable in the hippie communes of the West and New England. Young people may be smoking pot but they are also making bread, perhaps coarse and lumpy, but certainly unlike the styrofoam product we settle for in supermarkets. For adolescents, camp directors have noted the new enthusiasm for really primitive camps with tents set in bare fields and food foraged in the wilderness.

The sense of the mystery of life will perhaps never come to us as educators until we develop what Wordsworth called a "wise passiveness"—that gift which Blake suggested enables the untutored child and the mystic

> To see a world in a grain of sand
> And a heaven in a wild flower,
> Hold infinity in the palm of your hand
> And eternity in an hour.

Any retrospect of the Sixties must convince us that the younger generation (and here again I mean the cadre of the committed fringe) have richly contributed to American life. Substantial gains in civil rights, a new dynamism to American culture, the general liberation of films, new explorations in the arts, an increasing relevance and vitality in college curricula, growing dissatisfaction with the multitudinous hypocrisies of our lives, and the slow and painful reappraisal of our national values—these contributions have been real and positive. But the momentum of change is producing a period of crisis. To be sure, our lives continue in comfortably familiar routines. But we are living in a time of storm, and the beleaguered crew is required continually to jettison cargo. Only those articles will be retained to which we assign high value.

Among the things which are to go, I suspect, will be Junior-League Georgian suburbs and Eisenhower-ranch houses; big cars and combustion engines; billboards and main streets of Hardees and used car lots; Mantovani music and furniture reproductions; nondisposable beer cans and bottles; J. Edgar Hoover and the Mafia; the inanities of situation comedy on commercial TV; DDT, of course; prohibitions against birth control as well as against death control; religious fundamentalism of all kinds and much of established institutional Christianity as we now know it. People will be educated to think ecologically—to realize that one man's waste is literally another man's poison— and to think systematically so there will be decreasing distinction between public and private sectors. Sexual practices will become far more permissive and more and more people will question the value of the family unit. The examples of Sweden and England indicate that unmarried motherhood will become acceptable in most communities. Society will find a more efficient mind-transformer than alcohol. If no better substitute than marijuana is invented or discovered, it will become the favored mode of social intercourse.

As for education, if we can accept my notion that relevance requires our reaching down to the experience of the student, then the relevant school of the future will minimize the self-contained classroom. Talking to the young today means addressing them as individuals. The teacher will become increasingly democratic, recognizing that in education as in ethics the means shape the ends. The teacher will be reaching out to the students, increasingly using not the school so much as the city for primary learning resources.

A Unitarian seminary now in New York may point the pattern. Eschewing survey courses, classroom lectures, examination cramming, and the whole system of degrees and credits, the faculty instead are directing their students to live, work, and study in the city, developing specializations such as the dance for public worship, Oriental religions, poverty programs, or drug and alcohol therapy. Independent study through the study of great books—with supplemental learning in tutorials and seminars—forms the basis of an approach which internalizes learning and converts it to principle, insuring an enduring relevance to the whole educational process.

What I have attempted to do is to provide evidence for the assertion that we are living in a revolution, by which is meant a time of radical change. In times when we are no longer sure of anything, we must, privately and socially, create our own values and observe them lest we betray ourselves.

In the context of the new age signaled by the moonshot, why—once we grasp its awesomeness—should we continue the murderous struggles between Catholics and Protestants in Ireland, between Walloon and Fleming in Belgium, between Arab and Jew in Palestine, between Ibo and Yoruba in Nigeria? How long can human beings with a cosmic consciousness permit racism, whether in South Africa or South Carolina? Or in the subjugation of peoples in Czechoslovakia or Tibet?

In 1928, Yeats predicted that this civilization would be coming to a close, and a new man of a higher spiritual consciousness would displace the earth man of materialistic interests and absorptions. I find such a vatic prophecy interesting now. Arnold's lines about "wandering between two worlds, the one dead, and the other powerless to be born" no longer have the meaning today which gave them relevance before 1960.

For something *is* born, and there is a promise of what the new generation can offer, a promise poetically and sensuously adumbrated in the lyrics of the lead song in *Hair:*

> Harmony and understanding
> Sympathy and trust abounding
> No more falsehoods or derisions;
> Golden living dreams of visions
> Mystic crystal revelation
> And the mind's true liberation
> Aquarius
> Aquarius
> Aquarius. . . .

Ian Wilson, Oxford-bred observer of American life, offers some attitudinal and value shifts which he believes we should prepare for. Do you agree with his views? Can you give examples of these attitudinal shifts and of the reordering of our values which he cites? Would you anticipate serious conflicts and confrontations over the adoption of such a radically different value system?

THE NEW REFORMATION

Ian H. Wilson

We find ourselves today at the opening of a New Reformation—a major re-formation or re-ordering of our public and private value systems. Powered by the forces of affluence, education and technology, and forged in the crucible of our tense and changing times, this values reformation—perhaps more than any economic or technical change—is becoming perhaps the most distinctive, certainly the most pervasive, feature of the newly emerging "post-industrial society."

For society as a whole, a major implication of these trends is that the Seventies will be a decade of questioning, uncertainty, potential turmoil and confrontation. There will be substantial restructuring of many institutions; an effort to rethink their social purpose and objectives and reshape their operations and relationships, both internal and external. For business in particular, there will be the need to face up to the consequences of real questioning, challenge and modification of many basic business concepts—growth, technology, efficiency, profit, work, the legitimacy and authority of management.

It is important to stress at the outset, first, that we are not talking about "new" values, but rather about a restructuring of values systems; second, that we should not associate this movement merely with the new college generation, though they may be its cutting edge, but rather with a broader societal thrust.

QUALITATIVE RATHER THAN QUANTITATIVE WILL BE STRESSED

It would, indeed, be remarkable if after many millenia on this earth, mankind had discovered a new value. The more modest, but still revolutionary, assertion that we are moving toward a greater stress on the qualitative, rather than the purely quantitative, aspects of our economy and society reflects the developing picture more accurately.

Then, too, this movement is not limited to college students; nor are college students a monolithic body, with identical values, attitudes and opinions. It remains a fact, however, that it was the emergence of the "post-war generation" (the babies of 1946-49) on campus—a generation large in numbers, and significantly different in values—that brought into unified focus, in conspicuous locations, many of the diverse issues and problems of the Sixties.

There can be no doubt that the escalation of the Vietnam War, the urban explosions of minority groups and student unrest, were the events that catalyzed the turmoil,

Reprinted by permission from Ian H. Wilson, "The New Reformation," *The Futurist* 5 (June 1971): 105-8. *The Futurist* is published by the World Future Society, P.O. Box 30369, Bethesda Station, Washington, D.C. 20014.

doubts, and polarization of the late Sixties. The outbreaks in the cities and on the campuses might be interpreted as continuations of slowly growing disaffection—in one case, with progress toward integration and the elimination of poverty; in the other, with authoritarian structures and "irrelevant" education—that suddenly accelerated into an explosive burst. In varying degrees, both were sparked by, and focussed attention on, major discrepancies between the American ideal and present-day realities—equality, individual dignity, the "melting pot," brotherhood, "alabaster cities."

Minorities and youth might, therefore, be said to have started a major re-examination of social and individual values, even beyond the specific issues and demands of their causes. Thus, the minority rights movement, by focussing on the issue of inequalities, has opened the way for, and lent momentum to, the women's rights movement (though the two may clash at particular points). The riots have also finally riveted public attention on the general deterioration of urban living (for whites as well as blacks), and so been responsible for the initial escalation of efforts at urban renewal. And the youth movement, by focussing on the issues of materialism and individual choice, has led to some major questioning about the adequacy of the provisions made by "the system" (political, educational, business, etc.) for individual rights and choice.

SOCIETY BEGINS TO RECOGNIZE ITS LIMITATIONS

Though it is an undoubted oversimplification, there is some justification for seeing the mood of the late Sixties as setting the stage for new goals and new policies based on a recognition of current societal limitations:

The limitations of power: both of U.S. nuclear power in policing the world, and of domestic authority in preserving "law and order";

The limitations of affluence: in personal terms, awareness of the impact of inflation and (among some) a disenchantment with materialistic satisfactions; in public terms, a recognition that even an affluent society cannot afford "guns and butter," but has to make critical choices among national goals;

The limitations of technology: doubts about the benefits of unrestricted technological development, with its potential for social instability and environmental damage;

The limitations of our infrastructure: an awareness that a problem which had been supposed to be limited to underdeveloped countries also applied to the U.S.;

The limitations on equality: a broader recognition of the extent to which large segments of our population—women and nonwhites—did not enjoy true equality of opportunity;

The limitations on individualism: a questioning of whether there is an equitable "trade-off" between individual rights and institutional needs, and of whether organizations truly serve human needs;

The limitations of "the old values," or more accurately of the sincerity and adequacy of individual and social *performance* against these basic values.

For the future we may safely conjecture that the new challenge to our national will is in the qualitative sector of public expectations. It is not much of an exaggeration to say that we have largely solved the quantitative problems of our society. Two years ago *The Economist* of London put it this way:

"The United States in this last third of the twentieth century is the place where man's long economic problem is ending, but where his social problems still gape. On any rational view, the enormous fact of that approach to economic consummation should rivet all attention. It is almost certainly the most momentous news story so far in the history of the world. But people in the United States are at present wracked by the stretching to snapping point of too many of their temporary social tensions, so that this society which represents man's greatest secular achievement sometimes seems to be on the edge of a national nervous breakdown."

(The article, incidentally, was entitled "The Neurotic Trillionaire.")

POPULAR ATTITUDES WILL SHIFT

It is because of this probable future emphasis on quality that we, as futurists, need to be more keenly sensitive to social forces, and in particular to the attitudinal shifts of our population. It is these less tangible, more subtle forces that may work greater changes in our society than will the more obvious physical changes that we can expect. Some of the attitudinal shifts that we should prepare for are:

An emphasis on the "quality of life," from the quality of products to the quality of our environment;

Some modifications of the old Puritan work ethic, and a growing belief that leisure is a valid activity in its own right;

A new "self-image" that a rising level of education bestows on its graduates;

A rejection of authoritarianism as an acceptable style;

A growing belief in the values of pluralism, decentralization, participation, involvement;

A heightened respect for individual conscience and dignity;

An increased public impatience, a "lower frustration tolerance," with many forms of economic hardship (such as poverty and unemployment), and with social injustice in all its forms.

In sum, these (and other) changes would quite radically reorder our public and private values. Particularly among the young and the better-educated, we are likely to see a shift in emphasis:

From considerations of quantity ("more"), toward considerations of quality ("better");

From the concept of independence, toward the concept of interdependence;

From the satisfaction of private material needs, toward meeting public needs;

From the primacy of technical efficiency, toward considerations of social justice and equity;

From the dictates of organizational convenience, toward the aspirations of self-development of an organization's members;

From authoritarianism, toward participation;

From uniformity and centralization, toward pluralism and diversity;

From preservation of the systems' status quo and routine, toward promotion and acceptance of change.

What we are, and shall be, experiencing on a national scale is a progression up Maslow's hierarchy of needs. The late Abraham Maslow of Brandeis University postulated that man's needs could be arranged in a hierarchy of five levels—from the lowest level of the purely physiological needs (for food, clothing, shelter, rest), through security, social and ego needs, to the highest level of self-actualization needs (mental and spiritual growth, self-development, the fullest expression of *all* one's human potential). Viewed in this light, this New Reformation takes on a new significance. We can begin, I think, not merely to explain the present, but to predict the future.

Maslow's Hierarchy of Needs

Abraham Maslow, a Brandeis University psychologist, has postulated that all men share certain basic needs which can be arranged in a hierarchy of five levels, from the most fundamental physiological needs to the needs of intellectual and spiritual fulfillment. The five levels are:

1. *Physiological needs:* To survive, man needs food, clothing, shelter, rest. As the imperative requirements for staying alive, these represent the most elemental needs.

2. *Safety or security needs:* When physiological needs are satisfied, man wants to keep and protect what he has. He starts to try to stablilize his environment for the future.

3. *Social needs:* As his environment becomes more stable, he seeks to be part of something larger than himself. He has social needs for belonging, for sharing and association, for giving and receiving friendship and love.

4. *Ego needs:* These are the needs that relate to one's self-esteem (needs for self-confidence, independence, achievement, competence, knowledge) and one's reputation (needs for status, recognition, appreciation, deserved respect of one's peers).

5. *Self-fulfillment needs:* Finally comes the need for growth, self-development, self-actualization. As the capstone of all his other needs, man wants to realize the full range of his individual potential as a human being.

When discussing shifts on a national scale, some gross generalizations and over-simplifications have to be made. Yet it should be possible to predict major trends and changes in emphasis. In a society as complex and varied as the United States, the population cannot be slotted at one level only, for there are people operating at all levels. A profile of the population make-up, with its various modes of living, will thus be needed to represent the full range of needs; and future changes in this profile will be indicative of shifting value-systems.

MORE EMPHASIS ON SOCIAL, EGO AND SELF-ACTUALIZATION NEEDS

As a start, it is possible to predict that by 1980 there will be fewer people in the poverty class, and so a reduction of emphasis on survival and security needs nationally. At the other end of the spectrum, increasing affluence, more education and the changing composition of the work force will mean a rise in the number of high-income individuals, college graduates, professional and managerial personnel, and so an increase in emphasis on social, ego and (particularly) self-actualization needs.

The importance of this interpretation for our discussion lies in the seemingly simple statement that:

Needs determine values; and values determine goals.

At any given level, we tend to value what we need. If we are operating at the level of physiological needs, then we tend to value food and shelter. Attaining them becomes our goal. At the self-actualization level, we will be "turned on" by opportunities for self-expression, self-development, out-reach. It is not, of course, that we need food, shelter or any of the other intermediate needs any the less; but they are assumed or subsumed in the larger goal, rather than valued for themselves.

VALUES WILL BE INCREASINGLY DEBATED

One conclusion that we may draw from all the foregoing is that there will be greater importance, and greater complexity, attached both to the articulation of values and the formulation of more explicit goals—for ourselves, for our institutions, for our society. It should be evident, I think, that, as the "quality of life" becomes more and more our aim, so it becomes increasingly important that we identify and debate our values (an exercise in which few of us are adept or happy) for these will be major determinants of the specific goals we set.

"Better" requires more philosophizing, if you will, than "more." So long as our goals were mainly quantitative, there was less need to debate about the nature of the next steps for our society and economy. The immediate, physical needs had an obviousness and compulsion to them that made philosophizing largely irrelevant. They also, incidentally, generated a powerful unifying force in our society. To be sure, we have debated values-laden issues of the distribution of wealth and, increasingly, of the ordering of our economic priorities.

CHOICES MAY BECOME MORE DIFFICULT

As a society we are not yet—and shall not be within the foreseeable future—so affluent that we can afford to do everything at once; we have, in other words, to make choices. Indeed, it can be argued that increasing affluence and technology will enlarge our range of options, by bringing more of man's historical aspirations within the realm of the possible, and so make choices more, not less, difficult and important than in a poorer society in which options are strictly limited.

Establishing explicit goals will be a way of making these choices explicit, whether for the nation or for an institution. They will also be needed to create institutional focus and identity in an era of change. A search for meaning, purpose and identity—which we now think of primarily as an individual quest—will become necessary for organizational, and even national, vitality and self-renewal.

This need for identity and purpose was stressed by Max Ways in a recent *Fortune* article.

To a modern nation, especially one as fast-moving as the U.S., a sense of direction becomes the indispensable touchstone of the society's character, its identity. Specific issues of what is right for a modern society can no longer be referred back to some preceding condition considered as ideal.

The "normality" of a modern society has to be found in the unfolding of its fundamental values and principles, in the pattern of its movement, *in the broad characteristics of its forward reach.* [Emphasis added]

NEED TO SET GOALS MAY INCREASE CONFLICTS

It is perhaps worth stressing the obvious point that this new concern with values and goals does *not* usher in an era of tranquility, sweetness and light. To the contrary, as values have to be made more explicit, goals established and priorities selected, the potential for confrontation, conflict and polarization will be *increased.* Though I do not want to take issue too strongly with Daniel Bell, [author of *The End of Ideology,* 1960], I have the feeling that reports of the death of ideology have been greatly exaggerated.

Not only do we face the problem of how to define goals in a pluralistic, democratic setting, but we need to find answers to the question of how to bring about the degree of institutional change that I suspect our values and goals will call for. The answer, my friends, is not blowin' in the wind; we will not find it on the Beatles' magical mystery tour; it will not come to us with the dawning of the Age of Aquarius or the onset of Consciousness III. Indeed, if we rely on the presumed panacea of Charles Reich's phenomenon, we shall more likely experience the groaning than the greening of America. The developing tensions in our society cannot wait that long.

We must work, with speed, with passion, with competence, to build into our institutional systems the possibilities for a fuller expression of the values I have discussed. "The tasks of social change," John Gardner said, "are tasks for the tough-minded and competent." He added that "those who come to the task with the currently fashionable mixture of passion and incompetence only add to the confusion."

COLLECTIVE—NOT JUST INDIVIDUAL—INTELLIGENCE IS NEEDED

There is a valid question to be raised about the outcome of this venture. For centuries man has wondered, "Is there intelligent life on other planets?" However, when one considers the disarray in international relations, the tensions in our society and the physical decay of our cities, I feel there is a prior question we should ask ourselves: "Is there intelligent life on *this* planet?" I do not mean to sound cynical. I know that in this most educated of all societies there is an abundance of *individual* intelligence. But we all must question whether we have the same degree of *collective* intelligence to bring about the needed process of self-renewal and change required by the accelerated aging and rigidity of our institutions.

Yet we must make a beginning. And the beginning, I suggest, can be found in making this type of values-analysis and then building these newly-stressed values into the day-to-day working of our institutional systems. We are not perhaps fully aware of the extent to which these systems currently reflect certain values. We are more used to thinking of them as delivering a product or service than as reflections of our values. The current trouble—the trouble that puts so many of our institutions on a collision course with the future—is that they reflect almost exclusively organizational values such as order, routine, output, authority, efficiency. They reflect inadequately such other values as individualism, self-development, personal relationships, due process, equality.

Two experiences I have had suggest that this sort of institutional change is possible, but that it takes time, effort, clearly-defined goals and a systems approach:

In General Electric, two years ago, we made a corporate-wide effort to build equality of opportunity into the system. This is not just a matter of drafting a policy statement (we had had one for 35 years) or of hiring the "hard-core unemployed." It involved a year-long effort to examine every element of the manpower system—hiring, college recruiting, testing, orientation, training, motivation, promotion, union relations—to determine how it impeded or promoted equal opportunity. Then, and only then, was it possible to develop a set of integrated policies and programs for the needed changes to (in effect) build true equality into the system. This systems approach, incidentally, also involved looking beyond our plant walls to see what we could do to promote equality in, for instance, education, housing, and entrepreneurial opportunity.

In my home community I chaired a citizens committee on school goals that attempted to build into the educational system the values of individualization, diversity, innovation, teacher-student relationships, community relations. It took two years of concentrated committee work and a third year of community debate, but a new set of school goals based on a new set of values did emerge.

So the process is not easy, but this is the challenge that I offer you: to become catalysts of institutional change in your own organizations by making that dedication of time and effort to build new values, and so the process of self-renewal, into the system. Few would be better equipped for such a task than members of the World Future Society. As I challenged a group of corporate planners last fall: "If not you, who? If not now, when?"

Many critics have blasted our contemporary values of competition, racism, militarism, elitism and the vestiges of "rugged individualism." Few have offered viable alternative values. In the following article, Inlow sketches a sorely needed value synthesis. Do you like his new version of individualism? What parts of his synthesis would you object to?

A VALUE
SYNTHESIS

Gail M. Inlow

As the country continues to assess and revise its values in the coming years, I envisage the following evolving outcomes: (1) a new concept of individualism to take shape, (2) a new social ethic to unfold (3) the political order to become both more sensitive to the plight of the have-nots, and more world conscious, and (4) the system of formal education to become more value oriented.

INDIVIDUALISM

Self-Identity

I know who and what I am.

Self-Acceptance

I am able to accept myself at any given point in time.

Emergence

My goal is optimum growth. Thus, I shall maximize my positive attributes and eliminate or lessen as many of my shortcomings as I can.

Autonomy

I shall act and live independently, relying on others for social fulfillment, but I shall not exploit them.

Social Relatedness

My goal is to relate comfortably and warmly to associates, with altruism my ultimate aim.

Freedom From Guilt

I shall not dissipate my psychic resources by worrying about past errors of omission or commission. Rather, keeping those resources intact, I shall employ them in the pursuit of positive causes.

Reprinted by permission from Gail M. Inlow, *Values in Transition: A Handbook* (New York: John Wiley, 1972), pp. 186-95. Copyright © 1972 by John Wiley & Sons, Inc.

Flexibility

I shall avoid rigidity in reacting to life's problems.

Consistency

My goal is to avoid compartmentalization, applying my values consistently to life along its many fronts.

Frustration Tolerance

I shall assess frustrating situations realistically and relate to them authentically, not magnifying them out of proportion to their importance.

Openness

I shall look life in the face, understanding as much as I can of it and accepting the rest.

AN EMERGENT SOCIAL ETHIC

The social ethic, in actuality, incorporates the best in humanism but translates it into the following basic imperatives for today's world:

1. The brotherhood-of-man concept must leave the musty pages of theory and find its way into practice;
2. All, not just a favored few, must have the abundant life here and now; and
3. Altruism must win out over egocentric individualism.

VALUES AND THE POLITICAL ESTATE

The problem of gross economic disparity is political in that the government will have to act more vigorously than it ever has before if the economic gap is to be narrowed enough to prevent disaster. An essential first step is equitable tax legislation slanted in favor of those in greatest need of benefit. The more affluent in the society would obviously have to bear the cost of this step. A related second step is guaranteed employment for all and, by implication, full production at all times.

1. Full employment, maximum production, and an equitable income for all, guaranteed by the federal government (Leon Keyserling).
2. The government as an employer of last resort of people to work in such worthy and needy institutions as hospitals, schools, libraries, parks, forests, and so forth. (Garth Magnum).
3. The government to pay incentive bonuses, inversely related to salary, to the poorly employed or nonemployed.
4. The corporate structure to develop a more value-oriented conscience, leading to more extensive employment of the socially disadvantaged.

EDUCATION AND VALUES

With the country in a state of social turbulence, the goals, and functions of formal education need to be reassessed and updated. The underlying thesis in this connection is that education cannot operate on a business-as-usual basis at this critical time when the society is caught up in the throes of change. Avoiding pedagese, and deliberately condensing the substance of the presentation, I suggest that education needs to perform the following functions as it readies students to relate to the problems of today's world:

1. Educate for emotional and social as well as for intellectual outcomes,
2. Expose students in schools to the social facts of life as soon as they are ready for the exposure,
3. Take learners, insofar as possible, into the pulsating society to give them a firsthand view of social problems,
4. Teach learners to think critically.

Thus I contend that schools need to meet the following specifications:

1. Be inviting, not forboding, places.
2. Set reasonable guidelines of student behavior.
3. Develop and implement well-conceived curriculums that relate specifically to the growth needs of learners without neglecting the needs of society.
4. Develop the extracurriculum on a broad social base, and motivate *all,* not just *middle-class,* students to participate in it.
5. Develop, give active support to, and staff adequately for a counseling program the goals of which are emotionally healthy students, careful educational programming, and equally careful job placement.

If you will allow him five minutes of your time, Peter Wagschal will give you additional insights to the nearly universal student demands for relevance in their educational experiences.

ON THE IRRELEVANCE OF RELEVANCE

Peter H. Wagschal

Student activists and the faculty members they confront keep insisting that education is not "relevant" and must be made so. I must confess that for a while I participated wholeheartedly in this demand for "relevance," but at this point I find myself only confused by it. Without wishing to appear the picky grammarian, I am forced to admit that the clamor to "make education relevant" now strikes me as disastrously incomplete and unintelligible. I can't remember ever using the word "relevant" without adding "to x." Perhaps I am only thickheaded or overcome by my cultural conditioning, but whereas I can make sense out of the question, "Is ability to swim relevant to being a life guard?," I *can't* make sense out of the question, "Is ability to swim relevant?" Relevant to what?

So, when I read all the current articles on the relevance of American education, I always find myself filling something in to serve as the missing "x" in my "relevant to x" formula. Superficially, this is a very easy and satisfactory way to proceed. When a student says that education isn't relevant, it makes some kind of sense to add "to life in America of the twentieth century." If I were anything like the rest of my colleagues, I could leave it at that, nod my head in self-righteous agreement, and listen to the rest of the student's oratory. But, like a pin-ball machine, my mind flashes "tilt" at passing over what I see as a very ambiguous solution to the missing "x" problem. To say that education is not relevant to twentieth century American life and then move on to other considerations is, for me, to pass over the most crucial issue in America today, in or out of education: Do we want institutions, educational or otherwise, which are "relevant" to America as it is? As it probably will be if current trends prevail? Or as it *ought to be* if we could exert some control over the future?

With incredibly few exceptions, the students and educators I talk to and read about seem to be pushing for relevance in the context of America as it probably *will be,* and they seem to be reacting against the lack of relevance in the context of America as it *is.* Mind you, all of this is by implication only, since no one ever bothers to fill in the missing "x." But what frightens me is the absence of any talk, explicit or implicit, about making education relevant to what America *ought to be.* I for one am not willing to assume that my role as educator is to predict the directions which American society is taking and then design an educational system which has relevance to that society. There are social arrangements which I do not like and, more specifically, there are trends in American society which I do not like. I could not, even if I had the power, in good conscience design a system of education which would encourage and be relevant to an unhealthy society. Especially when education could, if it had visions of a more healthy social order, help to change America's course toward more viable directions.

Reprinted by permission from Peter H. Wagschal, "On the Irrelevance of Relevance," *Phi Delta Kappan* 51 (October 1969): 61.

To put the whole thing more bluntly than need be, I do not want to participate in the building of an educational system which is relevant to a nightmarish future even if that is the future which appears most likely to occur. I would rather build a system of education which is entirely irrelevant to that future in the hope of thereby avoiding the nightmare.

What I am reacting against is the way in which our society, and especially we educators who hide behind the "relevance" shield, is willing to relinquish control of, and responsibility for, the future. All the descriptions of the year 2000 which I encounter emphasize a world of enormously rapid change, large population, an infinity of technological gadgetry, and an overwhelming emphasis on people learning to "relate to each other meaningfully" (my essays on "the unrelatedness of relating" and "the absurdity of meaningfulness" are yet to be written). But who ever asks whether or not that is the world we want to live in? *Should* we move toward a future where change overwhelms us, where fellow humans abound on all sides, where gadgets literally fill the air, and where our sole concern in life is relating to other people? And if we do not want such a world, why are we so overwhelmed with its inevitability as to be unable (or unwilling) to prevent it from walking in on us like an unwanted houseguest?

It is in the context of such questions that my colleagues' harping on educational "relevance" stirs my blood and flashes my neon "tilt" signs. You see, I too want education to be "relevant"—to the cultivation of the most vital and enriching aspects of humanity—the capacities for joy, awareness, and self-direction that are the hallmarks of being human. The future ought to be—dare I say "must be"?—dedicated to the fulfillment of humanity's nature, and if the current trends of American society point in different directions, then education which is relevant to those directions is not only irrelevant but disastrous to boot. To be sure, we live in the age of pragmatism, cultural relativity, existentialism, and all those other trends of thought which encourage us to refrain from speaking of "human nature," "ought's," and "universal values." But wherein lies the greater wisdom? To continue our restraint before such global questions and thereby to give up all control of the future to the whims of circumstance—a world where relevance is always "to what *will be*"? Or to grope, however hesitatingly, toward a meaning for the nature and value of humanity, and thereby to gain a risky piece of control over the future—a world where relevance is always "to what *ought to be*"?

Have you ever wondered about the influences operating on an instructor in terms of his determination of grades? Did you ever feel your effort received a low evaluation when your own assessment was quite high? Conway relies on Rokeach's Dogmatism Scale in this article to identify students and faculty on having "open" or "closed" belief systems. How do you think an "open" institution relates to a "closed" student or vice-versa when it comes to the issuance of grades?

WHAT ARE
WE REWARDING?

James A. Conway

To most teachers the following remarks will sound familiar. In the process of reading examination papers (or compositions, or term papers) the instructor says:

I can't understand how John could have written such a poor paper. He's a good student, I'm sure of it. He's alert in class, asks questions, participates, a provocative student—but this paper just doesn't sound like him.

And here's Don's paper, another surprise! He really got to the point; his answers are clear and concise, surprisingly perceptive. I wonder why he never says anything in class? Come to think of it, I can't even picture which of my students Don is.

Now how am I going to grade these papers? Do I mark John down for this paper when *I know he's a good student?* Maybe he just had a bad day! Should I allow each student to select one test grade to be eliminated? Should I be putting so much weight on these written responses?

Whether the situation is familiar or not, it is one that exists. Ebel states, "Often a student's mark has been influenced by the pleasantness of his manner, his willingness to participate in class discussion, his skill in expressing ideas orally or in writing, or his success in building an image of himself as an eager, capable student."[1] Palmer indicates that marks are used as rewards or punishments for certain *kinds of behavior* manifested in the classroom.[2] The fact that grades may be tempered by classroom behavior is, perhaps, disturbing, but it is only half of the picture. My purpose here is to look at what we may be rewarding in such cases.

An incident that occurred while I was studying for my doctorate prompted me to pursue further the situation described above. I had administered a personality test to some 700 students enrolled in undergraduate education courses. The test was Rokeach's Dogmatism Scale, which purports to measure the degree to which a person's system of beliefs is open or closed to new or differing beliefs.[3] Rokeach points out that the basic characteristic that defines the extent to which a person's system is open or closed is:

... the extent to which the person can receive, evaluate, and act on relevant information received from the outside on its own intrinsic merits, unencumbered by irrelevant factors in the situation arising from within the person or from the outside.[4]

Reprinted by permission from James A. Conway, "What Are We Rewarding," *Phi Delta Kappan* 51(October 1969): 87-89.
[1]Robert L. Ebel, *Measuring Educational Achievement.* New Jersey: Prentice-Hall, Inc., 1965.
[2]Orville Palmer, "Seven Classic Ways of Grading Dishonestly," *English Journal,* October, 1962, pp. 464-67.
[3]Milton Rokeach, *The Open and Closed Mind.* New York: Basic Books, Inc., 1960.
[4]*Ibid,* p. 57.

From the pool of students tested, I selected a sample of extremes; that is, students predominantly open-minded and students predominantly closed-minded. To contact the subjects, I approached professors teaching the undergraduate education courses and asked them if I could talk to particular students. I would begin reading off the names. After no more than three or four, professors would invariably smile and say something like, "Yes, I can see why you are selecting those students—they are all sharp, perceptive." At this point I would check scores, finding, almost without exception, that these students were predominantly closed-minded as measured by the test. When I continued, reading names of the open-minded subjects, I found the professors having difficulty recalling them; in some cases they couldn't.

I was puzzled. Why were the closed-minded students easily identified and the open-minded students for all practical purposes anonymous? Rokeach noted that because the teacher only sees the student in a teacher-student context, the judgment may be quite unreliable.[5] This is understandable, but it doesn't explain the discrepancy between those who are recognized and those who are nameless.

Other investigators have reported related phenomena. Getzels and Jackson, as well as Alexander, indicate that conforming students seem to be rewarded with higher grades.[6] Dressel and Lehmann found that dogmatic and stereotypic students tend to receive higher grades from their instructors than the general academic aptitude of such students may warrant.[7] These and other studies suggest that the factor of dogmatism or open- and closed-mindedness may be directly involved in the biases that influence marks given as a result of teacher-pupil relationships in the learning situation.

Rokeach also argues for this position. He indicates that the dogmatic person is typically sensitive to the presence of authority in a social environment. In such an environment the closed-minded person is likely to adopt a respectful and acquiescent, yet at the same time enlightened and objective facade. He says further that the open-minded person's "equalitarian appreciation of his academic environment . . . may lead him to a greater willingness to venture sincere opinions which sometimes challenge or amend those made by his professors."[8] While Rokeach's position may be in agreement with the studies mentioned above, it is not consistent with my experience as the "questioning graduate student." Rokeach's "acquiescent student" was the individual I found the professors recognizing; the student who, according to Rokeach, *may* venture "sincere opinions and challenge professorial positions" was the unknown.

This apparent inconsistency prompted another investigation, made with John R. Dettre.[9] Its purpose was to determine the extent to which congruence (or noncongruence) of belief systems of students and of teachers influenced the final marks given in courses in teacher education on the undergraduate level. Twenty-six faculty members and 792 students at the State University College at Buffalo, New York, were administered Rokeach's Dogmatism Scale and also an adaptation of the life goals used by Getzels and Jackson.[10] Midway through the semester faculty members were asked to

[5]*Ibid.*

[6]Jacob W. Getzels and Philip W. Jackson, *Creativity and Intelligence.* New York: John Wiley and Sons, 1962.

Eugene O. Alexander, "The Marking System and Poor Achievement," *The Teachers College Journal,* December, 1964, pp. 110-13.

[7]Paul L. Dressel and Irvin J. Lehmann, "The Impact of Higher Education on Student Attitudes, Values, and Critical Thinking Abilities," *The Educational Record,* Summer, 1965, pp. 248-58.

[8]Rokeach, *op cit.,* p. 107.

[9]James A. Conway and John R. Dettre, "An Exploratory Study of the Relationship of Belief Systems, Goals, and the Evaluation of College Undergraduates," unpublished research sponsored by Research Foundation of the State University of New York, 1967.

[10]Getzels and Jackson, *op. cit.*

rate each of their students as being "above average," "average," or "below average." The ratings were to be general impressions of the student without reference to grade books or other sources. At the end of the semester final grades were recorded for each of the student subjects.

In order to magnify any differences, students and faculty whose scores on the Dogmatism Scale were in the top and bottom quarters were selected for analysis. Groups of closed-minded and open-minded students who had a closed-minded instructor, and also closed-minded and open-minded students who had an open-minded instructor, were formed for chi square analyses of grade distributions. Similar groups were also formed of high and low student-faculty goal agreements, as well as groups stemming from the interaction of belief systems with goal agreement as related to final grades. The last analyses were of the mid-semester estimates made by open- and closed-minded faculty members of their respective open- and closed-minded students.

Starting with the mid-semester estimates first, it was found (at the .01 confidence level) that closed-and open-minded faculty do rank their closed- and open-minded students differently. Closed and open faculty, considered together, assigned significantly more above-average ratings to the closed students than to the open students. When considered separately, it was found that the closed faculty ranked their closed students higher than their open students, but that the open faculty did not differ in their ranking of open and closed students. Agreement or lack of agreement on goals between students and faculty did not seem to influence the rank that students received in this mid-semester rating process.

When the distributions of final grades were analyzed, a slightly different picture emerged. Neither the variable of open- and closed-mindedness nor the variable of high and low goal agreement seemed to be related to the distribution of final grades among the students. However, when the interaction of the two variables was examined in relation to grade distributions, then a number of significant results appeared. The one outcome that seems to be of particular interest was that those closed-minded students who were in *low* agreement with their instructors received a significantly higher proportion of A's and B's than any other category of students, including those closed-minded students whose goal orientation was in *high* agreement with their particular faculty member. What is it about the variable of dogmatism combined with low goal agreement that influences the reported outcome? While no definitive conclusions may be stated at this time, I would like to consider the question and offer a tentative explanation.

Some of the topics treated in undergraduate education courses deal with such factors as "child-rearing practices," "permissiveness," "conditioning," "teaching machines," "authoritarianism," and so forth. It is possible that some of the areas of study may be in conflict with the beliefs of some students. A portion of the closed-minded students may find that their system of beliefs is threatened as they treat such topics in the classroom group. Rokeach points out that the closed-minded person will try to protect his threatened belief system by warding off the threats.[11] Conway found that, when all the members of a group were predominantly closed-minded, the individuals warded off threats by refusing to contribute to the situation. By refusing to discuss a concept or topic, the closed-minded members avoided having to take a stand on the belief in question. However, in mixed groups, which are more likely in the classroom situation, the closed-minded person cannot deter a conflicting belief through silence; instead, he

---

[11]Rokeach, *op. cit.*

must externalize irrelevant internal pressures, vocalizing or verbalizing frequently so as to direct the discussion away from the emerging threat.[12]

It may be that *low* agreement with the goal orientation of the professor is an indication of conflicting beliefs. When the low agreement is combined with a closed system of beliefs, then the situation is established for the argumentative verbalizations of the closed-minded person. It is almost a certainty that in almost all of the undergraduate education courses there is an attempt to foster the freedom to explore concepts and listen to opposing points of view; as such, the opportunity is created for exploitation by the closed-minded person. He is in effect, *expected* to defend his system of beliefs and prevent the alteration of that system.

On the other hand, the open-minded person, and the closed-minded person in high agreement with professorial goals, may react little if at all in the class situation. What reason is there to be vocal when you are in agreement with the beliefs stated? In those cases where the open-minded person is in *low* agreement with the instructor he may either internalize the new beliefs and integrate them into his open system; or he may ask for clarification and then act on the new beliefs. In either case his participation in the class "discussion" may be quite different from the threatened closed-minded student.

To summarize this speculation I would like to list the main points of the argument:

1. It is suggested that closed-minded students who are in low agreement with their instructor's goals act quite vocally in the classroom.

2. These vocal students become quite visible through their class participation and, as such, are looked upon with favor by their respective instructors.

3. The professor, regardless of whether he himself is open- or closed-minded, has a tendency to reward classroom participation by viewing vocal students as "above average," and then later by allowing such mid-semester estimates to influence the assignment of final grades.

Hopefully, the position offered in this paper will be clarified and strengthened or refuted through future research. However, in this interim period where we operate in the twilight zone of uncertainty, we might at the very least be aware of what we *may* be rewarding when we say, ". . . and finally, your grade will be influenced by your class participation."

---

[12]James A. Conway, "Problem-Solving in Small Groups as a Function of 'Open' and 'Closed' Individual Belief Systems," *Organizational Behavior and Human Performance,* November, 1967, pp. 394-405.

Grades continue to be a source of joy to some and frustration to others. Students would be surprised to learn that this is applicable not only to themselves but to many faculty as well. In the previous article by Conway ("What Are We Rewarding?") several conclusions were drawn regarding the basis on which many instructors grade. In this selection Simon also calls into question the value systems of many teachers and the effect those systems have when it comes to evaluation. Do you have any biases or prejudices that could influence your impartiality when it comes to evaluating a student's performance? Can you now begin to see the importance of value clarification as an initial factor in the way in which we view the world and other people in that world?

THE DAY THE CONSULTANT
LOOKED AT OUR GRADING SYSTEM

Sidney Simon
Howard Kirschenbaum
Rodney Napier

I

A controversy over the grading system has been raging among students and faculty at West High, a large suburban high school outside of one of America's largest cities.

It all began with an argument in one English class on the question, "Can you 'grade' poetry?" The argument spread and drew more and more teachers and students into rapidly polarizing camps.

Some of the students put out a position paper on the grading problem. It was circulated throughout the school. One class made a commitment to change the school's grading system, come hell or high water. A very successful alumnus came back to West High to address an assembly. He had won every academic honor in the book, but he caught everyone off guard with a speech consisting of reasons why he now felt that his formal education was a pointless charade because he had succumbed to the pressure to get grades.

He stirred up a lot of discussion. Students became enthusiastic and concerned. The faculty grew nervous, and the administration knew it was sitting on a powder keg. Rumors flew. Anxious parents called the school to warn Mr. Fusari, the principal, not to do anything to jeopardize their sons' and daughters' chances of getting into good colleges. Some faculty members quietly encouraged the students to bring about the revolution in marks.

Just before the action reported in this chapter, a group of moderate and concerned teachers approached Mr. Fusari, telling him that he must take action. They argued that grading practice was already a major issue for the students and that the faculty had better come to terms with the movement pretty quickly. They asked for a special faculty meeting to discuss the grading problem.

Mr. Fusari agreed to call such a meeting. His style was to bring in an old and trusted friend, Mr. Blanc, from the local state teachers college, who would give a solid, unexceptional talk to the faculty on what the research says, etc.—nothing controversial,

Reprinted by permission from Simon, Kirschenbaum, and Napier, "The Day the Consultant Looked at Our Grading System," *Phi Delta Kappan* 51(May 1970): 476-79.

fair to all sides. In his cliché-driven career, Mr. Fusari is firmly committed to the notion that "more light and less heat" is needed these days. But the special faculty meeting must be held this coming Friday if it's to be held at all.

As fate would have it, Mr. Fusari's education prof can't make it, but he finds a substitute, a younger member of the department. Mr. Blanc doesn't know much about the new fellow's views on grades, but he does know that the neophyte has a solid research background and "should do a very competent and professional job for you, Mr. Fusari."

The substitute is invited and he accepts. The meeting is announced the next day to the faculty. What follows is an account of the meeting.

II

The sun splashed through big windows and painted the library with pale yellow streaks. It was Friday, and Mr. Ingles looked down at the students filling the walkways and the grounds below.

"Lucky stiffs," Mr. Ingles muttered to no one in particular, as he turned from the window and headed for the tarnished metal coffee urn on the long center table.

"What's the matter, Mr. Ingles?" Miss Doyle said. "Don't you like donuts?"

"Not at 3:15 on a Friday afternoon," he told her, filling his clinical-white styrofoam cup with black coffee, "but since you insist." He fingered what he thought was a jelly-filled donut and bit into it.

"I don't insist," the lady answered, "but they were made by my fourth-period class especially for the faculty, and so I'll insist for *them.*"

Jelly spurted from the opposite end of the donut and dripped onto Mr. Ingles' hand. "Well, give them my compliments," he said, as he walked to a seat, licking the jelly from his fingers, "and an 'A' for effort."

"Thanks," she smiled back at him, and then turned to watch a stranger come into the room, flanked on both sides by Mr. Fusari and Mr. Crewson.

Mr. Ingles sat down, away from the other teachers, and sipped on his coffee, waiting for the meeting to get under way. He didn't like these faculty meetings, especially the ones that were called without notice, and even more especially when it was Friday. He had far more important things to do than listen to some college professor talk about grades.

"This is Dr. Richard Miller from Central State. He's in the Psychology Department there," Mr. Crewson was saying to Miss Doyle. "He's going to be talking to us this afternoon."

"Hi." Miss Doyle greeted the young-looking, slightly built man. "We have coffee and donuts. What can I get you?"

"I'd really like something," Dr. Miller said politely, "but I think I'd better go to work." He pointed to some equipment being wheeled in by two boys from the A-V Department. "So we can all get out of here at a reasonable hour." He smiled and nodded and then walked toward the boys. On the cart was an overhead projector. He directed the boys to set it up, then turned his attention to a small, strange-looking gadget that resembled a miniature version of a computer, somewhat similar to those one might see on television during election-night coverage.

Though a substitute for another speaker Mr. Fusari had originally invited, Dr. Miller felt assured. He was excited and as he worked he went over what he was planning to say to the West High faculty—or to any faculty he would ever get the chance to talk to on the subject of grades. He watched the teachers filing in. He heard one or two of them complaining about how late it was, a few outbursts of not too enthusiastic laughter. Then Mr. Fusari was introducing him. It was time. He turned and walked quickly up to the speaker's table, shook hands once more with Mr. Fusari, and then looked out at the teachers waiting for him to begin.

"I hope you are feeling experimental today," he said, "and I hope you don't mind being guinea pigs for the next half hour or so. Now I understand that you've been looking at the issue of grading here at West High during the past few days, and I'd like to put you and this computer (he patted the strange-looking machine beside him) to work on that subject for a few calculated experiments. Okay?"

A few groans came from the audience, and one or two of the teachers started to whisper to each other. Dr. Miller turned his eyes to the plywood lectern and studied the rather lively four-letter words carved into their surface. He smiled at the idea of reading out a few of them to the teachers to grab their attention. Instead, he waited a few seconds more, marveling at how some teachers could, without embarrassment, act just as they told their own students not to act.

"I'm going to give each of you one of these cards," he continued, holding up a handful of computer cards, "and then I'm going to ask some questions concerning your attitudes toward grading. We'll find out pretty quickly where you stand on the issue."

The A-V crew, finished with the overhead projector, had already started passing out the cards and special pencils. When the job was finished, they left the room.

Dr. Miller flashed on a transparency of the IBM card. "You'll notice," he said, "that there is no place for your name. This is so you'll be as honest as possible without intimidating yourself or anyone else. There's room for 20 answers on the card, as you can see, but I'm only going to ask 10 questions now. When we're done I'll run the cards through the computer. While they're being tabulated, I have another experiment which I think you'll find just as interesting. For that one I'll need all of you to sit with your own departments. And so after everyone is finished, please shift accordingly."

Dr. Miller turned back to the screen and explained that each of the questions required the teachers to consider a factor which they believed should or should not influence grading. "For example," he said, replacing the first transparency with the second one, "I might ask whether you think a student's race should affect his grade. You answer by coloring in one of the five possible replies printed on the card." His finger projected large and black on the screen and touched the scale to which he was referring:

TRANSPARENCY NO. 2—SCALE TO BE USED

A. It would be very important to consider this item when grading.
B. Somewhat important.
C. I have no strong feelings either way.
D. Should not be considered very heavily when grading.
E. Definitely should not be considered at all when grading.

"Should we answer that last question?" someone asked.

"No," said Dr. Miller quickly. And then, by shaking his head and crossing his forefinger against his lips, he indicated that the time for talking was over.

"Number one," he said, in a much louder and more impersonal manner, "Do you think a student's I.Q. should be taken into consideration in his grade?" He had written each question out on separate transparencies and he placed each of them on the projector in the order in which he asked them.

"Number two," he continued. "Should final exams be taken into consideration when grading at the end of the semester?"

"Number three: Do you think weekly quizzes should be used? By that," he clarified, "I mean one quiz a week, whether it is surprise or scheduled, but with perfect regularity."

"Four: Where do you stand on a monthly test—or at least one large test for each marking period?"

"Five: Should a student's popularity with other students enter into the grade?"

The young professor paused then and waited for the slower teachers (or perhaps the more contemplative ones) to catch up. Periodically, one or two of them glanced up at the screen or chewed nervously at the ends of pencils before marking the cards in front of them.

"Number six: Should class participation be considered in the grade?" And then quickly to seven: "Is the student's social class a factor? Eight: Should the student's ability to give you back exactly the same answers you want be considered? (A few ironic giggles rippled across the room, but Dr. Miller kept going.) Nine: Should the student's ability to take issue with what you say, to argue and sometimes to prove you wrong, be considered? (More giggles. A sigh. A groan.) And the last one: Where do you stand on the idea of a curve? I mean on the premise that there should be an equal number of people receiving low and high grades?"

The screen contained all 10 questions now, in addition to the rating scale, and Dr. Miller gave the teachers a few more seconds to check their answers before he called for the cards.

Mr. Ingles scraped his chair against the hardwood floor and joined the other teachers moving around the room to gather with the people from their own departments. He glanced at his watch, shook his head, and thought about the lawn he would not be mowing that afternoon. At least it was not a straight lecture—at least there was something to do, he mused to himself as he joined his fellow science instructors. They were all sitting and discussing their answers, but Mr. Ingles remained silent.

"Through the light-fingered efforts of some of my students," Dr. Miller was saying, "I have obtained some actual test papers written by students from other high schools in the city. Now these have been duplicated, and I'm going to give all members of each department a copy of the same paper. You grade the paper as if it had been written especially for you. The idea, of course, is to see just how close your marks will be to those of your colleagues."

Mr. Crewson and Mr. Fusari were already passing out the papers and red pencils. "Any predictions?" Dr. Miller queried softly.

Mr. Ingles seemed to come to life for the first time that afternoon. His hand shot up. "I'll bet that the English teachers have a spread of 30 or more points, but those of us in math and sciences will be as close as five points straight down the line." Mr. Ingles was grinning and his associates around him were nodding their heads. Not a word came from the English Department. Mr. Ingles grinned even more.

Smiling, Dr. Miller said: "Are you ready? Remember, consider this test paper a real one and grade it as you would if it belonged to any one of your students." He paused for a second, smiled once more, and continued with his instructions: "Eyes on your own paper. Do your own work."

The large room grew silent; only the sounds of turning pages and the efficient clicking of the little computer could be heard. Outside a truck passed. A car horn blared.

"Finish up now," Dr. Miller's sharp voice sliced through the silence. "Actually, I've given you about twice the time you would take if you had a whole stack of papers in front of you."

There were a few *sotto voce* remarks as the teachers placed pencils on the table and sat upright once more.

"Put a grade on the paper," Dr. Miller told them, "but not your name, and hand them in face down. One person from each table please collect them and trade them for a batch from a table not in your subject matter."

Mr. Ingles' table had traded with the English Department. "Hey," he said loudly, looking over the paper he had been handed. "Somebody in English misspelled *commitment* in his marginal notes."

Dr. Miller interrupted the laughter almost before it started. It was getting late and he still had quite a lot to do. "Okay. Since English seems to be considered so vulnerable, let's hear the spread of grades you gave that essay question paper on *Macbeth.*"

He asked for the hands of those people holding English papers. He nodded. Then he asked for hands of people with English papers graded below 70 or "C." Two went up. "What were the actual grades?"

"I have 68," one teacher said from the back of the room.

"This one has a large 'C' with a small minus circled in blue ink." It was Miss Doyle. "Maybe it means one is for content and one is for grammar."

"You get an 'A'," someone from the English table quipped.

"Okay, hold on," Dr. Miller called for quiet. Then he asked for people with an English paper with an "A" or with 90 or more. Three more hands went up.

"Aha! What did I tell you," Mr. Ingles said triumphantly, now very much interested in what was going on.

"What are the actual grades and comments?" Dr. Miller asked.

" 'A—Very thought-provoking.' "

" 'Couldn't agree with you less,' " came the second answer, " 'but I admire the way you put it.' "

"I've got an even better one than that, said a third teacher. " 'A– and B– equal B+.' "

"That's separate grading for grammar and content, then figured together," someone said stonily from the English Department. No one looked too happy there.

"Well, now," said Dr. Miller slowly, pacing back and forth in front of the lectern, "who is right and who is wrong? Is it an 'A' paper or a 'C' paper? Or is it somewhere in between? And for that matter," he continued, "what would have happened if you had known the student? And what if this were the 35th paper you read at one sitting instead of the first? And perhaps even more relevant, would the grade have been the same, say, if this were a Monday instead of a Friday? I wonder . . ."

"Look, Dr. Miller," Mr. Ingles stood up quickly. He was no longer smiling. "You may be making some points where it concerns the English Department, but I'd like to see the spread among the science papers if you don't mind."

The professor nodded. "Okay. I suppose that's a fair request. Let's do it with a show of hands. How many science papers were marked lower than 'C,' 69 or under?" he asked. Two hands went up. "Between 70 and 79?" Two more hands. "Over 90?" One hand.

"Why, this is ridiculous," Mr. Ingles shot up again. "I don't believe it. There are only seven of us in the department and that paper deserved a solid 'B.' "

"You're crazy," Cliff Harper stood up and faced him. "Just because the kid has the right answers doesn't mean he knows how he got them. Unless a student goes through the entire process, I take off points. Doesn't everybody?"

"I don't know about everybody," Mr. Ingles sputtered back, his face turning pink. "I only know about me. I don't worry about cheating or about collecting scrap paper.

I worry about whether a student has a right answer or a wrong one, and this kid did the job."

The debate between the two science teachers was drowned out by a hubbub of controversy that had erupted around the room. Dr. Miller allowed the teachers to argue among themselves a bit longer as he said something in Mr. Crewson's ear. Mr. Crewson nodded, then Dr. Miller walked back and slammed his fist on the table for quiet.

"Hold on now," he said. "It's quite obvious that grades mean different things to different people—even in the so-called objective disciplines like math and science. Now let's try one more experiment before we call it a day."

He didn't wait for comments. He asked the teachers to get out a piece of scrap paper and put numbers on it from one to 10.

"This is a quiz," he said, "and may be used to determine your next salary increase."

Mr. Ingles glared up at the professors, along with a few other teachers. This time there was no laughter. Dr. Miller ignored the hostile faces and launched right into the questions. "Question one: What is a standard deviation?"

"You must be kidding," Miss Doyle said loudly.

He was not kidding.

"Question two: Explain what a mean is. Three: Define median. Four: What is a normal distribution? Five: What is a reliable test?"

Mr. Ingles threw down his pencil. "This is ridiculous," he said. "What's he trying to do?" His face had now turned a glowing red. Dr. Miller ignored the remark and the groans and sighs of disgust. Inexorably, he asked his questions in a cold and confident staccato:

"What is validity? What is objectivity? List the measurements you use to determine the reliability of one of your own tests. How do you know that the last quiz you gave was valid? And finally, tell me please—just tell me—what right you have to grade other people's children."

The room was silent as Dr. Miller looked out across the plywood lectern at the West High faculty. He wanted to look at their eyes, he wanted to ask them these questions again and again until he got his answer, the only answer that they could possibly give. But no one—not one teacher—would look back at him. Fingernails were being studied. Desks and papers and the floor were under examination. And looking out at those hiding faces, Dr. Miller was angry.

He had told himself that he would be cold and scientific and calculating, that he would try to be objective and understanding and impersonal. But he was also angry. He was vitally concerned with the way these people in this room on this Friday would from now on confront the problems of evaluating their students.

"I suppose I should apologize," he said finally in a very soft and controlled tone, "for the harsh way I asked those questions. But my own objectivity, where grading is concerned, is sometimes very strained. You see, grades to you are just incidental letters and numbers, but to students—especially students today—grades mean much more. Don't you see?"

He walked around the table toward the faculty, "Grades can and often do determine who is sent to Vietnam; grades can systematically screen out lower-income children from getting some of the benefits that their more wealthy peers take for granted.

"I think that there's nothing—nothing that more effectively separates students and teachers—that drives them actually into warring camps—than grades. The student has his crib sheets, his rote memorization, his apple polishing. Teachers combat these devices with Mickey Mouse assignments, surprise quizzes, notebook checks, tricky multiple-choice questions.

"Grades have made us into overseers driving the most reluctant group of field hands ever known. Grades have made us puppeteers pulling the emotional strings of live marionettes. Grades have made our students believe that *wadjaget* is the most important word to be used when summarizing their own education."

Dr. Miller turned and walked quickly to the miniature computer. He picked up the printout and held it in his hand without looking down at it.

"I think there are serious problems in this high school—as there are in so many other high schools—problems that both teachers and administrators need to face. We can see it in this printout," he said, pointing down at the long white sheet coming from the machine. "I see a tremendous spread of opinion about which kinds of things should be considered in grading."

"Take Question Seven," he continued. "More than 80 percent of you said that social class should not be considered when grading. And yet you are all aware that students in the general section of this high school are there because of their social class. You justify not putting them into college entrance sections on the grounds that they are too lazy or that they supposedly cannot read. Those general students have been neatly 'classed out' of the rewards of this school and you and teachers like you have done it to them.

"Let's go to Question Eight. 'Should the student's ability to give you back exactly the answers you want to hear be considered in his grade?' Ninty-five percent of you said that it should not be given much weight; it should definitely not be considered when grading. But I wonder. Do your students have this understanding?"

"I recently interviewed 50 of your students in the context of a research on student dissent I am doing. I am convinced—*I was told*—that students think that not giving *your* answer—the answer they think you want—leads to a lower grade. You may not have tried to do it, but that's what you have accomplished. 'Give them what they want to hear,' your students say of you, 'and do it neatly, without erasures.' "

Suddenly Dr. Miller felt very weary. His suitcoat, the bright library lights, even the weight of the printout in his hand seemed to put unbearable pressure on his arms and shoulders.

"I'll leave this printout with Mr. Fusari," he said quietly, "and I'm hoping that he'll want to call another meeting about this topic in the near future. Thank you very much for your time and attention."

Dr. Pearl addresses himself to the demise of the university and says, because it is out of place with external realities the university has established internal structures and procedures that are as resistant to change as those established by an advanced schizophrenic as a defense against the threat of reality." Rather than address itself to the resolution of the problems suffered by our population the university has been largely responsible for the creation and continuance of these problems. The current ecological craze is singled out by Pearl as an excellent example of the culpability of higher education in contributing to the delinquency of a society. Can you envision any changes in the institutional structure that would improve with change and not, as the author suggests, "become worse"?

THE MORE WE CHANGE,
THE WORSE WE GET

Arthur Pearl

The call for change in the American university ranges today from nonnegotiable demands to polite requests, and from complete exchange of power to some minor tinkering with the curriculum. Every college and university is prideful of its willingness to innovate. And yet what has all this noise and activity achieved? Not very much; and the little that has been changed isn't even desirable.

The need for fundamental change in the university is obvious. Both outside and inside its hallowed halls the evidence fairly shrieks out at us. In the outside world there are mounting unresolved problems that threaten man's survival, and the university provides neither the men nor the ideas for solving them; worse yet, there is not even a promise that solutions will be forthcoming. Not unrelated to this is the nonsensical struggle for power that goes on within the university in which various factions, distinguished only by their lack of qualification to lead, joust for hegemony. To make matters worse, the majority in the university ignores both the outside concerns and the internal upsets, and continues business as usual. The majority would have you believe that their indifference reflects maturity. In truth, they are the walking dead—the zombies whose condition is ascribed in the horror flicks to voodoo. Now we know better. They are merely well-educated, conformist students, teachers and administrators.

The main failing of the university is that it has become an alien institution: it does not relate itself to anything of importance. Its processes are corrupted because the university itself is not pertinent to man's tenuous hold on life. At rock bottom the university is alien to nature, and as a consequence it is also alien to any defensible world of work, politics, culture and individual growth.

Now at a crossroads, the university faces a classical dilemma. Because it is out of phase with external realities the university has established internal structures and procedures that are as resistant to change as those established by an advanced schizophrenic as a defense against the threats of reality. The geography, the logistics, the normative behavior, the tolerance of ways of life, the admission policies, the evaluative systems, the content and sequence of courses, the hiring practices, the promotion system, the access to funds, the financial support of students, the administrative apparatus, the relationships of students with employers and recruiters, the "experimental

Reprinted by permission from Arthur Pearl, "The More We Change, the Worse We Get," *Change* 2 (April 1970): 39-44.

innovations"—all become mechanisms to insulate the university from outside influences, regardless of their urgency. The university system, moreover, with all its convolutions, impedes change because the organization itself has a vitality which enhances and extends itself with the Parkinsonian vigor of a metastasizing cancer. No wonder some critics of the university conclude that the only hope lies in a restart of the university, after it is destroyed. This conclusion is not greeted enthusiastically by most university teachers and administrators. As one of them, I too shy from the ultimate solution, but not because I find anything to defend in the contemporary form of the institution. Rather, I fear that its replacement would look god-awfully similar to that which was ostensibly destroyed.

Man has tinkered with ecological balance nearly to the point of no return. The equilibrium between death and birth has been seriously disrupted. The population of the world, now calculated to be in excess of three billion, is projected to double again in thirty-seven years. The resources necessary to sustain life are being depleted. Pollutants are ravaging our air and water resources. The most fertile land is being covered with concrete. The university has not only failed to help solve our ecological crises, it has contributed significantly to them: technology, one of education's most prized contributions, is the major polluter and destroyer of life-sustaining resources. Related to the problems of the ecological equation is the deflection of energy to anti-human activities; the most obvious examples are war and racism. In both of these areas, the university's record is similarly dismal: the scientists' most significant accomplishment of the twentieth century was the creation of the super-weapon. If the university, as an institution, has been involved in any major peace-making activities, that activity must stand as one of the best-kept secrets of all times.

Because we are a credential society, because we portion out wealth, prestige and status disproportionately to those who successfully complete a formal education, the university has become the primary vehicle for the maintenance of racism. The precious few numbers of poor minority youth who obtain degrees camouflage the university's apparent true function, which is to help maintain the current inequitable distribution of power and wealth. The continued existence of poverty, the developing of "behavioral sinks" in the inner cities where overcrowding and dilapidation contribute to the degeneration of human relationships, the muddling of our attempts to build model cities— all reflect the failure of the university and its self-proclaimed scholars to come to grips with major social problems. Even some ecologists fail to appreciate the extent to which war, racism, poverty and urban blight relate to the environmental crisis.

Consider that minorities are asked to join with the rest of us and limit population, but they are also told that their political impotence is caused by their lack of numbers. Minorities are asked to join in the common cause of survival, but they are also told to be content with a barely livable existence, and for God's sake, don't get militant about it. War and threat of war preclude international cooperation on population growth and preservation of the environment; war and threat of war destroy and pollute, divert enormous power resources and manpower into wasteful activity, and energize nations to stimulate population growth. Poverty destroys hope, and without hope there is no concern for the future. Seeing no future, we see no point in taking the time or the trouble to prevent population growth. The mess of the metropolis impedes rationality in family planning, but also is profligate in the use of energy resources and devastating in the matter of pollution.

Leadership and ideas are needed to solve all such problems, and every aspect of university life is to some extent involved. The involvement should pervade university concerns with work, politics, culture and human competence. But functioning as it does, the university (and its advertised innovations) is guilty of malfeasance, misfeasance and nonfeasance. To illustrate, the student government at the University of Oregon recently asked the faculty at that institution to approve a one-week moratorium on business as usual to permit discussion of the responsibilities of colleges and universities to help eliminate the ecological crises. The students requested that every department justify its activities in the context of man's survival. After some extensive and acrimonious debate over procedure, one of the more esteemed science professors arose and in stentorian tones dismissed the request, proclaiming that it was absurd for a department of romance languages, for example, to justify itself ecologically. The sad thing is he thought he had said something profound.

The university is primarily in the business of vocational training. It turns and tailors the student to meet the specifications of the business, medical, legal, educational and engineering industries. The procedures used reinforce all prevailing prejudices and deny opportunity to the poor and the non-white. But the reinforcement of racism is, perhaps, not the university's primary evil; it is conceivable that even more devastating is the low level of competence that results from the process. In the end, the credentialed professional is either palpably unable to perform (trained incapacity, as in the case of the teacher in the ghetto), or he has deceived himself and others that he possesses the requisite skills (delusional competence, as in the case of the teacher in the suburbs).

Every aspect of professional training suffers from inertia. Neither the training nor the profession relates to physical or human ecological problems. The university trains in obsolete procedures for a world which long since has gone out of existence. Lawyers are unable to deal with anomic responses to legal statutes or with the argument that justice takes precedence over law and order; and they are unable to deal with the fact that a world unable to provide adequate food, water and air for its people cannot possibly develop a stable pattern of law. Medical doctors are unprepared to treat chronic diseases associated with an urban ecology. Social workers become completely unraveled when they confront anything not explainable by generic casework theory. Businessmen are so taken with their discovery of group dynamics that they forget that the economic theory on which they pin their enterprise is puerile.

The university responds to the challenges of training for work by offering curriculum "innovation." Field placement is the most prevalent and exalted of these reforms. Earlier and earlier in their college careers, students are paroled from campus and placed in schools, in welfare and probation offices, in recreation departments, in local and federal government, and in business and law offices. The practice is justified on the grounds that the student thus is tethered to reality, learns the ropes and as a consequence becomes a better trained, more valuable practitioner.

But both logic and evidence suggest that field placement only serves to initiate the prospective employee into the ritual of the system. Ever more efficiently he becomes a frictionless cog in a well-oiled bureaucratic machine totally removed from problems of livability. The student is trained to be just as bad a probation officer as the current group of bad probation officers, because he is going to be trained by them. The tenuous commitment to humanistic principles that school teachers evince in their pre-service training evaporates soon after they get on the job. The police cadet in the academy displays more respect for laws of evidence and the rights of the accused than he manifests after he is in the squad car—his partner, the senior officer who wises him up, educates him to forget all the mickey mouse crap he learned in the academy. The supervisors in the employment and parole offices do much the same thing. Why doesn't the university ask what it can do to help the student retain the little good which derives from a university association after he gets into the field?

To withstand the pressures to conform, incipient professionals must be a tougher, smarter breed of animal than those currently mass-produced. Innovation must be directed toward developing persons who can change the system, not reinforce it. Nevitt Sanford, among others, has become so disheartened that he doubts whether there is enough gumption in publicly subsidized educational institutions to even try to develop such leadership. James Ridgeway suggests that the corruption of the university by military and business is so complete that its staff and administration are perfectly willing to prostitute their limited talents for the loot derived by serving the system. (I think he treats my colleagues much too kindly. They are not prostitutes. From what I know of them, they will gladly *give* their favors away.)

The university has the capacity to produce change-agents. To be sure, there is risk in the venture; but since the ruptures in the university are becoming increasingly apparent and because there are more adventurous students on campus, true innovation in training for work is possible. It would require that professional preparation be far more "educational" than it is now. Professionals must be much more theoretical. They must have a theory of change in which strategies and tactics are specified. They must verify the efficacy of their theory through case study, simulation and field test. They must use the broadest issue of man's survival as the star by which to steer.

University innovation in the realm of work preparation is piddling at best; the university is even more derelict in the area of work planning. Work in this country is not determined by plan. Systems develop which need manpower, and away they go. Large numbers of persons are not allowed to participate in the design; many others obtain little gratification from the work itself. Products and services produce comfort for some, but many are unable to become effective consumers. The concept of a free market was clouded by monopoly and collusion, which eliminated competition. There was, and is, much to criticize about the system, simply in terms of distribution of wealth and concern for the human being, but even these considerations pale beside the considerations of ecology.

The basic work systems developed by this society can no longer be tolerated because they are wasteful. Our number one product is pollution. We subsidize industry to pollute even more. We generate pollution by depleting our power resources. We build, ship, warehouse, display, advertise and sell products we should never have produced in the first place. We don't need a society which doubles its electrical output every ten years: we need a society which discourages people from using electricity to cut a turkey or open a can or shave; we need houses which provide convenience and livability and at the same time conserve energy. We cannot afford to employ millions to build automobiles which are the primary polluters not only of air but also of space.

If people are not going to work in industries dedicated to waste, then where shall they work? How will new industries develop? What will be *their* logistics? The university has not even begun to ask such questions, let alone teased out any answers. Indeed, the university is the greatest single obstacle to new thoughts about work. It is not merely that new ideas are ignored in the university; worse, the ideas are forbidden. At the University of Oregon, for example, a curriculum committee is resisting inclusion of course numbers which would permit community colleges to offer new career training that could be transferred to the university. Inclusion of these courses would in no way affect standards. It would neither hinder nor hamper any existing irrelevancy. It would cost the university no money. But at this moment, after months of haggling, the curriculum committee is adamant against even this tiny change.

In a modern, complex, overcrowded world, change is political. Everything done in the university is political. The curriculum committee operates politically, so does the admission committee, the space committee, the search committee for a new dean, the committee which selects the search committee to search for the new dean. Everything revolves around political consideration. Everything that happens outside of the university and which affects the university is baldly political. (Any faculty member who doesn't believe that after what has gone on in California doesn't really deserve his status.) And any change, either within or without the university, in the direction of ecological validity will require political action, will demand the mobilization of power.

For the first time in the history of any nation, our colleges and universities have the potential power to make a difference. The power is both in numbers (there are in the United States at least nine million students and faculty members) and in strategic position (every enterprise in the country depends upon the university). It is no longer possible even to go to war without relying on the brains of the university to design sophisticated weaponry. If united, the university is in a marvelous bargaining position, and yet it refuses to exert its force. Worse yet, it fails to debate, discuss, analyze or study the legitimate uses of its power to produce change. In almost all its activities, the university is either anti-or non-intellectual, and nowhere does it demonstrate this more clearly than in the area of politics. If the university-based scholar enters politics at all, he prefers to be an Iago, planning and scheming for or against the administration he serves, rather than to be a leader and state unequivocally the principles for which he is prepared to fight.

An ecologically valid world would require new kinds of political decision-making. The current system is too turgid and too chaotic. Too many groups are forced into powerlessness, and with no possibility for them to gain power through coalition. The university must begin to provide leadership for political growth. Because of the enormity of the problems facing us, the arguments in favor of totalitarian efficiency may be hard to resist. If the university reneges in its obligation to help make democracy work, democratic principles undoubtedly will be a casualty of our increasingly complex world. Since it is hardly possible to have an ecologically valid world—or an ecologically valid university—in a totalitarian society, we must struggle for new models of effective politics based firmly on democratic principles. Most particularly, we must build a system based on respect for individual rights.

The university should represent a model democratic community. It could, and should, develop a political structure which would be the beachhead for larger political entities. Its political system should be consistent with every concern for livability. It must reject dehumanization through bureaucratic intransigence and racism, provide alternatives to the wastage of a war mentality, and provide for the sharing of power among all concerned. It should be accountable to outside forces and influence, and it should show how it is possible to unite in an effort to gain things for which there is consensus. That kind of innovation does not exist. Instead, we display our shabby student governments and other mockeries of viable political practices, which some people have the audacity to call innovation.

Another aspect of logical university innovation in the arena of politics is the development of leadership consistent with democratic principles. We should be able to develop leadership which respects diverse and pluralistic populations, which holds itself accountable to all groups over which it presides, which willingly negotiates with the opposition, which treats grievances on merit, which recognizes that conflict is inevitable and thus is not traumatized by its existence, which recognizes that in a rapidly changing society all rules are means, not ends, and therefore are subject to change as the world changes. That type of development—that kind of innovation—is not taking place in the university either.

The most trivial and traditional means of teaching are called "innovations." One of the most popular ones for undergraduates takes the form of performance goals and programmed learning. These "innovators" take for themselves the mantle of science. They claim for themselves a tough-mindedness, they argue that the university has gone to hell because it is aimless, and as a remedy they propose performance goals. But there is no accountability in their "system." The goals cannot be justified. They accept all that is now being taught as valid, and claim only that they can teach it more efficiently. The goals consist of test passing; they feel they have accomplished something if they improve the efficiency of memorization of names and dates: their concern is "right answer" learning.

Anything based on such a behavioral goal does not belong in the university. It is intellectually stultifying. Leave it perhaps for a six-week training program run by the Department of Labor, but remove it forever from university curriculum and admit that there *are* no Right Answers. If we do not begin with that assumption, we can only hinder the university. For our ecological problems inform us that all which we do, we do wrong, and that we need to struggle for entirely new answers.

Another alleged innovation is the honors college—the curricular invention by which we provide a few select persons with an enriched and diversified education. We allow them options not available to other students. We give them unique independence and unmatched choices. Yet still the fare is limited. The university cafeteria is simply not very diversified: the "honors" student is offered spinach or broccoli. And where the university offers only garbage, the choice is even more restricted. In short, there is no independence in independent study if all the choices are worthless.

The university is involuted. Its students, who come from restricted environments and limited experiences, are further restricted and limited because they are allowed to interact only with each other. The university as a whole lacks sufficient stimulation from minority groups and other populations with diverse experiences. But bad as that is in the university, it is worse in the honors college, whose students mingle only with each other. Thus is prevented even limited personal contact with the problems of black people and the social ecology of the ghetto, or Mexicans and the social ecology of the barrio, or what happens to people when they are crowded more and more into less and less livable space. At best, the student in the honors college gets the information which is emitted from a sanitized computer. If racism is a major problem in our society, and if it is related to the question of survival, then the bias in higher education could be the disease which destroys us all. The honors college, protector of our academic elite, may provide more of a problem than a solution. The "elite" is distinguished because it is whiter, more middle class and more restricted in background than any other group in the university. "Honors" college is a misappellation.

Why don't we require all our students to write a different scenario than Paul Ehrlich provides in his book, *The Population Bomb?* Ehrlich predicts that the future will bring either atomic war or a series of local calamities—famine, local wars, things of that nature—which would reduce the world population from three and a half billion to a billion and a half. Every student should try to write his own scenario, basing it on what he knows about economics, psychology, sociology, social organization, theater, art, music, literature, etc. Once we begin to direct student attention to such major problems, perhaps we will begin to eliminate our bickering.

The world as currently constituted distorts character and personality, and people who are unable to live harmoniously with themselves or their neighbors distort even further their physical and social environment. The university has the obligation to develop areas of interpersonal and intrapersonal competence, to test out its theories, and to develop experiments based on them. The most logical place to begin is in the university itself. But no such innovation is taking place.

The university has an obligation to update personality theory. Today there is preoccupation with obviously outdated mechanistic learning models and psychodynamic theories. At the practical level, the university not only fails to develop model living communities, but is itself becoming a "behavioral sink." It is overcrowded, bureaucratically organized, fragmented, depersonalized and computerized. At yet another level—the level of leadership development—the university has failed even to identify the attributes of a person: the intellectual, social, communicative, emotional characteristics which are necessary if we are to move from where we are now to where we must go to survive.

Leadership in the university is similar to that exemplified by the captain of a luxury liner who, after five or six days at sea, told the passengers: "I've got some good news and bad news. The bad news is that we are lost, we haven't any idea where we are, our electronic compass is broken, we've lost radio contact with the mainland, because of overcast conditions we can't use celestial navigation—we are hopelessly lost. Now for the good news: We are two hours ahead of schedule." The trouble with the university is that it is aimless. It can justify itself only because it has not specified its goals (As it says in the Talmud, if you do not know where you are going, all roads will get you there.)

Because the university has reached no consensus as to its purpose, the delusion that it has gotten someplace is easily believed. Because it has lost its sense of direction, because it survives to exist and exists to survive, because it generates leadership through perverted politics, because it prefers to model its leaders after the mayor of Chicago rather than to provide leadership for the city of Chicago, all those things which are called innovations in the university are trivia. And since the world and its problems worsen every minute, the more we change, the worse we get.

What messages are contained herein for some of our concerns about relevant school curricula? Why has education been so reluctant and so lethargic in using the new media on a large scale?

CURRICULUM AND CHANGE

This is a story of civilization of some thousands of years ago. The people lived in the warm lands, covered by streams fed by glaciers far to the north. They supported themselves by spearing fish and by trapping tigers.

The glaciers moved south. The lands became cold. The tigers left and sediment from the glaciers choked the rivers. Still, the people remained.

Before the advent of the cold weather the people had prospered and in their prosperity they felt that they should embellish their society and they set up a school system. In that school system, quite logically, they taught the spearing of fish and the trapping of tigers. Then the cold came and the fish left and the tigers left. The people of this area now survived by snaring eel and hunting bear. And they prospered again. They went back to examine their school system. They asked the headmaster what he taught. And he said, "I teach spearing fish and trapping tigers." And they said, "Well, do you not teach snaring eels and hunting bears?" He said, "Well, of course, if you want a technological education; but for a well-rounded education I prefer the classics."

Let us assume that by some highly selective catastrophe, all the schools and universities in this country were destroyed last night. Our task now is to build a new system.

Would we recreate the present educational system? Would we use the present assortment of architectural, administrative, curriculum and teacher-training assumptions? Would we install the same instructional materials and teaching practices?

The answer is clearly "No." Education is said to be the mirror of a society. Our schools do not reflect ours. Where the blame for this lies is not pertinent at this time; our objective now must be to get from our schools what we need to survive and prosper —in freedom and dignity and happiness—in the present and future worlds.

To achieve this we are going to have to do these things:

1. We must now initiate studies leading toward a far better understanding than we now possess of the function and future structure of our school systems.

2. We must develop methods that will make it possible for our education systems to adopt and benefit from innovations and discovery—in all related fields, including the fields of technology and communications as quickly and as easily as our industrial and commercial sectors. We have this curious anomaly in our present world of innovation and invention—industry and commerce depend on these forces and thrive on them: our educational systems receive them with unbelievable slowness and frequent hostility.

If the people themselves are so clearly responsive for example, to modern communications and devices—films, television, tape recordings, and even computers—why aren't the schools?

Do the real rewards in teaching come from working with young people and from the feeling that one is contributing to youth and to society? Or is monetary reward also an important motivating factor and a needed impetus for educational innovation? Jack Frymier takes a forthright stand in the following selection.

BARRIERS TO
EDUCATIONAL CHANGE

Jack R. Frymier

Under our present ways of working, those of us who seek to foster improvement in education in effect say to the teachers involved:

Here is a new idea. Try it out. Work hard. Learn all of the new factors and skills and knowledge which are involved. If you really try and really put yourself into it, children will learn more at the end of the year, and you will feel good about it.

For all practical purposes, we assume that altruism is an adequate motivational base from which to encourage teachers to adopt or incorporate important educational change into what or how they teach each day. But is this assumption reasonable? That is, is it reasonable to suppose that teachers can be encouraged to incorporate important kinds of educational change into their own teaching repertoire if all that we can promise them at the end of the year is a good feeling if improvement occurs?

Altruism is a powerful motivational force, that much is sure. However, in the business of working to foster widespread and significant educational change, is the promise of "a good feeling" and "an increase in satisfaction" from helping others enough to insure adoption of the new techniques or materials?

No other group in our society presupposes such a complete dependence upon altruism as a basis for change. If the farmer tries a new fertilizer and grows more bushels of corn per acre, he obtains a financial gain. If the physician or attorney is more successful, his practice improves and his income goes up. If the private in the Army does a better job, he can hope to be promoted and reap a monetary gain. Even ministers who do a better job end up with bigger churches and larger salaries. With the exception of Catholic priests and nuns who take the vow of poverty, almost no one in our society is expected to do an ever-better job on the assumption that an increase in satisfaction from helping others will suffice to encourage them to change. No one except public school teachers, that is.

It would appear that the concept of "merit pay" is somehow related to educational change. In a society permeated with materialistic concerns, a complete dependence upon altruism ought to be questioned, at least.

Reprinted by permission from Jack R. Frymier, *Fostering Educational Change* (Columbus: Charles E. Merrill, 1969), pp. 24-25.

Many educators predict that sweeping changes will occur in education in the next decade. Some of the most likely and most significant changes are explored in the following article. Do all these predicted changes appear to be positive? Which changes strike you as invidious and potentially harmful to youngsters?

FORECAST FOR
THE 70's

Harold G. Shane
June Grant Shane

During the last five years, there has been a marked increase in long- and short-term speculation regarding possible educational futures that may lie before us in the remaining years of the twentieth century. For the past three years, we have studied approximately 400 published and unpublished articles and books in which such conjectures and projections occur.

These current writings clearly indicate that education and schools, as they exist today, will change drastically during the 1970's and will be modified almost beyond recognition by the end of the century. The paragraphs that follow summarize some of the more important developments that could occur in the next decade and propose some of the new roles in which the teacher is likely to be cast. In conclusion, we give thought to the question: For what kind of world should children who will live most of their lives in the twenty-first century be prepared? Here, then, as many scholars see it, are some of the possible designs of educational futures in the seventies.

Education will reverse its traditional pattern of expenditure. From the beginning, more money has been spent per student in higher education, with secondary education coming in a strong second and elementary education, a poor third. Preschool and kindergarten programs have not even been in the race for funds. But now, major support for early childhood education seems highly probable because of our belated recognition that we have spent literally billions at the upper-age ranges to compensate for what we did not do at the two- to seven-year age levels.

Now priorities for education of the youngest will bring to public education nonschool preschools, mini-schools, and a preprimary continuum. As nonschool preschool programs begin to operate, educators will assume a formal responsibility for children when they reach the age of two. We will work with parents of young children both directly and through educational TV programs for young mothers. And we will offer such services as medical-dental examinations and follow-up, early identification of the handicapped and deprived, attacks on nutritional needs, and—of major importance—early referral to cooperating social agencies for treatment of psychobehavioral problems.

New programs for two-year-olds will involve the coordination of community resources, under school auspices, to equalize educational opportunity for these children before cultural deprivation makes inroads on their social and mental health.

The minischool, as envisioned here, is one that provides a program of carefully designed experiences for the three-year-old—experiences deliberately devised to in-

Reprinted by permission from Harold G. Shane and June Grant Shane, "Forecast for the 70's," *Today's Education: NEA Journal,* January 1969, pp. 29-32.

crease the sensory input from which the children derive their intelligence. Each mini-school presumably would enroll six or eight children under a qualified paraprofessional. A professionally prepared childhood environmental specialist would directly supervise clusters of approximately six minischools.

We will probably build these small schools into housing projects, make them part of new schoolhouse construction, or open them in improvised space in convenient buildings.

The preprimary continuum is a new creation intended to replace contemporary kindergartens for the four- and five-year-old. This program presupposes that the young learner will spend from one year to four years preparing himself to perform effectively in a subsequent primary continuum, the segment of education now usually labeled grades one through three. The preprimary interval should sharply reduce the problems of widely varied experience and social adjustment encountered by children who are arbitrarily enrolled in grade one at age six regardless of their previous cultural environment.

Major environmental mediation for two- to six-year-olds, as described above, will permit schools to abandon the current transitional concept of nongrading. In the coming decade, a seamless primary, middle-school, and secondary continuum of coordinated learning experiences will begin to replace the nongraded programs of the sixties.

Here, progress and the time spent on a given topic will become completely individual matters, as one emergent design for learning serves all ages. The intellectually advantaged child, for instance, might spend only two years in the primary or intermediate continuum, accomplishing what most children would accomplish in three or four years.

In this personalized educational continuum, the question of how to group children will no longer be relevant. The child will simply work with others in ephemeral groupings during whatever time certain shared learning experiences happen to coincide.

Admission age quibbles, too, will become irrelevant after several years of minischool and preprimary experience. There is no need to group children for first grade at the magic age of six, since they would be phased into their primary school year at any time from age four at one extreme to age eight at the other.

Promotion problems will also vanish, since in a continuum of learning there are no specific points at which a student passes or fails; he merely moves ahead at his own pace. Grade cards are likewise destined to disappear: Evaluation of progress will be continuous, and a progress report can be made in a parent conference whenever pupil performance analysis is in order.

The school will provide more learning experiences that parallel or accompany conventional academic content. The creative and enjoyable will begin to vie strongly with the utilitarian and academic dimensions of education. Such paracurricular ventures as educational travel, school camping, informal dramatics (including sociodrama), enlarged intramural sports programs that stress mass participation, and engaging youth in useful service to the community are due to increase in frequency and extent.

Biochemical and psychological mediation of learning is likely to increase. New drama will play on the educational stage as drugs are introduced experimentally to improve in the learner such qualities as personality, concentration, and memory. The application of biochemical research findings, heretofore centered in infra-human subjects, such as fish, could be a source of conspicuous controversy when children become the objects of experimentation.

Enrichment of the school environment in the seventies—especially in the ghetto—to "create" what we now measure as intelligence by improving experiential input also will become more accepted. Few are likely to make an issue of efforts to improve educational opportunities for the deprived child. However, there could be a tinderbox quality to the introduction of mandatory foster homes and "boarding schools" for children between the ages of two and three whose home environment was felt to have a malignant influence. Decisions of the 1970's in these areas could have far-reaching social consequences. Although it is repugnant to permit a child's surroundings to harm him, there is no clear social precedent for removing a child from his home because it lacks the sensory input needed to build normal intelligence and, therefore, in effect condemns him to a lifetime of unskilled labor.

The next decade will see new approaches to "educational disaster areas." Most of America's large cities, and some suburban and rural sections, contain a central core that can only be described in this way. Damage surrounding this core decreases from severe to extensive, to moderate, to negligible.

Up to now, perhaps, we may have spent too much energy and money on just the worst schools of these central cores. In such neighborhoods, we cannot create a decent educational opportunity until the *total* social setting is rehabilitated. In the early 1970's, we may find it both more efficient and more educationally sound to direct our attention initially to improving those areas and schools where educational damage is moderate to extensive rather than drastic. For such areas, immediate attention may prevent their deteriorating in the near future into severe disaster areas. Once the deterioration in these outer ring schools is reversed, greater educational resources will become available to help us close in on the ghetto schools where damage is severe or total.

It would be unthinkable to ignore the children who live in our worst educational disaster areas until we can mobilize the greater forces needed to bring these schools up to necessary standards of excellence. Therefore, until inner cities regain their socioeconomic and educational health, we often will transport their children to outlying areas. In the next decade, this will involve a rapid buildup of facilities in these areas both in terms of enlarging existing schools and of creating new types of learning environments. Removing children from inner-city problem areas has the added merit of stimulating them through contacts with children from other social groups.

Later in the seventies, the elementary school changes will cause the junior and senior high schools to modify their programs. Their curriculums will presumably become more challenging and interesting. Wider age ranges, increased pupil interchange within and between schools, and individualized programs built around new instructional media will inevitably influence emerging secondary school organization.

In the late 1970's or early 1980's, it is not unlikely that students will graduate from high school with knowledge and social insight equal or superior to that of the person who earned a bachelor's degree in the 1960's.

On entering college, these students will be ready to begin postbaccalaureate studies, and our undergraduate college programs *in their present forms* will be unnecessary.

If this seems farfetched, bear in mind that the young person pictured here will have had the benefit of carefully developed learning opportunities in a skillfully mediated milieu since he was two or three years old.

During the next 10 years, business will participate in education to a greater extent. Although many of their activities are neither widely known nor generally understood, major corporations are already contracting to tackle pollution, teach marketable skills to the deprived, administer police protection, reclaim slums, and manage civic governments.

John Kenneth Galbraith has noted that the modern corporation already has the power to shape society. Frank Keppel commented recently that the revival of U.S. metropolitan schools depends as much on the action of leaders of finance and commerce as it does on educators. And Hazel Henderson commented last summer in the *Harvard Business Review* that industry's expansion into such areas as housing, education, and dropout training is probably the best way to handle our central needs if suitable performance standards and general specifications are properly controlled.

The growth of a cooperative business-and-education relationship will be of great portent in the seventies as corporations both expand the production activities of the education industry and assume more management and control responsibilities.

The roles and responsibilities of teachers will alter throughout the next decade. Future-think suggests that between 1970 and 1980 a number of new assignments and specialties will materialize if present trends continue.

For one thing, the basic role of the teacher will change noticeably. Ten years hence it should be more accurate to term him a "learning clinician." This title is intended to convey the idea that schools are becoming "clinics" whose purpose is to provide individualized psychosocial "treatment" for the student, thus increasing his value both to himself and to society.

In the school of the future, senior learning clinicians will be responsible for coordinating the services needed for approximately 200 to 300 children. In different instructional units (an evolution of the "team" concept) we will find paraprofessionals, teaching interns, and other learning clinicians with complementary backgrounds. Some will be well-informed in counseling, others in media, engineering, languages, evaluation, systems analysis, simulation, game theory, and individual-need analysis.

But on the whole, the learning clinican will probably not be appreciably more specialized in subject matter disciplines than he was in the 1960's except for being more skilled in using educational technology. He will do more *coordinating* and *directing* of individual inquiry and will engage in less 1968-style group instruction. He will be highly concerned with providing and maintaining an effective environment, skilled in interpersonal transactions, and able to work with persons of different ages and learning styles.

Ten years from now, faculties will include—

Culture analysts, who make use of our growing insights into how a subculture shapes the learning style and behavior of its members.

Media specialists, who tailor-make local educational aids, who evaluate hardware and software and their use, and who are adept in the information sciences of automated-information storage and retrieval, and computer programing.

Information-input specialists, who make a career of keeping faculty and administration aware of implications for education in broad social, economic, and political trends.

Curriculum-input specialists, who from day to day make necessary corrections and additions to memory bank tapes on which individualized instructional materials are stored.

Biochemical therapist/pharmacists, whose services increase as biochemical therapy and memory improvement chemicals are introduced more widely.

Early childhood specialists, who work in the nonschool preschool and minischool programs and in the preprimary continuum.

Developmental specialists, who determine the groups in which children and youth work and who make recommendations regarding ways of improving pupil learning.

Community-contact personnel, who specialize in maintaining good communication, in reducing misunderstanding or abrasions, and in placing into the life of the community the increased contributions that the schools of the 1970's will be making.

As educators turn a speculative eye on the next decade, they must seek to answer a question that most of them have hesitated to face. For what kind of world should we strive to prepare children and youth who will spend most of their lives in the next century? We say this question is crucial because educational policy decisions in the 1970's will not only anticipate tomorrow, they probably will help to *create* it.

Recent publications in the physical, natural, and social sciences suggest emerging changes in society that seem likely to characterize the world of 2000 A.D. A number of future-think writers agree that unless unforeseen catastrophes intervene, such developments as the following are probable:

The individual's personal freedom and responsibility will be greater.

The IQ of the average child will be 125, perhaps 135.

Cultures throughout the world will be more standardized because of the impact of mass media and increased mobility.

Access to more information will carry us toward an international consensus as to what is desirable in family life, art, recreation, education, diet, economic policies, and government.

Cruelty will be more vigorously rejected and methodically eliminated.

Leaders will be those who are the most able, regardless of their racial origins, religious beliefs, family backgrounds, or lack of great wealth.

The worldwide status and influence of the female will greatly increase.

Differences in wealth and ownership between haves and have-nots will narrow.

Through the mediation of trends, society will begin to design or give direction to the future so that the years ahead will better serve human welfare.

The changes described above will open many more doors for educational leadership. During the coming decade, however, education must do more than just lengthen its stride to keep pace with trends and innovations. We must bring social perception and long-range vision to the task of designing and planning schools that can help bring about the best of many possible tomorrows.

In the past few years there has been a good deal of publicity about the sudden, and it seems unexpected, surplus of teachers. Many graduates report difficulty in finding a desirable teaching job. As of spring 1972 there were an estimated seven teachers for every four jobs available. Explanations for this situation are not difficult to find: many of today's teachers were part of the World War II baby boom; the 1960s saw a sharp drop in the birth rate, and now the number of children entering first grade is leveling off; and some schools, particularly in the big cities, have experienced budget cuts and have been forced to reduce teaching staffs or limit normal expansion. On the other hand, educators see the present supply of teachers as a golden opportunity to make such needed changes as reducing class sizes, avoiding split sessions, expanding kindergarten and pre-school programs, and really making a serious attempt to improve the educational quality of our ghetto schools.

At the heart of the problem is our nation's economy. Presently the economy is not expanding and new jobs are not being created in nearly any field. To assume, however, that this situation will continue is short-sighted. In the article which follows, M. M. Chambers argues that we will make needed educational changes and that the American public will be willing and able to pay the increased costs for education in the future.

The Gallup Poll of Public Attitudes Toward Education, 1971, provides some data on the willingness of the public to support tax increases for the public schools: School bond issues fared no better in 1971 than they did in 1970. The public is reluctant to vote for additional funds; in fact, a majority of all school bond issues throughout the nation lost out at the voting booths. The percentage of issues voted upon favorably changed little during the year; it is still in the low forties.

To gauge voter sentiment toward voting tax increases for the public schools, this question was framed:

Suppose the local public schools said they needed much more money. As you feel at this time, would you vote to raise taxes for this purpose, or would you vote against raising taxes for this purpose?

When this question was asked in 1970, the results showed:

For raising taxes	37%
Against raising taxes	56%
No opinion	7%

When the same question was asked in 1971, the results were substantially the same:

For raising taxes	40%
Against raising taxes	52%
No opinion	8%

The pattern of those who vote favorably on tax increases for the public schools and those who vote against remains constant.

Those who are most inclined to approve tax increases are the better educated, the younger age groups, business and professional people. This probably augers well for future educational support.

The greatest opposition comes from the poorly educated, persons over 50 years of age, low-income groups, and manual laborers.

At the very least we can hope for a marked change in the priority that education now has among the nations of the world. UNESCO figures reveal that the world spends $100 a year per pupil and $7,800 a year per soldier. The $100-a-year figure applies only to developed countries; underdeveloped nations manage $5 annually. The world spends $110 billion per year on public education and $159 billion on armaments.

With the dawning of the age of Aquarius, the resources of the world could well be allocated toward the fulfillment of the human potential rather than to control or destroy one's fellow man. Is this too optimistic?

NO TEACHER
SURPLUS

M. M. Chambers

Sensational headlines in newspapers and widely circulated national magazines have shrilly trumpeted an oversupply of teachers. They quote college placement officers as reporting fewer jobs open this year than last year, and city school systems inundated with incredible floods of applications.

They quote the U.S. Commissioner of Labor Statistics who recently estimated that the total of new teachers likely to be needed between now and 1980 is 2½ million, while the number of fully credentialed new applicants will probably be 4¼ million.

The constructive feature of Commissioner Geoffrey H. Moore's comments is often entirely overlooked or concealed in a fine-print footnote. Among other things, he said: "More communities may introduce or expand kindergartens, nursery schools, and curriculums for the handicapped and for the gifted. Local school officials may feel they can improve the quality of education by hiring additional teachers to reduce class size."

The facts are that although the nation-wide annual number of births began to level off in 1957, there was no really substantial decline until 1962. This means there is already a little decrease in enrollments in the first three grades of the elementary schools. It also signals that high school enrollments will continue to rise until about 1978 (when babies born in 1962 will be aged 16); and college enrollments will go right on up until about 1982 (when those born in 1962 will reach age 20).

This is reinforced by at least three practically impregnable reasons: (1) There was no significant drop in number of births until 1962. (2) The percentage in the appropriate age-groups actually attending high school and college will continue to rise; the higher the level, the greater the percentage of rise. (3) In high school and college there will be smaller percentages of quick drop-outs and larger percentages of longer stays in school. In college and in graduate and professional schools, the presence of mature adult students will increase. The swift establishment and expansion of hundreds of two-year junior colleges will fortify and augment these trends.

Even now the public schools in some "inner cities" of huge population are so far short of doing their jobs well that there is desperate talk of the "demise" of public schools, and serious argument about such expedients as diverting state tax funds to private schools or adopting the weird "voucher plan" under which tax support would go to the parents rather than to the public schools. There are also incipient experiments involving the turning of whole local school systems, or selected parts of their programs, over to profit-seeking private corporations in the apparent naive hope that they will produce better results for less money.

Admittedly there is low morale in many schools and colleges, with some distrust and hostility between students, teachers, and administrators. Admittedly some elementary and high schools in many instances accomplish less than optimum educational results. We blame economic and cultural deprivation in the families of pupils, and impersonal bureaucracy in the schools. The remedy is not in repression, regimentation, and harsher

Reprinted by permission from M. M. Chambers, "No Teacher Surplus," *Phi Delta Kappan* 52 (October 1970): 118-19.

"discipline" in the schools; it is in the recruiting and holding of more and better teachers and auxiliary educational personnel, to make possible decent and humane person-to-person relationships between teachers and counselors and students.

A student-teacher ratio of 30 to 1 may be traditional, but it is absurdly high. It compels teachers to act like drill-sergeants and prevents them, for sheer lack of time, from giving the personal attention to each student and his work that a good job requires. Twice as many well-educated teachers as we now have, reducing the ratio to 15 to 1, would be none too many.

At about this point, unless you have thought this through thoroughly, you will be plaintively asking "Where would the money come from?" The answer is, "From the taxpayers—the masses of citizens who want the best of education for oncoming genera-tions, and are willing and able to pay for it!" State and federal support of public schools and colleges is increasing at a great rate, and will continue to grow.[1] Cities and other local subdivisions are no longer able to provide their own public services without state and federal financial aid, it is true; but the states are not up against a ceiling; and the federal support of domestic programs will expand enormously within a few years. There are occasional slowdowns that come with the advent of inept or reactionary state and federal administrations, but the long-term upward trend is irreversible.

Of course we can scarcely employ twice as many teachers in 1971 as we have in 1970. An estimate released by the U.S. Office of Education and published in a periodical of wide national circulation,[2] shows the gap between the estimated numbers of new elementary and secondary school teachers needed and the projected numbers of creden-tialed new candidates for each of the next five years as being:

1971	*1972*	*1973*	*1974*	*1975*
19,000	29,000	32,000	45,000	55,000

For a mythical average state of approximately 4 million people these figures would reduce to about 380, 580, 640, 900, and 1,100. Meeting these modestly graduated upward steps would hardly be a bankrupting burden for a state of 4 million population. The new money required for 1971 would be something like $1½ million. For California or New York it would be about $7 million. For any of 14 states having less than one million people it would be generally about $300,000 or less. Expressed in another way, in any state it would be about 35 cents per citizen.

This would accentuate the positive and take advantage of an opportunity that has not been available for a generation. There is no surplus of teachers. There is a rare opportunity to start to remedy a deficit of teachers. Theodore G. Mitau of the Minne-sota State Colleges has said this so-called national emergency is really a national opportunity. Allan W. Ostar of the American Association of State Colleges and Univer-sities says: "This is an opportunity, not a calamity. I call on our state and federal governments to take immediate steps to find new resources to enable our school districts and our colleges to utilize our supply of educated manpower for the improvement of the education of our children."

Mere panicky repetition of the fact that the shortage of teachers is now beginning to be less acute than it has been for many years, as though this were a misfortune, can

---

[1] For statistics in detail of the increases in state appropriations for annual operating expenses of higher education 1960–1970 see *Higher Education in the Fifty States* Danville, Illinois 61832: Interstate Publishers, 1970, 453 pp.

[2] *U.S. News and World Report,* July 6, 1970.

be a self-fulfilling prophecy of gloom. It can contribute to a downward spiral of fewer graduate students, poorly staffed schools, and general standstill or decline in the quality of education at all levels. It is reminiscent of the mindless "share the work" slogan during the Great Depression forty years ago, which would have put everybody on half-time, until it was recognized that there is always enough productive work to keep us all busy for a thousand years. That the difficulty was not lack of work to be done, but only failure in the allocation and distribution of resources.

We have passed from the nineteenth century economy of scarcity into the latter-day economy of abundance. Bold public investment in the expansion and improvement of education is necessary for continued progress in economic growth and quality of life. Placement officers could perform a great service if, whenever they report any tendency toward a surplus of well-qualified teacher-applicants, they would invariably add that this is the opportunity of the century to improve the schools and colleges, by expanding their overworked staffs of teachers and counselors.

The alleged forthcoming "glut of Ph.D.'s" is an especially wrongheaded concept. Eight hundred public junior colleges will be twelve hundred before 1980, and will enroll four million students. At present their faculties include only a negligible sprinkling of holders of doctoral degrees. Conceding that some doctoral programs other than the currently prevalent strait-jacketed mathematical research Ph.D are needed for college teachers and are now being developed, can we imagine the junior colleges frozen into the past mold of no doctorate holders on the faculties? Even the high school faculties need a substantial infusion of holders of doctoral degrees who have looked forward to scholarly careers in teaching. The secondary schools of France, middle Europe, and Scandinavia are largely staffed with persons at that level.

There are places for the esoteric Ph.D. research specialist, but we need ten times as many people somewhat more broadly educated up to the doctoral level to staff the schools and colleges. The theory of this is simply that teachers should be educated persons. This is far and away the most important factor in improving the quality and productivity of schools. It is unhealthy and counterproductive for graduate schools and departments to become panicky about the future market for doctorate holders, and become constrictive about admissions and generally fearful about the expansion of their own programs. This is another form of contribution to the possible downward spiral of discouraging graduate students, choking off the build-up of the supply of educated persons, and depressing the advancement of education for the present and future generations.

In my opinion we should and will adopt the positive stance, and convince the legislatures, state and national, that more and better-educated teachers, counselors, and administrators are essential. The people of this nation are not about to abandon public schools, or to allow the growth of universities and colleges to languish. Our confidence in education is not disappearing. It is moving upward. It behooves us to catch the vision and keep it in view.

Have you ever repeated a course taught by a different teacher? Could you immediately identify one teacher's approach as more conducive to learning? Given that both knew their content, what factors can you ascribe to each that account for their different classroom environment? What makes you feel more "at home" in some classes; notwithstanding subject matter competency, what factors can you cite that contribute to the successful creation of a healthy learning environment?

GIVE THEM
A PERFORMANCE

Elaine G. Denholtz

When I was a little girl, my mother taught me a lesson outside the classroom which has a direct bearing on my teaching career today. It was not the kind of lesson that was formal, structured, or clearly spelled out. My mother knew nothing of "the methodology madness." It was simply her passing remark in reply to an observation I made to her about the Treasurer's Report she delivered before a meeting at our home.

The reports by the officers preceding mother were full of facts, accurate to the third decimal point, and—alas—dreadfully dull. No one bothered to listen. But when mother got up, she wowed them! Her report was not nearly as meaty; she was off by 27 cents; and when she searched for the chart that she had crayoned as a visual aid, she remembered with horror that she had left it at the beauty parlor.

Yet she delighted them all. They hung on her words; they followed every gesture. She was warm, direct, earthy, and charming. And if she had absconded with all their funds, I think they would have cheered her on. Why?

"They really went for your speech. How did you make it so good?" I asked her.

She aimed her radiant smile straight at me. "Honey," she said, "I'm not the best treasurer in the world, but I guess they liked it because they could understand it. And," she winked broadly, "I gave them a performance."

Give them a performance was the lesson. I carry that into my class each day. Make them purr with your performance.

Let's admit it. Every teacher—whether he teaches sixth grade chorus or a graduate seminar in Advanced Comparative Anatomy of the Vertebrates—wants to get to his students, to make them care about the subject, to engender excitement and involvement; in their language: to turn them on.

I try to turn my students on by preparing for a performance each time we meet. Before class, I consider the theme (of the lesson, lecture, discussion), the costumes, the scenery, the pacing, the setting, the plot, the dramatic effects, the music, the lighting —the entire production. Impossible? I think not.

Consider this. I know a woman, a full professor. She has a Ph.D., three fellowships, and one grant under her belt and is chairman of her department. Her knowledge of her specialty is inexhaustible. She has a brilliant, incisive mind capable of dealing with the larger abstractions and also with remembering the picayune details. She should be a superb teacher. She isn't. She's a dud. Why?

First of all, her out-of-date appearance turns them off. As soon as she enters the room, in her lacquered hairdo, frilly dress, pointed toe shoes, and sequined harlequin

Reprinted by permission from Elaine G. Denholtz, "Give Them a Performance," *Today's Education: NEA Journal* 59 (October 1970): 55.

eyeglasses, she turns them off. Am I suggesting that she don a mini skirt and love beads, that she frug as she enters stage left? Certainly not. But why not get with it? That's costume! They want a *now* professor—someone of the seventies.

Second, while she is informative, accurate, and thorough, she is unbearably dull, doggedly unrealistic about young people, and completely unengaging. Her students respond with a "Who cares?" attitude. None of what she says seems relevant to their lives. It is all a badly performed, Grade B movie, so they switch her off.

The list of crimes committed by "competent teachers" against students is endless. The amazing thing is that in most cases they are the most obvious, hit-you-over-the-head type. Is there any excuse for a teacher to lecture by reading his notes? An author whom I had admired for years did this at a Princeton Writers Conference I attended, and fell from grace in the first five minutes of his talk. Because he didn't bother giving a performance, few bothered to listen to his erudition.

A teacher sells himself first. Of course, he must be competent, knowledgeable, scholarly. That's content. But what about his performance? Does he understand timing, or does he spit out information at an unvarying rate like a teletypewriter? Is his voice dull and unchanging in pitch and volume? Is he content with assigning Chapter II, Exercise 4, and giving a true-false quiz every Monday? Or does he employ various media—music, records, film, tape, student projects—and a variety of techniques to put across the production? Can he make his students laugh, make them angry, make them argue, make them *find out?* Does he pull out *all* the stops on occasion, or is he content to just soft-pedal the whole thing?

Make them purr with your performance!

What I am calling for does not require a combination of Raquel Welch and Judith Anderson. However, it does call for the kind of teacher who understands the excitement and drama of a good learning experience, and who is ready and able to put on a show. Such a person will enjoy the delicious taste of verbal applause when a student, lingering after class, says, "Hey, that was cool. I really dig it. Uh, could I talk to you about it some more?"

Meadow Heights is an upper-middle-class suburb of approximately 25,000 people. The leadership of the community has come to rest in a group of rising young business executives, some of whom compose the majority of the school board. The community takes great interest in its schools and the schools reflect it. The school system has a fine reputation. Its salary schedule is somewhat higher than others in the area and thus many good teachers have come to teach in Meadow Heights.

Recently a new superintendent of schools, Dr. Rice, was hired by the school board. Rice was reputed to be an efficient administrator and often claimed that he "applied business methods to educational problems."

One of Rice's first recommendations to the board was that a system of merit pay replace the salary schedule as the basis for teachers' salaries. Rice contended that paying the *same* amount to all teachers of equal training and experience with an automatic annual salary increment offered no incentive for teachers to excel. A system of merit pay would reward the hard working and creative teacher and introduce much needed competition into the school system and into the consideration of a teacher's salary. "It was just like selling," Rice said. "The energetic, creative, producing teacher should receive more in commissions than others on the staff. Making salary commensurate with ability and accomplishments would result in more teacher initiative, attract better young people into teaching and give the school system new life and morale," he concluded.

The head of the local teachers organization appeared before the board and argued for the retention of the salary schedule. "Many of the teachers were opposed to merit pay," he said.

So the Superintendent, with the cooperation of the board and the principals of the schools, planned a program of classroom observation and rating of each teacher. Principals were to make regular classroom observations of teachers and confer with the teacher after each observation. The rating of the teacher was to be given at the close of the year by the principal. The salary of the teachers for the next year was to be determined by the rating he or she was given. The criteria to be used in teacher rating were as follows:

1. Provides for the learning of students (55%):
   Uses psychological principles of learning.
   Uses principles of child growth and development.
   Manages classroom effectively.
   Organizes classroom for democratic living.
   Evaluates pupil achievement.
2. Counsels and guides students effectively (10%):
   Maintains effective relations with students individually and in groups.
   Makes significant use of counseling materials.
   Maintains effective relationship with parents.
   Maintains appropriate relations with guidance personnel.
3. Aids students to understand and appreciate our cultural heritage (5%):
   Transmits to students our cultural heritage, recognizing that most of such heritage is embodied in the school curricula.
4. Participates effectively in the other than formal teaching activities of the school (15%):

Works with others to maintain a unified learning process.

Assumes a full part of the responsibility for school activities.

Maintains harmonious personal relations with colleagues.

5. Works on a professional level (15%):

Gives evidence of the importance of the profession to its members, students, parents, and others in the community.

Assists in maintaining good relations between the school and others in the community.

Contributes to the profession by membership in the professional organizations and participates in their activities.

Assumes responsibility for his own professional growth.

Aids in the orientation of teachers coming into the system.

Complies with rules and administrative requests.

It was agreed by the board and the local teachers organization that the plan be submitted to a vote of the total teaching staff of 350 teachers. The teacher vote was to be the deciding factor in adopting or rejecting the merit pay system.

How would you vote? What are the pros and cons of merit pay?

It has been suggested in your elementary school system that the regular academic marks on the report card can be supplemented by a checklist on traits of effective citizenship. Among the traits which have been suggested are such things as "keeps desk neat at all times"; "prompt in turning in work"; "always in seat when bell rings"; "seldom absent"; "settles disputes by discussion"; "listens to opinion of others"; "plans work ahead"; and many more. If you were limited to some eight traits, what traits would you favor listed on the report card? On what grounds would you make this decision?

RADICAL
PERSPECTIVES

"Acceptance of the present condition is the only form of extremism which discredits us to our children."

Lorraine Hansberry

Contemporary critics point to the socio-educational scene largely with dejection and abandonment. There are those who would dismantle; those who would reconstruct; those who would courageously lead while others cautiously follow and ultimately those who would defer and suffer a malaise not unlike atrophy. This section is devoted to a glimpse into a society in which "school" would be redefined, perhaps assume the qualities of an existential utopia.

Attempts to radicalize education occur daily when any teacher in any school bravely dares to challenge outdated and outmoded curricular traditions, and these attempts are not limited to polemical outbursts by highly touted leftists. One need not be nearly as renowned as any of the authors in this section to be a driving force in the humanization of one of our most human endeavors. Presently we are witnessing an unprecedented attack on the technology which has vaulted our nation into material prominence. But can any society be so praised on the basis of what it does *to* people and not *for* people? Can the neutralization of eager, young, creative minds be considered a worthy accomplishment? Are the consequences of technocratic activity to be desired above those of existential encounter? How long must teachers be cowed into submission by defectors from the classroom whose only notion of education rests in discipline, order, quiet, corridor duty, lavatory duty, ad infinitum?

The readings contained herein express a glimmer of hope for those who dare to be human, who dare to explore the frontiers of awareness with their students. The rest may receive assurance that the list of the disenchanted grows longer and the hope lies not in the length but in the strength of the few to challenge effectively the many. The hope lies in the knowledge that those imbued with power among the many have acquired that power due largely to their refusal to challenge, to dare, to stand and fight. There is comfort in the knowledge that the adversary is weak, that his cause is not that of justice but that of expedience and that in our society the cause of right, not might, does at times prevail.

Beatrice and Ronald Gross in "Radical School Reform" analyze and articulate some of the changes of education's and society's toughest critics like Goodman, Friedenberg, Henry and Kozol. The inhuman character that many classrooms assume becomes the focal point of the critics' concerns. Barth raises some vital questions concerning the merits of the "open classroom," especially the personnel involved in their creation and management.

The Silberman article has been excerpted from the contemporary classic, *Crisis in the Classroom,* in which the author summarizes a few of his more significant research conclusions. The Goodman article, "Freedom and Learning: The Need for Choice," is a devastating attack on our compulsory educational system which Goodman "would largely dismantle." The prescriptions continue with "What the Kids Want," written by an unidentified New Jersey high school student, a refreshing piece of advice by a recipient of much of the advice heretofore offered.

The Robinson ("Alternative Schools: Challenge to Traditional Education?") and Fantini ("Options for Students, Parents, and Teachers: Public Schools of Choice") articles offer concrete proposals for learning about what's happening in the "alternative schools" movement as well as seven options that are within the realm of possibility for students, parents, and teachers sincerely concerned with the provision of alternatives to our mechanistic system.

The remainder of the articles, by Wertheimer, "School Climate and Student Learning"; and the Grosses, "A Little Bit of Chaos," are living examples of the merits of a humanistic style of teaching and learning. The articles cover elementary through secondary school and tell about the successes of several experimental programs. Jonathan Kozol concludes this section with an insightful analysis of the problems that plague "free schools." His perspective is especially refreshing for its frankness and sensitivity to the real needs of children and teachers.

Beatrice and Ronald Gross are two of the most articulate and responsible spokesmen for the increasing numbers of educational critics who advocate radical change in our elementary and secondary schools. The selection which follows provides a brief historical sketch of the most influential criticisms of American education over the past thirty years. They define radical education for us and describe it as the most far-reaching demand for change ever to challenge the prevailing educational system and indeed, the very nature of the contemporary American culture.

RADICAL
SCHOOL REFORM

Beatrice Gross
Ronald Gross

We have bungled badly in education. Not merely in the ways noted by most school critics—too little money for education, out-dated curricula, poorly trained teachers—but in more fundamental ways. It is not just that our schools fail to achieve their stated purposes, that they are not the exalted places their proponents proclaim. Rather, many are not even decent places for our children to be. They damage, they thwart, they stifle children's natural capacity to learn and grow healthily. To use Jonathan Kozol's frightening, but necessary, metaphor: they destroy the minds and hearts of our children.

The school crisis finally has broken through to basics. The debates of the 1950's about academic rigor and "life adjustment," the Sputnik-sparked worries that we were falling behind the Russians in producing scientists, James Conant's concerns about marketable skills, and Rudolph Flesch's formulas to make Johnny read—all suddenly seem irrelevant.

In the large urban centers, the black communities are demanding full control of their schools; in the suburbs, the students are demanding control of theirs. In the cities, the power structure is under attack; in the suburbs, the value structure. Reforms are debated which would have been branded anti-American and "unconstructive" 10 years ago, *e.g.,* abandonment of public education in favor of a competitive system of private and public alternatives, black schools in the ghetto as preferable to integrated schooling, political and economic reform as a prerequisite to better education, schools run by students themselves, or schools without subjects and teachers. To affirm such propositions would have put a writer beyond the pale of "responsible criticism" in the late 1950's. But today we have many examples where the existing system of public education has failed, and such alternatives have succeeded—street academies in the ghettos, Freedom Schools, experimental colleges, and Free Universities. In a few short years, men who were considered wild-eyed romantics have begun to sound like the most realistic voices in education.

The sharpness of the crisis has made the most basic questions the most relevant, and the most radical answers the most cogent. Radical means going to the root, posing the fundamental problems, and responding with theories and practices which are genuine alternatives to present theory and practice.

The term radical has many meanings, in fact. In politics, radical means revolutionary: black parents in the ghetto taking control of their schools. In social relations, radical means libertarian: an affirmation of the autonomy of the individual against the demands of the system. In a school situation, radical means unorthodox ways of promoting learning that fall outside the scope of conventional, or even innovative, school practice.

Radical thought and practice cover a wide range: from the grand demand that compulsory public education be repealed and the formal educational system dismantled, to intensely practical teachers working constructively within the existing system, but nevertheless, using truly unorthodox teaching techniques. But all of those involved share the belief that we will not have significantly better schools until we have radically different schools.

It is important to distinguish these radical theories and practices from those "innovations"—team teaching, teaching machines, the New Math and other "new curricula," teaching via television, and non-graded classes—which have appeared in many American schools in the past decade.

By the mid-1950's, Americans increasingly realized the importance of education in the economic sense. For the individual, it meant a chance for college and, thereby, an opportunity to find a job or occupation or profession in a world of work which was being transformed by automation and bureaucracies. A diploma was the passport to the affluent society.

For the nation, education was clearly the key to strength in a scientific and technological age. Sputnik, that superb visual aid, riveted home the practical relevance of Whitehead's dictum: "In the conditions of modern life the rule is absolute, the race which does not value trained intelligence is doomed." The ensuing sense of national urgency rallied an unprecedented corps of master plasterers to patch up the outmoded and intellectually disreputable facade of American education.

These "innovative" programs were undertaken in well-established schools with fairly conventional philosophies. They were not based on new ideas about the role of education, or the nature of the child, or the place of culture in a democratic society. They focused on practical methods of achieving the traditional end of schooling—the mastery of basic skills and subject matter—in schools strained by burgeoning enrollments and shortages of first-rate teachers. For the most part, they were ingenious new techniques rather than radical reforms.

These innovative approaches changed the climate of American public education in the late 1950's and early 1960's. So pervasive were they that the idea of "innovative education" was embodied in the most notable piece of Federal legislation aiding schools —the Elementary and Secondary Education Act of 1965. One of the titles of that act specifically mandated money for innovative demonstration projects. What these innovations achieved has been important; but what they failed to achieve, unfortunately, has been even more important.

Even as these innovations relieved the rigid programs in many schools, a deeper malaise in American education was developing unnoticed. The seemingly enlightened educators who had pressed these changes toward flexibility and enrichment had focused their energies entirely on making the process of learning in school more lively and rewarding. But they had not perceived that larger social forces were calling into question the relevance of the entire enterprise of formal education.

In the urban ghetto schools, starvation budgets, the impact of the slum environment, and teacher indifference and sometimes unconscious racism had reduced the schools to mere disciplinary institutions. In the suburbs, the shadow of college preparation and social conformity had blighted the process of growing up less brutally, but with comparable efficiency. In all schools, the excitement of learning seemed somehow to shrivel from the time the child entered till the time he left.

By the mid-1960's, black parents in the ghettos and white students on the campuses and in the suburban high schools began to revolt against the educational system. "Innovative" approaches, enlightened and humane as they were, simply did not seem to get at the deeper causes of the educational malaise. The riots in the urban slums and the demonstrations on the campuses of the multiversities made it shockingly clear that the educational system had reached a point where it no longer could continue without basic, radical changes in its structure, control, and operation. Radical reform is a vigorous recoil and response to realities too long suppressed.

The call for radical reform takes many forms. Social critics like Paul Goodman, Kenneth Clark, Edgar Friedenberg, and Marshall McLuhan articulate its theory. Teachers like Herbert Kohl, John Holt, Sylvia Ashton-Warner, and Jonathan Kozol describe a whole new way of teaching. Others of lesser renown report radically new programs spotted around the country, from the ghettos of Harlem and Watts to rural schools of Oregon and Kentucky. They draw insights and ideas from Rousseau, Dewey, Pestalozzi, Montessori, and A. S. Neill; from schools in Canada, England, and Africa. They can not be subsumed—theorists or practitioners—in any neat set of underlying principles.

For example, black leaders in the ghettos want radical political reform of education —changes in who says what goes. They feel they must have this control because the schools under white control have failed to teach their children those basic skills of reading and writing which spell survival in the American economy today. For them, radical educational attacks on the existence of schools *per se* or extensive questioning of pedagogical assumptions are often not the most compelling priority. Their children cannot read, and, until they have power over their children's education, no more basic criticisms can be meaningful to the ghetto parents they represent.

On the other hand, the most radical theorists—Goodman, Friedenberg, Jules Henry, McLuhan—are not critics of the educational system in the usual sense, because they are not interested first and foremost in schooling. They are interested less in teaching and learning than in growth, dignity, autonomy, freedom, and the development of the full range of human potentialities.

Despite these divergencies, there is a spirit that informs this thought and action as a whole, and that spirit has some distinguishable components. The radical criticism of America as a sick society. They come at it from many angles: its competitive ethos, its cultural vulgarity, its neglect or suppression of minority groups, its inherent racism and imperialism, and its failures in compassion, let alone enterprise, in regard to the wretched within its own boundaries and throughout the rest of the world. Their critique of the schools derives from this questioning of society, for they see the schools as the mere agents of society.

The radical critics then look at the schools. What they find in the classroom is suppression, irrelevance, uncaring, inhumanity, manipulation, and the systematic stultification of most of what is promising in children and youth. The concept of "miseducation" covers much of this, and additionally distinguishes the tone of their writings. Whereas some of them score the schools' failures to accomplish what they set out to do, or what the needs of society require them to do, the most radical attack them for being entirely too successful in doing the wrong things. From McLuhan to Holt, these writers agree that more of the same is worse than nothing. Like Goodman, they would not give one cent to bolster education as it now proceeds, but first would require dismantlement of the entire enterprise and its reconstitution along basically different lines.

Many of you are no doubt attracted to the open classroom concept championed by such notables as A. S. Neill and Herbert Kohl. As products of the usual traditional, rigid American elementary and secondary schools, you are probably greatly attracted by the ideas of freedom within the classroom and the students' freedom of choice in terms of curriculum and other activities. A teacher working with enthusiastic youngsters in an unstructured learning situation seems to be the ideal teaching-learning situation.

The authors have experienced a number of young teachers, steeped in the literature, language and crusading zeal of the radical school reformers, who became authoritarian, subject-centered traditionalists when they themselves begin to teach. What happened? A partial explanation is that many public schools are not easily changed and the young, idealistic teacher soon falls victim to the powerful cadre of traditional teachers on virtually every school faculty.

There is a further reason, however. Many young teachers appear to overlook or misunderstand the assumptions involved in an open classroom situation. Thus, when actually confronted with the teaching situation they revert to their earlier underlying assumptions about learning, youngsters, and human nature and become traditional classroom teachers.

In the article which follows, Roland Barth offers you an opportunity to test your assumptions about learning and knowledge. Take his test and see if your assumptions are compatible with an open classroom philosophy.

SO YOU WANT TO CHANGE TO
AN OPEN CLASSROOM

Roland S. Barth

Another educational wave is breaking on American shores. Whether termed "integrated day," "Leicestershire Plan," "informal classroom," or "open education," it promises new and radical methods of teaching, learning, and organizing the schools.[1] Many American educators who do not shy from promises of new solutions to old problems are preparing to ride the crest of the wave. In New York State, for instance, the commissioner of education, the chancellor of New York City schools, and the president of the state branch of the American Federation of Teachers have all expressed their intent to make the state's classrooms open classrooms. Schools of education in such varied places as North Dakota, Connecticut, Massachusetts, New York, and Ohio are tooling up to prepare the masses of teachers for these masses of anticipated open classrooms.

Some educators are disposed to search for the new, the different, the flashy, the radical, or the revolutionary. Once an idea or a practice, such as "team teaching," "nongrading," and (more recently) "differentiated staffing" and "performance contracting," has been so labeled by the Establishment, many teachers and administrators are quick to adopt it. More precisely, these educators are quick to assimilate new ideas

Reprinted by permission from Roland S. Barth, "So You Want to Change to an Open Classroom," *Phi Delta Kappan,* October 1971, pp. 97-99. The Assumptions also appear in Barth, *Open Education and the American School* (New York: Agathon, 1972).
[1]For a fuller description of this movement, see Roland S. Barth and Charles H. Rathbone, annotated bibliographies: "The Open School: A Way of Thinking About Children, Learning and Knowledge," *The Center Forum,* Vol. 3, No. 7, July, 1969, a publication of the Center for Urban Education, New York City; and "A Bibliography of Open Education, Early Childhood Education Study," jointly published by the Advisory for Open Education and the Education Development Center, Newton, Mass., 1971.

into their cognitive and operational framework. But in so doing they often distort the original conception without recognizing either the distortion or the assumptions violated by the distortion. This seems to happen partly because the educator has taken on the verbal, superficial abstraction of a new idea without going through a concomitant personal reorientation of attitude and behavior. Vocabulary and rhetoric are easily changed; basic beliefs and institutions all too often remain little affected. If open education is to have a fundamental and positive effect on American education, and if changes are to be consciously made, rhetoric and good intentions will not suffice.

There is no doubt that a climate potentially hospitable to fresh alternatives to our floundering educational system exists in this country. It is even possible that, in this brief moment in time, open education may have the opportunity to prove itself. However, a crash program is dangerous. Implementing foreign ideas and practices is a precarious business, and I fear the present opportunity will be abused or misused. Indeed, many attempts to implement open classrooms in America have already been buried with the epitaphs "sloppy permissivism," "neo-progressive," "Communist," "anarchical," or "laissez-faire." An even more discouraging although not surprising consequence has been to push educational practice further away from open education than was the case prior to the attempt at implementation.

Most educators who say they want open education are ready to change *appearances.* They install printing presses, tables in place of desks, classes in corridors, nature study. They adopt the *vocabulary:* "integrated day," "interest areas," "free choice," and "student initiated learning." However, few have understanding of, let alone commitment to, the philosophical, personal, and professional roots from which these practices and phrases have sprung, and upon which they depend so completely for their success. It is my belief that changing appearances to more closely resemble some British classrooms without understanding and accepting the rationale underlying these changes will lead inevitably to failure and conflict among children, teachers, administrators, and parents. American education can withstand no more failure, even in the name of reform or revolution.

I would like to suggest that before you jump on the open classroom surfboard, a precarious vehicle appropriate neither for all people nor for all situations, you pause long enough to consider the following statements and to examine your own reactions to them. Your reactions may reveal salient attitudes about children, learning, and knowledge. I have found that successful open educators in both England and America tend to take similar positions on these statements. Where do you stand?

ASSUMPTIONS ABOUT LEARNING AND KNOWLEDGE

INSTRUCTIONS: Make a mark somewhere along each line which best represents your own feelings about each statement.

Example: School serves the wishes and needs of adults better than it does the wishes and needs of children.

strongly agree	agree	no strong feeling	disagree	strongly disagree

1. Assumptions About Children's Learning

Motivation

Assumption 1:   Children are innately curious and will explore their environment without adult intervention.

| strongly agree | agree | no strong feeling | disagree | strongly disagree |

Assumption 2:   Exploratory behavior is self-perpetuating.

| strongly agree | agree | no strong feeling | disagree | strongly disagree |

Conditions for Learning

Assumption 3: The child will display natural exploratory behavior if he is not threatened.

| strongly agree | agree | no strong feeling | disagree | strongly disagree |

Assumption 4:   Confidence in self is highly related to capacity for learning and for making important choices affecting one's learning.

| strongly agree | agree | no strong feeling | disagree | strongly disagree |

Assumption 5:   Active exploration in a rich environment, offering a wide array of manipulative materials, will facilitate children's learning.

| strongly agree | agree | no strong feeling | disagree | strongly disagree |

Assumption 6:   Play is not distinguished from work as the predominant mode of learning in early childhood.

| strongly agree | agree | no strong feeling | disagree | strongly disagree |

Assumption 7:   Children have both the competence and the right to make significant decisions concerning their own learning.

| strongly agree | agree | no strong feeling | disagree | strongly disagree |

Assumption 8:   Children will be likely to learn if they are given considerable choice in the selection of the materials they wish to work with and in the choice of questions they wish to pursue with respect to those materials.

strongly agree	agree	no strong feeling	disagree	strongly disagree

Assumption 9: Given the opportunity children will choose to engage in activities which will be of high interest to them.

strongly agree	agree	no strong feeling	disagree	strongly disagree

Assumption 10: If a child is fully involved in and is having fun with an activity, learning is taking place.

strongly agree	agree	no strong feeling	disagree	strongly disagree

Social Learning

Assumption 11: When two or more children are interested in exploring the same problem or the same materials, they will often choose to collaborate in some way.

strongly agree	agree	no strong feeling	disagree	strongly disagree

Assumption 12: When a child learns something which is important to him, he will wish to share it with others.

strongly agree	agree	no strong feeling	disagree	strongly disagree

Intellectual Development

Assumption 13: Concept formation proceeds very slowly.

strongly agree	agree	no strong feeling	disagree	strongly disagree

Assumption 14: Children learn and develop intellectually not only at their own rate but in their own style.

strongly agree	agree	no strong feeling	disagree	strongly disagree

Assumption 15: Children pass through similar stages of intellectual development, each in his own way and at his own rate and in his own time.

strongly agree	agree	no strong feeling	disagree	strongly disagree

Assumption 16: Intellectual growth and development take place through a sequence of concrete experiences followed by abstractions.

strongly agree	agree	no strong feeling	disagree	strongly disagree

Assumption 17:   Verbal abstractions should follow direct experience with objects and ideas, not precede them or substitute for them.

strongly agree	agree	no strong feeling	disagree	strongly disagree

Evaluation

Assumption 18:   The preferred source of verification for a child's solution to a problem comes through the materials he is working with.

strongly agree	agree	no strong feeling	disagree	strongly disagree

Assumption 19:   Errors are necessarily a part of the learning process; they are to be expected and even desired, for they contain information essential for further learning.

strongly agree	agree	no strong feeling	disagree	strongly disagree

Assumption 20:   Those qualities of a person's learning which can be carefully measured are not necessarily the most important.

strongly agree	agree	no strong feeling	disagree	strongly disagree

Assumption 21:   Objective measures of performance may have a negative effect upon learning.

strongly agree	agree	no strong feeling	disagree	strongly disagree

Assumption 22:   Learning is best assessed intuitively, by direct observation.

strongly agree	agree	no strong feeling	disagree	strongly disagree

Assumption 23:   The best way of evaluating the effect of the school experience on the child is to observe him over a long period of time.

strongly agree	agree	no strong feeling	disagree	strongly disagree

Assumption 24:   The best measure of a child's work is his work.

strongly agree	agree	no strong feeling	disagree	strongly disagree

II. Assumptions About Knowledge

Assumption 25: The quality of being is more important than the quality of knowing; knowledge is a means of education, not its end. The final test of an education is what a man *is*, not what he *knows*.

strongly agree	agree	no strong feeling	disagree	strongly disagree

Assumption 26: Knowledge is a function of one's personal integration of experience and therefore does not fall into neatly separate categories or "disciplines."

strongly agree	agree	no strong feeling	disagree	strongly disagree

Assumption 27: The structure of knowledge is personal and idiosyncratic; it is a function of the synthesis of each individual's experience with the world.

strongly agree	agree	no strong feeling	disagree	strongly disagree

Assumption 28: Little or no knowledge exists which it is essential for everyone to acquire.

strongly agree	agree	no strong feeling	disagree	strongly disagree

Assumption 29: It is possible, even likely, that an individual may learn and possess knowledge of a phenomenon and yet be unable to display it publicly. Knowledge resides with the knower, not in its public expression.

strongly agree	agree	no strong feeling	disagree	strongly disagree

Most open educators, British and American, "strongly agree" with most of these statements.[2] I think it is possible to learn a great deal both about open education and about oneself by taking a position with respect to these different statements. While it would be folly to argue that strong agreement assures success in developing an open classroom, or, on the other hand, that strong disagreement predicts failure, the assumptions are, I believe, closely related to open education practices. Consequently, I feel that for those sympathetic to the assumptions, success at a difficult job will be more likely. For the educator to attempt to adopt practices which depend for their success upon general adherence to these beliefs without actually adhering to them is, at the very least, dangerous.

At the same time, we must be careful not to assume that an "official" British or U.S. government-inspected type of open classroom or set of beliefs exists which is the

[2]Since these assumptions were assembled, I have "tested" them with several British primary teachers, headmasters, and inspectors and with an equal number of American proponents of open education. To date, although many qualifications in language have been suggested, there has not been a case where an individual has said of one of the assumptions, "No, that is contrary to what I believe about children, learning, or knowledge."

standard for all others. Indeed, what is exciting about British open classrooms is the *diversity* in thinking and behavior for children and adults—from person to person, class to class, and school to school. The important point here is that the likelihood of successfully developing an open classroom increases as those concerned agree with the basic assumptions underlying open education practices. It is impossible to "role play" such a fundamentally distinct teaching responsibility.

For some people, then, drawing attention to these assumptions may terminate interest in open education. All to the good; a well-organized, consistent, teacher-directed classroom probably has a far less harmful influence upon children than a well-intentioned but sloppy, permissive, and chaotic attempt at an open classroom in which teacher and child must live with contradiction and conflict. For other people, awareness of these assumptions may stimulate confidence and competence in their attempts to change what happens to children in school.

In the final analysis, the success of a widespread movement toward open education in this country rests not upon agreement with any philosophical position but with satisfactory answers to several important questions: For what kinds of people—teachers, administrators, parents, children—is the open classroom appropriate and valuable? What happens to children in open classrooms? Can teachers be *trained* for open classrooms? How can the resistance from children, teachers, administrators, and parents—inevitable among those not committed to open education's assumptions and practices—be surmounted? And finally, should participation in an open classroom be *required* of teachers, children, parents, and administrators?

Silberman's massive study has become one of the classic works dealing with American education. No stone is left unturned, no problem unexposed. In a very Deweyan sense, Silberman speaks of the need for considering consequences, for the value of the study of education in all areas of the liberal arts curriculum. In an era when the study of education has come to imply something less desirable than the study of sociology or philosophy, Silberman maintains these disciplines cannot avoid confronting the educational institution in pursuit of what constitutes the "good life" or "the good society." Of what value do you find the study of education? Is a conception of man more central to the study of life and society than the study of education or are they bound together interminably?

MURDER IN
THE SCHOOLROOM

Charles E. Silberman

"The most deadly of all possible sins," Erik Erikson suggests, "is the mutilation of a child's spirit." It is not possible to spend any prolonged period visiting public schools without being appalled by the mutilation visible everywhere: mutilation of spontaneity, of joy in learning, of pleasure in creating, of sense of self. The public schools, those "killers of the dream," to appropriate a phrase of Lillian Smith's, are the kind of institution one cannot really dislike until one gets to know them well. Because adults take the schools so much for granted, they fail to appreciate what grim, joyless places most American schools are, how oppressive and petty are the rules by which they are governed, how intellectually sterile and aesthetically barren the atmosphere, what an appalling lack of civility obtains on the part of teachers and principals, what contempt they unconsciously display for children as children.

And it need not be! Public schools *can* be organized to facilitate joy in learning and aesthetic expression and to develop character—in the rural and urban slums no less than in the prosperous suburbs. This is no utopian hope; there are models now in existence that can be followed.

What makes the change possible, moreover, is that what is mostly wrong with the public schools is not due to venality, or indifference, or stupidity, but to mindlessness. To be sure, teaching has its share of sadists and clods, of insecure and angry men and women who hate their students for their openness, their exuberance, their color, or their affluence. But by and large, teachers, principals, and superintendents are decent, intelligent, and caring people who try to do their best, by their lights. If they make a botch of it, and an uncomfortably large number do, it is because it simply never occurs to more than a handful to ask *why* they are doing what they are doing—to think seriously or deeply about the purposes or consequences of education. This mindlessness—the failure or refusal to think seriously about educational purpose, the reluctance to question established practice—is not the monopoly of the public school; it is diffused remarkably evenly throughout the entire educational system, and indeed the entire society.

The solution must lie in infusing the various educating institutions with purpose; more important, with thought about purpose, and about the ways in which techniques, content, and organization fulfill or alter purpose. And given the tendency of institutions to confuse day-to-day routine with purpose, to transform the means into the end itself, the infusion cannot be a one-shot affair. The process of self-examination, of "self-renewal," to use John Gardner's useful term, must be continuous. We must find ways of stimulating educators—public school teachers, principals, and superintendents; college professors, deans, and presidents: radio, television, and film directors and producers; newspaper, magazine, and TV journalists and executives—to think about what they are doing, and why they are doing it. And we must persuade the general public to do the same.

Students need to learn far more than the basic skills. Children who have just started school may still be in the labor force in the year 2030. For them, nothing could be more wildly impractical than an education designed to prepare them for specific vocations or professions or to facilitate their adjustment to the world as it is. To be practical, an education should prepare a man for work that doesn't yet exist and whose nature cannot even be imagined. This can be done only by teaching people how to learn, by giving them the kind of intellectual discipline that will enable them to apply man's accumulated wisdom to new problems as they arise, the kind of wisdom that will enable them to *recognize* new problems as they arise.

Education should prepare people not just to earn a living but to live a life: a creative, humane, and sensitive life. This means that the schools must provide a liberal, humanizing education. And the purpose of liberal education must be, and indeed always has been, to educate educators—to turn out men and women who are capable of educating their families, their friends, their communities, and most important, themselves.

Of what does the capacity to educate oneself consist? It means that one has both the desire and the capacity to learn for himself, to dig out what he needs to know. It means that one has the capacity to judge what is worth learning. It means, too, that one can think for himself, so that he is dependent on neither the opinions nor the facts of others, and that he uses that capacity to think about his own education, which means to think about his own nature and his place in the universe—about the meaning of life and of knowledge and of the relations between them. "To refuse the effort to understand," Wayne Booth, dean of the College of the University of Chicago, argues, "is to resign from the human race." "You cannot distinguish an educated man," he continues, "by whether or not he believes in God, or in UFO's. But you can tell an educated man by the way he takes hold of the question of whether God exists, or whether UFO's are from Mars."

To be educated in this sense means also to know something of the experience of beauty, if not in the sense of creating it or discoursing about it, then at the very least, in the sense of being able to respond to it—to respond, that is to say, both to the beauty of nature and to the beauty of the art made by our fellowmen.

To be educated also means to understand something of how to make our intentions effective in the real world, of how to apply knowledge to the life one lives and the society in which one lives it. The aim of education, as Alfred North Whitehead has written, "is the acquisition of the art of the utilization of knowledge." Indeed, "a merely well-informed man is the most useless bore on God's earth."

In all of this, the schools fail utterly and dismally. They fail in another and equally important way. Education is not only a preparation for later life; it is an aspect of life itself. The great bulk of the young now spend a minimum of twelve years in school; with kindergarten attendance, and now preschool programs, becoming more widespread, more and more of the young will have spent thirteen to fifteen years attending school by the time they have finished high school. The quality of that experience must be regarded as important in its own right.

The most important characteristic that nearly all schools share is a preoccupation with order and control. And one of the most important controls is the clock. Things happen because it is time for them to occur. This means that a major part of the teacher's role is to serve as traffic manager and timekeeper, either deciding on a schedule himself or making sure that a schedule others have made is adhered to.

Several things follow from this. Adherence to a timetable means that a great deal of time is wasted, the experiencing of delay being one of the inevitable outcomes of traffic management. No one who examines classroom life carefully can fail to be astounded by the proportion of the students' time that is taken up just in waiting. The time is rarely used productively. Hence in the elementary grades, an able student can be absent from school for as long as two to three weeks and, quite literally, catch up with all he has missed in a single morning.

Adherence to the schedule also means that lessons frequently end before the students have mastered the subject at hand. As Herbert Kohl points out, "the tightness with time that exists in the elementary school has nothing to do with the quantity that must be learned or the children's needs. It represents the teacher's fear of loss of control and is nothing but a weapon used to weaken the solidarity and opposition of the children that too many teachers unconsciously dread."

ITEM: An elite private school in the East, once a bastion of progressive education. A fifth-grade teacher is conducting a mathematics class, demonstrating a technique for quick multiplication and division by recognizing certain arithmetic patterns. A few students grasp the point instantly; a few ignore the teacher altogether; most struggle to grasp the concept. Just as they are beginning to catch on—mutterings of "I get it, I get it," "I think I see," "Oh, that's how it works" can be heard all over the classroom—the lesson ends. No bell has rung; bells would violate the school's genteel progressive atmosphere. But the time schedule on the board indicates that math ends and social studies begins at 10:40, and it is now 10:37; the teacher tells the children to put away the math worksheets and take out their social studies texts. Some of the children protest; they're intrigued with the patterns they are discovering, and another five or ten minutes would enable them to consolidate what they have only begun to grasp. No matter; the timetable rules.

ITEM: All over the United States, that last week of November, 1963, teachers reported the same complaint: "I can't get the children to concentrate on their work; all they want to do is talk about the assassination." The idea that the children might learn more from discussing President Kennedy's assassination—or that, like most adults, they were simply too obsessed with the horrible events to think about anything else—didn't occur to these teachers. It wasn't in that week's lesson plan.

It is all too easy, of course, for the outsider to criticize. Unless one has taught (as this writer and members of his staff have), or has studied classroom procedures close up, it is hard to imagine the extent of the demands made on a teacher's attention. Philip W. Jackson's studies of teacher-student interchange, for example, indicate that "the teacher typically changes the focus of his concern about 1,000 times daily," with many shifts of interest lasting only a few seconds, most of them less than a minute.

There are occasions when it is wise to depart from the lesson plan—surely the assassinations of a President, a distinguished civil rights leader and Nobel Laureate, and a senator contending for the presidency are such occasions—but there are also times when the teacher may be well advised to resist the seduction of talking about the day's headlines.

The trouble, then, is not with the schedule or the lesson plan per se, but with the fact that teachers too often see them as ends in themselves, rather than as means to an end. Even when children are excited about something directly related to the curriculum, teachers ignore or suppress the interest if it is not on the agenda for that period.

ITEM: A scholar studying curriculum reform visits a classroom using a new elementary science curriculum. Arriving a few minutes before the class was scheduled to begin, he sees a cluster of excited children examining a turtle with enormous fascination and intensity. "Now children, put away the turtle," the teacher insists. "We're going to have our science lesson." The lesson is on crabs.

The tyranny of the lesson plan in turn encourages an obsession with routine for the sake of routine. School is filled with countless examples of teachers and administrators confusing means with ends, thereby making it impossible to reach the ends for which the means were devised.

ITEM: A fourth-grader is discovered by his parents to have abandoned reading E. B. White and the Dr. Doolittle books in favor of Little Golden Books—at his teacher's request. The young teacher—a dear, sweet, loving human being—explains that students are required to submit a weekly book report on a 4 x 6 filing card. If the student were to read books as long as *Charlotte's Web* or *Dr. Doolittle,* he wouldn't be able to submit a weekly report, and his reports might be too long to fit on the file card. "I urged him to continue reading those books on his own," the teacher explains, "but not for school." The youngster does not continue, of course; he has learned all too well that the object of reading is not enjoyment, but to fill out file cards.

ITEM: A suburban community boasts of its new three-million-dollar elementary "school of the future," with classrooms all built around a central library core, which one piece of promotional literature describes as "the nerve center of all educational processes in the school." There is not even a full-time librarian, and children are permitted to use the library only during scheduled "library periods," when they practice taking books from the shelves and returning them. They are not permitted to *read* the books they take off the shelves, however; they are there to learn "library skills," and the librarian will not permit them to "waste time." Nor are children permitted to borrow books to read over Christmas or Easter vacation; the librarian wants her books "in order." If a parent protests vigorously enough, the librarian makes an exception—after warning the child that "you'd better take care of that book and bring it back on time."

ITEM: A junior high school in a West Coast city. The day after a student has thrown a book out of a classroom window, a distinguished professor of education doing research in the school reports, all the teachers received a memorandum from the principal: "Please keep all books away from students."

ITEM: With considerable fanfare, a New York City school district introduces what it calls "The Balanced Class Project" in a neighborhood containing a rich mixture of black, white, and Puerto Rican youngsters. The experiment, which involves heterogeneous grouping of children in classes, is designed to demonstrate the values of diversity. But instead of the English-speaking youngsters learning Spanish from their Puerto Rican classmates and teaching them English in turn, all children are taught French.

Administrators tend to be even guiltier of this kind of mindlessness and slavish adherence to routine for the sake of routine. It is, in a sense, built into their job description and into the way in which they view their role. Most schools are organized and run to facilitate order; the principal or superintendent is considered, and considers himself, a manager whose job is to keep the organization running as efficiently as possible.

This preoccupation with efficiency, which is to say, with order and control, turns the teacher into a disciplinarian as well as a timekeeper and traffic manager. In the interests of efficiency, moreover, discipline is defined in simple but rigid terms: the absence of noise and of movement. "When we ask children *not* to move, we should have excellent reasons for doing so," the English psychologist and educator, Susan Isaacs, of the University of London, argued in 1932. "It is stillness we have to justify, not movement." But no justification is offered or expected. Indeed, there is no more firmly rooted school tradition than the one that holds that children must sit still, at their desks, without conversing at all, both during periods of waiting, when they have nothing to do, and during activities that almost demand conversation. Yet even on an assembly line, there is conversation and interaction among workers, and there are coffee breaks and work pauses as well.

ITEM: A new suburban elementary school is being hailed in architectural circles for its "open design." The building has no corridors; the sixteen classrooms open instead onto "project areas" with worktables, sinks, et al., connected to a central library core. What the architects don't know, however, is that in most classrooms, the project areas go unused: if some children are in the project area and some are in the regular classroom, the teacher might not be able to see every child, and so some of them might be carrying on a conversation without detection.

ITEM: In lecturing the assembled students on the need for and virtue of absolute silence, an elementary school principal expostulates on the wonders of a school for the "deaf and dumb" he had recently visited. The silence was just wonderful, he tells the assembly; the children could all get their work done because of the total silence. The goal is explicit: to turn normal children into youngsters behaving as though they were missing two of their faculties.

ITEM: A high school in a New England city is very proud of its elaborately equipped language laboratory, with a new "Random Access Teaching Equipment" system touted as "tailored to the individual student's progress, as each position permits the instructor to gauge the progress of all students on an individual basis." To make sure that its expensive equipment is used properly, the high school gives students careful instructions, among them the following:

No one is an individual in the laboratory. Do nothing and touch nothing until instructions are given by the teacher. Then listen carefully and follow directions exactly.

The equipment in the laboratory is not like ordinary tape recorders. The principles involved are quite different. Please do not ask unnecessary questions about its operation.

You will stand quietly behind the chair at your booth until the teacher asks you to sit. Then sit in as close to the desk as possible.

The instructions for the lab assistants are equally explicit. They include the following:

1. Keep watching the students all the time.
    a) By standing in the middle of the lab on window side you can see most of the lab.
    b) Walk along the rows to make sure all arms are folded; politely but firmly ask the students to do this.

ITEM: A first-grade classroom has the following sign prominently posted:

RULES FOR CLASSES 1-7

1. Keep your hands at your sides.
2. Raise your hand to speak.
3. Be polite and kind to all.
4. Fold hands when not working.

The sign does not indicate how a child can fold hands that are required to be at his side. . . .

*Have you ever wondered about the possibility of a public school curriculum designed in
such a way as to accommodate a number of different academic lifestyles? More often than
not we are led to believe that a commitment to one type of educational program cannot
provide accommodation for methods and techniques not within the purview of the
philosophy of education to which one has made a commitment. Diane Divoky presents a
refreshing insight into the public school system of Burlington, Vermont and its attempt to
humanize the curriculum of its high school. Dr. Harvey B. Scribner, Vermont Commissioner
of Education, was the moving force behind the unorthodox approach to secondary education
in Burlington. Before you decide that the "open classroom" is the right approach for you,
take the time to consider the consequences of that approach, especially in terms of the
successes and failures of the students and teachers in Vermont.*

YOUNG IDEAS IN
AN OLD STATE

Diane Divoky

In Burlington, Vermont, it's different. When people talk about their schools, they talk
about how kids learn. There is a sense among them that all things are still possible for
youngsters growing up. If one program doesn't work, try a different kind. If schools
themselves seem wrongheaded, try learning in the community. If there are no easy
answers, at least there are alternatives.

Possibilities are open, because, in spite of industrial and population growth, Burlington remains a community where real people with faces and names run things, where
daily life is manageable, where nothing is farther away than a walk down Church Street
or a five-minute drive across town. People and institutions connect and intertwine: The
woman doctor who heads the child health services for the state is also chairman of the
board of a private school, when her friend, the minister's wife, calls her about the
possibility of setting up a free community school. The sixteen-year-old activist serves
on the Governor's Committee on Education, and the proper-looking chap in the back
of the meeting of long-haired kids in a coffeehouse is the state's Lieutenant Governor.
Roles are loose.

There is another influence. Whenever people talk with excitement about experimental schools, new forms, the possibilities of change, the name Scribner comes up as a
reference point, a footnote, a hero. Dr. Harvey B. Scribner, Vermont Commissioner of
Education, is an anomaly—an unorthodox schoolman in a conservative state.

Now almost three years in the job (he came to Vermont after gaining a national
reputation for integrating the suburban Teaneck, New Jersey, schools), Scribner seems
to enjoy the controversies that surround him. He wears his sideburns long—longer than
most high schools in the state would allow—and talks a language refreshingly free of
educational platitudes: "What we need are new forms, not just reforms. . . . I'd like to
have twenty-five approaches, not one solution. . . . School is merely a place where you
resolve the problems met outside of school. . . . But teachers really believe that children
don't learn unless they teach them. . . . We promise kids defeat: grades, marks. . . .
Sports is the way we finance hostility between small towns. . . . If only we'd put as much

time into thinking about learning as we do into thinking about how kids dress. . . . Don't fight about terminology—don't say you're going to ungrade a school—just ungrade it. . . . I keep telling the poor that the schools aren't serving them, that they've got to stand up and start making demands."

A tireless worker who will travel anywhere in the state to talk to anyone, Scribner keeps his staff small ("You've got to wipe out the bureaucracy") and contracts with outsiders for special projects. One of his favorites is DUO, which allows the state's highschoolers to do volunteer work in the community for academic credit.

Currently he is trying to convince small school districts to contract with his department to become demonstration districts, to translate into practice the concepts set forth in Scribner's *Vermont Design for Education.* Presented to the public in a pleasant little publication complete with cartoons, the *Design* contains premises considered so radical or subversive by some Vermonters that requests for its recall appear frequently in the legislature and newspapers. ("The emphasis must be upon learning, rather than upon teaching." "A student must be accepted as a person.")

The kids and the change-makers love Scribner. An informal state-wide network of teachers and administrators actively working for school reform—known as the Stowe Caucus—considers him their patron saint. "We feel more comfortable here because he's there," a teacher at a Burlington free school said. "He's the most beautiful thing that's ever happened to Vermont," is the word at another. A disgruntled Burlington High School senior confesses: "Whenever I'm really discouraged, I just think about Harvey Scribner and read the *Vermont Design,* and then I feel better."

Burlington is not the only place where Scribner's influence is felt, but as the largest city in the state (population: 40,000), it's a good indicator. The city has, as even the critics will tell you, excellent public schools: a 1,600 student high school, two junior high schools, ten elementary schools. Partly because the system hasn't had to worry about a race problem or even a militant teachers' union, it's been able to focus elsewhere: on an elementary school with child-centered, open classrooms; on new structures within the junior high schools; on making change attractive and desirable to the public. The associate superintendent said: "We've got lots of time in Burlington. And we've got reasonable people."

Moreover, the climate and the times are fostering a new educational pluralism. Counter-institutions are beginning to emerge. BEAM School is a haven, an educational experiment for bright students growing disenchanted with the very schools that have pronounced them successful. Shaker Mountain School is a free school for poor youngsters pushed out of the public schools as "unmanageable." And the ASPIRE program, operating within the high school for near dropouts, is a recognition by the institution that its style and routines do not suit at least one group of its students.

For the kids, the existence of new options and new styles creates all kinds of questions. Is the BEAM School a spur for change in the high school, or is it simply a safety valve for student unrest? If the kids at Shaker Mountain were rejected by the public schools, are those schools doing their job? Should the high school simply try to serve some nebulous "typical student," or should it really value diversity? "How come I somehow feel intimidated every time I walk into the high school, yet there is no fear at BEAM?" asks the boy who is the high school's pride. "Why can't I take two courses at the high school and the rest wherever I want?" The clientele is learning to be discriminating about the process of education.

Burlington High School, enrolling a diverse student body, in fact, offers a good deal. Built in 1964, the school is a series of two-story buildings, connected by glass-walled passageways, that climb a hillside. The fifty-three-acre campus abuts Lake Champlain northeast of the city. The linear and fragmented spread of the buildings provides a degree of physical and psychological elbowroom found in few institutional buildings. The school has adopted, rather unself-consciously and with little fanfare, innovations still in the works at renowned suburban high schools. A house plan divides the student body into four administrative units to facilitate counseling, communication, and supervision. (The fact of "so many people in one place" still runs counter to the Vermont sensibility.)

Flexible scheduling and the "collegiate mode" stagger the length of courses and class hours based on actual need, provide individualized programs for students, and loosen up the use of building space. This year the English department went "nongraded," offering students twenty-three elective courses in seventy-nine sections (for example, Semantics, The Rebel in American Literature, Afro-American Literature). Pass/fail began cautiously this semester. Enterprising upperclassmen are beginning to take courses for credit at the University of Vermont on the other side of town. The reforms are not just for the college-bound. American Studies, an experimental, interdisciplinary course for slow students, uses a humanistic, team-teaching approach. A sophisticated and relevant program of vocational-technical training is available in the high school's newest addition, the area vocational center serving seven high schools.

What is striking about the high school is not so much its model programs as its relaxed sense of itself. The top three administrators are all under thirty and all recent newcomers to the system. There are no bells, although pop music is heard in the entrance hall. Students come and go as they please between classes, to a learning center, a student lounge, or off campus.

The dress code died after some friendly negotiations last fall. "We knew if we waited a couple of weeks the change would come through the democratic process. So we did," a student protester said. A bulletin board announces an all-day happening on the environment; a poster invites students to drop by at a "talk-in" on education. A sign nearby says: "I would rather have a school produce a happy street cleaner than a neurotic scholar."

In spite of all this, Burlington High School still is heir to many of the assumptions and manners that make learning and schooling somewhat incompatible, that keep high school a place once removed from the world outside. The daily "base period" requires students to herd into assemblies to be counted and read at. A student report on the blues and B. B. King grows strangely de-charged in the blandness of a classroom. A creative writing class becomes a long list of "dos" and "don'ts," and across the hall literary images are extracted lifelessly from a novel. A student leader calls his round of clubs and activities the "sugar coating" that makes his courses bearable. A handful of resourceful and capable kids designed a student-run seminar for this semester; it died when the cool caution and qualifications the plan met in administrative offices quenched the enthusiasm that had gone into the proposal. "It's like working in Jello," a senior said. "You suggest an idea, they put you on a committee, and nothing happens." There is an acceptance that school is a place you get through, but you're happy to get out of. The kids reveal their ambivalence: "It's the best high school in the state. It's a bitch."

And so, even in Burlington High School, out of a sense that there must be alternatives, other ways to treat kids have developed. One of the people who started thinking about the problem was Jim Carter, who metamorphosed over a few years from junior high school disciplinarian into the high school's leading reformer. Carter started looking for a way to talk to one group of kids the schools obviously were failing: the students barely hanging on as they reached high school. ASPIRE was the result.

At ASPIRE headquarters—a suite of rooms at the center of Burlington High—the day begins slowly. At 8:30 the rock music blares before the lights go on. Three sleepy eyed, fifteen-year-old girls gossip in a corner, another pokes away at a typewriter, a boy fusses with a guitar. Two students design a psychedelic poster for a wall. "Evie, does this look all right?" one asks a tiny, birdlike woman as she comes in.

In half an hour, Evie Carter (Jim Carter's wife) and burly, gentle-faced Chick Ash, ASPIRE's teachers, call their students together—fifteen of them present this day—for a meeting to decide plans for the week. They push their chairs into a ragged circle—the kids who, in another place, could go through school without ever stating an opinion or being noticed by anyone. Kids who look a bit more blank-faced, sullen, fidgety, a little less acceptable than the clichés about teen-agers allow. In the meeting they bait and jockey each other ("You stupid jerk." "This class is fruity."), get sidetracked, grow shy and then boisterous, and find the business of planning and suggestion-making awkward. Evie and Chick hold back, then prod a little, then let the students carry the meeting. ("We're getting together slow.") The meeting over, the kids drift off—a handful to a photo-shooting trip, two to glaze pottery. One sits over a programed workbook, another does a crossword puzzle. Evie and Chick—kind, low-keyed, re-spectful—stay available to talk with kids, settle disputes, work with problems. It is hard, sloppy work without pattern or precedent. In the afternoon, the kids gone, they contact the day's absentees by phone and plan strategy for the next day. Evie writes in ASPIRE journal: "Ups and downs, cohesive days and fragmented days, content and irritation, but a thin thread of direction runs through it all."

ASPIRE (A Student Planned Innovative Research Experiment) was conceived as a way to help unmotivated, alienated kids with often critically poor school records get a toe hold on the high school ladder as they entered tenth grade. Give them a year away from the pressures and competition met in high school, the plan went. No formal courses, no requirements, no grades. Let them talk out and accept how rotten the school system has been for them, let them plan their own curriculum based on real interests, let them see that education can be more than bad grades, and they'll go back into the main stream with changed attitudes and initiative. The plan has gone through many variations in ASPIRE's three years of operation: no structure, minimal structure; large group projects, individual projects; limited contact with the rest of the school, no contact. The constants have been a group dynamics approach with all students asked to participate in planning common goals and activities.

Kids considering joining the program are often wary of the freedom from daily assignments, routine classwork. "What about English? Will I get all my credits?" This concern came from a girl who had dropped out of school the year before because she "didn't like it." The freedom continues to be a difficulty for some—they want to impose the very standards which have made them failures.

The program's obvious successes are many. A full-scale model of a World War I Sopwith Camel biplane (made famous again by Charles Schulz's Snoopy) sits in a hangar nearby, the work of a completely engrossing prospect that took math, engineer-ing, and a lot of carpentry. Trips to Expo and the Florida Everglades grew out of geography projects. (ASPIRE's report to the state Department of Education about their midwinter Florida trip stated somewhat naïvely: "There has been a rather poor acceptance of our trip-program by many members of the faculty . . . an undercurrent of criticism was felt, the reasons for this not being entirely clear to those involved in the program.")

This year the emphasis has been on photography. A group of self-selected students work with a commissioned free-lance photographer, John Williams. Nikkomats in hand, they take shooting trips to the lake nearby or all the way to Boston, and then learn film processing, developing, and printing. Groups of students have made a movie, worked with ceramics, volunteered at an orphans' home, gone to the ballet, bowled, skied, and climbed mountains. A pollution-environment project is developing this semester. ASPIRE's records show that twenty of each year's class of thirty or so go on to graduate with their class two years later. The program's graduates occasionally return like evangelists to urge enrollees to work hard so "they can make it like I did."

This year Mike promises to be one of ASPIRE's successes. He came to the program with reports from former teachers that he was "slow," and his quiet reserve seemed to verify this. ASPIRE staff discovered early in the fall that archaeological diggings were his passion. They let him be the new source person for natural science field trips and digging expeditions. In November, he had opened up enough to teach a first-grade class studying Indian artifacts. In January, he was making copies of Iroquois pots; the talent in his specialty was being transferred to other areas. "He works with the same intense concentration he shows in so many of his efforts," the journal notes. "Perhaps one of the reasons for Mike's difficulties in school is that he needs time—long quiet expanses of time—in which to develop slowly whatever ideas come to him. Maybe he just can't be chopped into forty-five-minute chunks."

But for every Mike, there is a student ASPIRE loses. One enlists in the Army to get away from a family in which he serves as whipping boy. Another troubled boy is declared unmanageable by his parents and sent to reform school. A girl makes a decision to drop out of school and go to work so she can move out of her home—her drunken father has tried to rape her one time too often.

"This year we seem to have young people to whom school problems, which they no doubt have, pale beside the immediacy of their difficulties at home," an ASPIRE teacher explains. The personal problems are often overwhelming, and can color the entire program. The group becomes disruptive as the result of the contagious edginess of a classmate who must negotiate a truce between his parents and a delinquent younger brother. Occasionally a situation thrusts itself into ASPIRE's realm: Last fall participants in a feud between two families descended on the ASPIRE meeting room to continue the battle.

ASPIRE has not hit upon any formula for balancing academic work with personal therapy, nor even discovered where one leaves off and the other begins. Threatened with extinction when Title III funds end this June, ASPIRE may be dropped because it has strayed too far from a course that is defensible in conventional school terms. "You undermine everything we try to do," one teacher complained. "We set up standards for the kids and expect them to live up to them, and then you come along with all this freedom and set an example that these kids don't need. What these kids need is more structure with absolute opportunities for success."

A critic in the vocational education department says: "Life is not the way ASPIRE is. You can't get along in society that way. You have to have a vocation and you have to adjust, to learn to conform." He insists the same kids would do better in the "low-level programs" in his department.

Evie Carter agrees in part: "You couldn't teach auto mechanics or any specific skill the way we teach in ASPIRE." Increasingly, she believes that basic skills can't be belittled, that reading problems are a cause as well as a result of the ASPIRE student's personal feelings of inadequacy. But she wonders, at the same time, whether the school really understands anything about the lives of the students she teaches, and whether

—at this point—school can make a difference in their lives at all. Three years ago there seemed to be some ways to a solution. Today ASPIRE knows that many of the questions haven't even been raised yet.

In Burlington, as everywhere else, there are kids who never make it to high school, who find at ten or fourteen that they and the conventional institutions designed for their education have nothing left in common. Their homes are the material of social pathology: broken families, alcoholism, welfare checks. In school, they get labels stuck on them—"deprived," "behaviorally disordered," "delinquent," "unteachable"—are put in special programs, pushed out, or quietly disappear on their own.

A dozen of these kids, once headed for reform school, are the students of Shaker Mountain School, a crazy idea that seems to be doing well. The school began on a whim last year. Jerry Mintz, a freewheeling young man with a Master's in education, picked up a boy hitchhiking who didn't want to get back to school. On the spot they decided to start their own. "We had $30 and a car," Mintz, now the headmaster, recalls. "It was a Plymouth; so we thought about calling it 'The Plymouth School,' but we finally named it after the mountain behind our farm."

Shaker Mountain occupies the entire first floor and basement of the former Hotel Breton on Church Street, Burlington's main thoroughfare. Rent is $125 a month. Inside there are a comfortably cluttered meeting room, mechanics room, art room, recreation room—even a cubbyhole with drawings on the wall and a mattress on the floor for being alone. Mintz's farm in Starksboro is the country location of the school. The five full-time teachers live there, and that is where "some classes are held, where some kids stay most of the time, and where most of the kids stay some of the time," giving the school a semi-boarding arrangement.

In the meeting room, the students look like nothing so much as the orphans in *Oliver Twist*—scruffy young rowdies, but charming. Long, stringy hair topped by a perky cap. Skinny bravado. A cigarette butt hanging out of the corner of a twelve-year-old mouth. Two play chess. A girl—one of three in the school—plays a word association game with a teacher. A boy paints a sign warning: BEWARE, TROUBLE MAKERS, and next to him a friend begins to weave a rug that will say: "Let there be peace in this school." Next to a rack of specially selected paperback books, a boy—his feet up on a table—reads aloud to two others. The words come slowly and painfully, but there is no embarrassment. The kids seem both tougher and younger than their counterparts in public school. One moment a boy will be insolent; the next, he'll be hugging a teacher, needing someone to hang on to. When a favorite teacher arrives, the group welcomes him wildly.

Last year, the school got by on $6,000 in small donations from foundations and friends (including one from Scribner, who tithes for favorite causes). To earn money, students have made and sold gravestone rubbings, metal sculptures, candles, and paintings. The school comes on like a cheerful beggar. The teachers, all with respectable academic credentials, work for room and board, and occasional expense money. There is no tuition for students.

Ironically, although the school isn't the Plymouth, the car seems to be its central symbol. Particularly in the long, bitter winter, the daily twenty-two-mile commute between the farm and city quarters is a continuing struggle with ailing vehicles, gas, and repair bills. In addition, the school has traveled more than 10,000 miles by car on trips this year. As members of the school community (three of the kids serve as trustees), the students are part of the effort that goes into keeping everything in motion. Asked what project he would like to take on next, a student replied: "Get the bus fixed." Real transportation problems become educational experiences. The students went comparison-shopping for a new school car, and then visited the bank to decide on the best financing plan—a full day's math lesson.

"The kids are turned on to doing anything with their hands," a teacher said. "Abstract concepts don't make it, but then they don't make it with any kids. They're turned off to anything that looks like education. We have to make it fun. We do a lot in art, and now one kid is digging electronics."

Perhaps more than anything else, the kids are turned on by Indians. The interest began first through Buffy Sainte-Marie records, and then by a newspaper account of a protest by St. Regis Mohawks on the U.S.-Canadian border. With no advance notice, the group drove up to the reservation and were given a full welcome, with dances, by the Mohawks. Since then, they've traded visits regularly, and recently several of their Indian friends came to Burlington for the weekend as the main attraction in an Indian festival at a local junior high school.

Shaker Mountain students receive scholastic accreditation through the state's equivalency program. Last year, Vermont requested that the students take standardized reading tests at the beginning and close of the term. The students averaged a 2.1-year increase in reading ability over the period. Mintz is not particularly proud of the gain. "You can't test the most important changes."

In January, Mintz received an achievement award from the Governor's Committee on Children and Youth. The community seems pleased that because of Shaker Mountain there are fewer kids "in trouble" these days in Burlington. But whether or not the public schools will be able to come to terms with the Shaker Mountain kids in the future, no one can now predict.

A block down Church Street from Shaker Mountain is a trip to a different world: the BEAM School, an alternative for the kids for whom the public schools are ostensibly designed. The paneled walls of the second-floor offices, across from City Hall, are covered with announcements, statements, questions. A poster asks: "What is BEAM School?" And answers: "Democratic. Individual. Ageless. Fun. Community. Noncompulsory. Organic." BEAM is for the verbal.

In a small room a cluster of teenagers—some of high school age, some younger—are dissecting the *Communist Manifesto* in a seminar on Marxism. "How could it ever work with people?" one asks. "How could he ever have so much faith in people?" In another room, twenty students and a few adults gather for a meeting of the education class. The Vermont education law is up for revision, and a fifteen-year-old girl discusses potential changes in statutes, and explains the procedures by which BEAM members will testify before a legislative committee the following day. "God, that's really important," someone breaks in. "Why didn't I know about this?"

BEAM is the hangout, the afterschool school for the kids born to succeed in the school system. The children of the university professors, the professionals, the middle class. The students who always swim through the grades, thrive on books and competition, and—until recently—have made everyone feel good about the public schools.

The school is the child of an older experiment with which it shares its offices, the Burlington Ecumenical Action Ministry. Big BEAM—as the kids call it—is supported on an inter-faith basis, spawns task forces on social concerns within the community, and is headed by the Reverend William H. Hollister. He came to Burlington out of seminary fifteen years ago to build a new Presbyterian church. Instead, he established a unique city-wide congregation that gets tough about social problems and celebrates at "festivals" once a month in a converted TV studio. (A typical member of his congregation told Hollister: "I don't believe in God, but there's a spirit around here that's really great.") Somewhere along the way, the need for a church building was forgotten.

A year ago, BEAM's education task group, sensing something in the wind, called in a group of bright, articulate kids to talk about their attitudes toward school. The open sessions, which sometimes included the long-time chairman of the Burlington school board, revealed a lot: "What I don't want to know I can be taught for years and not learn." "School does not provide the experience in the community to get you involved in life." "School is turning people off. If that's education, thanks, but no thanks." Then the kids dreamed out loud about the kind of school they'd like, if they had a choice.

Out of these sessions grew the concept of the BEAM School. It would be democratic. ("Kids and grown-ups on same level. Caste system done away with. Everyone will help everyone else. Yeah!" a journal notes.) It would use the community, the "real world," as its classroom. And everyone would learn as an individual, moving in his own direction.

The group (kids and adults) thrashed through the practical problems of developing the school through the spring and summer. There would be no teachers, the kids decided, just "enablers," adults who would guide the learning and administer the programs. They interviewed candidates for the job. "It was a terrifying experience," recalls Sally Smith, one of two full-time enablers. "For fifteen minutes the kids told me what the school would be like. Then they set up problem situations and listened critically as I explained how I'd handle them."

In operation since September as an independent supplement to the public schools, BEAM School has thirty kids and adults who make up its core group, another thirty who float in and out. At first, projects emphasized social service to the community, through VISTA, OEO, and the Visiting Nurses Association. Since that time, "the kids have learned they're not as dedicated to saving the world as they talked," Sally Smith said. "They realize they're more selfish than they thought, that they need things for themselves." Much of the rhetoric used in BEAM's development has disappeared as the kids have had the responsibility for "building" their own school. But the process goes on, and everyone learns. "It's important for them to be free to make the mistakes that come with power," said Dr. Joan Babbott, a BEAM School founder.

Arts projects have grown very popular at BEAM, and the school is even "limping into" academic courses, for which a few students receive credit at the high school. But what is most significant about BEAM School is not so much the projects, which run from blacksmithing to black studies, but the tension it creates with the public schools, and the somewhat unnerving questions it asks of the community. What turns kids on at BEAM, and turns them off at the high school with its array of courses, clubs, activities? Why are these kids here? What are they saying?

The former football star who dropped out of "that scene," let his hair grow long, and became critical of a school system that's "clearly not doing what it's supposed to do for kids, by any standard." The fresh-faced fellow from Rice Memorial, Burlington's Catholic high school, who's figured out that the main goal of his school is "to teach people to conform," and who likes the feeling of "being himself" at BEAM. The girl who said: "The world is real and all around us, if we can see it. Before BEAM, I had been learning within four walls, and the world was outside. The BEAM School has opened my eyes to the world just outside the door that I could not quite open by myself." They are hopeful, moderate kids who call themselves "liberals"; who explain that the school system, whatever its shortcomings, "has a hard job on its hands"; and who agonized over whether to cut a math test to attend a Vietnam Moratorium Day rally. (Most didn't.)

Because of their mutual financial problems, both BEAM and Shaker Mountain are being forced to think hard about their futures. At a BEAM meeting in January, the kids confronted Howard Goodrich, associate superintendent of schools, with the ways BEAM might receive public funding. (It's not uncommon for a representative of "the system" to show up at BEAM strategy sessions.) He seemed pessimistic about the possibilities. Since then, there's been a change of heart. Goodrich is now proposing that BEAM and Shaker Mountain live under the same roof in an old, vacant school building outside of Burlington, and become a community school under ESEA Title III funds obtained through the school systems. BEAM would undertake full-time schooling for some participants, and would be required to impose greater structure on itself to meet minimal state and local demands. The community school, as outlined by Mark Smith, a BEAM enabler, would draw heavily on community resources, use a tutorial group as a working unit, and maintain the democratic practices begun in BEAM and Shaker Mountain. Such a proposal, which would ally the two experiments with the system, does not smack so strongly of co-optation in Burlington as it might elsewhere. In Burlington, the Establishment is still a nice guy, reasonable, and likable. "I'm one of you," Goodrich tells the BEAM kids. They look quizzical, half-believing him, half not.

Perhaps Shaker Mountain and BEAM can become an annex of the system without losing their vitality, perhaps they can remain a force for change inside them as well as out. But if ASPIRE dies, and Shaker Mountain and BEAM are subsumed into the school system, there are still people in Burlington uncomfortable enough with the status quo to try something else, something new. Play your hunches for all they're worth. Take the risks. Learning is an adventure, remember? The kids get the message.

Paul Goodman has been hailed as one of the patriarchs of the educational left for many years now. In this selection Goodman provides an overview of his position that has established him as one of the most popular among contemporary educational radicals. His simple notion of educating ". . . the young entirely in terms of their free choice . . ." is an appealing one. Summerhill operates solely on this principle and has achieved its share of greatness in so doing. This reading gives you a great deal to consider. Most of you by this time have given some thought to the less traditional forms of schooling and Goodman should be able to be of valuable assistance in the encouragement of abandoning those traditional ideas and embracing a more human approach to the education of the young.

FREEDOM AND LEARNING:
THE NEED FOR CHOICE

Paul Goodman

The belief that a highly industrialized society requires twelve to twenty years of prior processing of the young is an illusion or a hoax. The evidence is strong that there is no correlation between school performance and life achievement in any of the professions, whether medicine, law, engineering, journalism, or business. Moreover, recent research shows that for more modest clerical, technological, or semi-skilled factory jobs, there is no advantage in years of schooling or the possession of diplomas. We were not exactly savages in 1900 when only 6 per cent of adolescents graduated from high school.

Whatever the deliberate intention, schooling today serves mainly for policing and for taking up the slack in youth unemployment. It is not surprising that the young are finally rebelling against it, especially since they cannot identify with the goals of so much social engineering—for instance, that 86 per cent of the federal budget for research and development is for military purposes.

We can, I believe, educate the young entirely in terms of their free choice, with no processing whatever. Nothing can be efficiently learned, or, indeed, learned at all—other than through parroting or brute training, when acquired knowledge is promptly forgotten after the examination—unless it meets need, desire, curiosity, or fantasy. Unless there is a reaching from within, the learning cannot become "second nature," as Aristotle called true learning. It seems stupid to decide a priori what the young ought to know and then to try to motivate them, instead of letting the initiative come from them and putting information and relevant equipment at their service. It is false to assert that this kind of freedom will not serve society's needs—at least those needs that should humanly be served; freedom is the only way toward authentic citizenship and real, rather than verbal, philosophy. Free choice is not random but responsive to real situations; both youth and adults live in a nature of things, a polity, an ongoing society, and it is these, in fact, that attract interest and channel need. If the young, as they mature, can follow their bent and choose their topics, times, and teachers, and if teachers teach what they themselves consider important—which is all they can skillfully teach anyway—the needs of society will be adequately met; there will be more lively, independent, and inventive people; and in the fairly short run there will be a more sensible and efficient society.

Reprinted from Paul Goodman, "Freedom and Learning: The Need for Choice," *Saturday Review,* May 18, 1968, pp. 73-75. Copyright 1968, Saturday Review, Inc.

It is not necessary to argue for free choice as a metaphysical proposition; it is what is indicated by present conditions. Increasingly, the best young people resolutely resist authority, and we will let them have a say or lose them. And more important, since the conditions of modern social and technological organization are so pervasively and rigidly conforming, it is necessary, in order to maintain human initiative, to put our emphasis on protecting the young from top-down direction. The monkish and academic methods which were civilizing for wild shepherds create robots in a period of high technology. The public schools which did a good job of socializing immigrants in an open society now regiment individuals and rigidify class stratification.

Up to age twelve, there is no point to formal subjects or a prearranged curriculum. With guidance, whatever a child experiences is educational. Dewey's idea is a good one: It makes no difference *what* is learned at this age, so long as the child goes on wanting to learn something further. Teachers for this age are those who like children, pay attention to them, answer their questions, enjoy taking them around the city and helping them explore, imitate, try out, and who sing songs with them and teach them games. Any benevolent grownup—literate or illiterate—has plenty to teach an eight-year-old; the only profitable training for teachers is a group therapy and, perhaps, a course in child development.

We see that infants learn to speak in their own way in an environment where there is speaking and where they are addressed and take part. If we tried to teach children to speak according to our own theories and methods and schedules, as we try to teach reading, there would be as many stammerers as there are bad readers. Besides, it has been shown that whatever is useful in the present eight-year elementary curriculum can be learned in four months by a normal child of twelve. If let alone, in fact, he will have learned most of it by himself.

Since we have communities where people do not attend to the children as a matter of course, and since children must be rescued from their homes, for most of these children there should be some kind of school. In a proposal for mini-schools in New York City, I suggested an elementary group of twenty-eight children with four grown-ups: a licensed teacher, a housewife who can cook, a college senior, and a teen-age school dropout. Such a group can meet in any store front, church basement, settlement house, or housing project; more important, it can often go about the city, as is possible when the student-teacher ratio is 7 to 1. Experience at the First Street School in New York has shown that the cost for such a little school is less than for the public school with a student-teacher ratio of 30 to 1. (In the public system, most of the money goes for administration and for specialists to remedy the lack of contact in the classroom.) As A. S. Neill has shown, attendance need not be compulsory. The school should be located near home so the children can escape from it to home, and from home to it. The school should be supported by public money but administered entirely by its own children, teachers, and parents.

In the adolescent and college years, the present mania is to keep students at their lessons for another four to ten years as the only way of their growing up in the world. The correct policy would be to open as many diverse paths as possible, with plenty of opportunity to backtrack and change. It is said by James Conant that about 15 per cent learn well by books and study in an academic setting, and these can opt for high school. Most, including most of the bright students, do better either on their own or as apprentices in activities that are for keeps, rather than through lessons. If their previous eight years had been spent in exploring their own bents and interests, rather than being continually interrupted to do others' assignments on others' schedules, most adolescents would have a clearer notion of what they are after, and many would have found their vocations.

For the 15 per cent of adolescents who learn well in schools and are interested in subjects that are essentially academic, the present catch-all high schools are wasteful. We would do better to return to the small preparatory academy, with perhaps sixty students and three teachers—one in physical sciences, one in social sciences, one in humanities—to prepare for college board examinations. An academy could be located in, and administered by, a university and staffed by graduate students who like to teach and in this way might earn stipends while they write their theses. In such a setting, without dilution by nonacademic subjects and a mass of uninterested fellow students, an academic adolescent can, by spending three hours a day in the classroom, easily be prepared in three or four years for college.

Forcing the nonacademic to attend school breaks the spirit of most and foments alienation in the best. Kept in tutelage, young people, who are necessarily economically dependent, cannot pursue the sexual, adventurous and political activities congenial to them. Since lively youngsters insist on these anyway, the effect of what we do is to create a gap between them and the oppressive adult world, with a youth subculture and an arrested development.

School methods are simply not competent to teach all the arts, sciences, professions, and skills the school establishment pretends to teach. For some professions—e.g., social work, architecture, pedagogy—trying to earn academic credits is probably harmful because it is an irrelevant and discouraging obstacle course. Most technological know-how has to be learned in actual practice in offices and factories, and this often involves unlearning what has been laboriously crammed for exams. The technical competence required by skilled and semiskilled workmen and average technicians can be acquired in three weeks to a year on the job, with no previous schooling. The importance of even "functional literacy" is much exaggerated; it is the attitude, and not the reading ability, that counts. Those who are creative in the arts and sciences almost invariably go their own course and are usually hampered by schools. Modern languages are best learned by travel. It is pointless to teach social sciences, literary criticism, and philosophy to youngsters who have had no responsible experience in life and society.

Most of the money now spent for high schools and colleges should be devoted to the support of apprenticeships; travel; subsidized browsing in libraries and self-directed study and research; programs such as VISTA, the Peace Corps, Students for a Democratic Society, or the Student Nonviolent Coordinating Committee; rural reconstruction; and work camps for projects in conservation and urban renewal. It is a vast sum of money—but it costs almost $1,500 a year to keep a youth in a blackboard jungle in New York; the schools have become one of our major industries. Consider one kind of opportunity. Since it is important for the very existence of the republic to countervail the now overwhelming national corporate style of information, entertainment, and research, we need scores of thousands of small independent television stations, community radio stations, local newspapers that are more than gossip notes and ads, community theaters, high-brow or dissenting magazines, small design offices for neighborhood renewal that is not bureaucratized, small laboratories for science and invention that are not centrally directed. Such enterprises could present admirable opportunities for bright but unacademic young people to serve as apprentices.

Ideally, the polis itself is the educational environment; a good community consists of worthwhile, attractive, and fulfilling callings and things to do, to grow up into. The policy I am proposing tends in this direction rather than away from it. By multiplying options, it should be possible to find an interesting course for each individual youth, as we now do for only some of the emotionally disturbed and the troublemakers. Voluntary adolescent choices are often random and foolish and usually transitory; but they are the likeliest ways of growing up reasonably. What is most essential is for the youth to see that he is taken seriously as a person, rather than fitted into an institutional system. I don't know if this tailor-made approach would be harder or easier to administer than standardization that in fact fits nobody and results in an increasing number of recalcitrants. On the other hand, as the Civilian Conservation Corps showed in the Thirties, the products of willing youth labor can be valuable even economically, whereas accumulating Regents blue-books is worth nothing except to the school itself.

(By and large, it is not in the adolescent years but in later years that, in all walks of life, there is need for academic withdrawal, periods of study and reflection, synoptic review of the texts. The Greeks understood this and regarded most of our present college curricula as appropriate for only those over the age of thirty or thirty-five. To some extent, the churches used to provide a studious environment. We do these things miserably in hurried conferences.)

We have similar problems in the universities. We cram the young with what they do not want at the time and what most of them will never use; but by requiring graded diplomas, we make it hard for older people to get what they want and can use. Now, paradoxically, when so many are going to school, the training of authentic learned professionals is proving to be a failure, with dire effects on our ecology, urbanism, polity, communications, and even the direction of science. Doing others' lessons under compulsion for twenty years does not tend to produce professionals who are autonomous, principled, and ethically responsible to client and community. Broken by processing, professionals degenerate to mere professional-personnel. Professional peer groups have become economic lobbies. The licensing and maintenance of standards have been increasingly relinquished to the state, which has no competence.

In licensing professionals, we have to look more realistically at functions, drop mandarin requirements of academic diplomas that are irrelevant, and rid ourselves of the ridiculous fad of awarding diplomas for every skill and trade whatever. In most professions and arts there are important abstract parts that can best be learned academically. The natural procedure is for those actually engaged in a professional activity to go to school to learn what they now know they need; re-entry into the academic track, therefore, should be made easy for those with a strong motive.

Universities are primarily schools of learned professions, and the faculty should be composed primarily not of academics but of working professionals who feel duty-bound and attracted to pass on their tradition to apprentices of a new generation. Being combined in a community of scholars, such professionals teach a noble apprenticeship, humane and with vision toward a more ideal future. It is humane because the disciplines communicate with one another; it is ideal because the young are free and questioning. A good professional school can be tiny. In *The Community of Scholars* I suggest that 150 students and ten professionals—the size of the usual medieval university—are enough. At current faculty salaries, the cost per student would be a fourth of that of our huge administrative machines. And, of course, on such a small scale contact between faculty and students is sought for and easy.

Today, because of the proved incompetence of our adult institutions and the hypocrisy of most professionals, university students have a right to a large say in what goes on. (But this, too, is medieval.) Professors will, of course, teach what they please. My advice to students is that given by Prince Kropotkin, in "A Letter to the Young": "Ask what kind of world do you want to live in? What are you good at and want to work at to build that world? What do you need to know? Demand that your teachers teach you that." Serious teachers would be delighted by this approach.

The idea of the liberal arts college is a beautiful one: to teach the common culture and refine character and citizenship. But it does not happen; the evidence is that the college curriculum has little effect on underlying attitudes, and most cultivated folk do not become so by this route. School friendships and the community of youth do have lasting effects, but these do not require ivied clubhouses. Young men learn more about the theory and practice of government by resisting the draft than they ever learned in Political Science 412.

Much of the present university expansion, needless to say, consists in federal-and corporation-contracted research and other research, and has nothing to do with teaching. Surely such expansion can be better carried on in the Government's and corporations' own institutes, which would be unencumbered by the young, except those who are hired or attach themselves as apprentices.

Every part of education can be open to need, desire, choice, and trying out. Nothing needs to be compelled or extrinsically motivated by prizes and threats. I do not know if the procedure here outlined would cost more than our present system—though it is hard to conceive of a need for more money than the school establishment now spends. What would be saved is the pitiful waste of youthful years—caged, daydreaming, sabotaging, and cheating—and the degrading and insulting misuse of teachers.

It has been estimated by James Coleman that the average youth in high school is really "there" about ten minutes a day. Since the growing-up of the young into society to be useful to themselves and others, and to do God's work, is one of the three or four most imporant functions of any society, no doubt we ought to spend even more on the education of the young than we do; but I would not give a penny to the present administrators, and I would largely dismantle the present school machinery.

The selection which follows examines the "alternative" school movement. Though widely varying viewpoints on curriculum and methodology abound in the "alternative" schools, there is a preponderance of "super Summerhills." What is your reaction? Why do so many of these schools die?

"ALTERNATIVE SCHOOLS":
CHALLENGE TO TRADITIONAL EDUCATION?

Donald W. Robinson

Over 700 independent schools have been founded during the past three years, as teachers, parents, and students seek alternatives to the stultifying climate of so many public schools. Two or three new "alternative" schools are born every day, and every day one dies or gives up its freedom, claims Harvey Haber, founder of the New Schools Exchange.

In existence less than a year, the New Schools Exchange (2840 Hidden Valley Lane, Santa Barbara, Calif. 93103) describes itself as the only central resource and clearinghouse for all people involved in "alternatives in education." The exchange publishes a directory of experimental schools, acts as a placement bureau for teachers, and publishes a newsletter (29 issues to date, 2,000 subscribers, $10 per year).

The exchange provides a sense of community among radical educators. As one visitor recently expressed it, "The information that is moving through things like the *New Schools Exchange Newsletter* is primarily a feeling, and only incidentally a body of data. It's that Woodstock complex, a ritual magic to ward off the stunning desolation that sweeps across the land sometimes like a cold wind. But then feelings are very powerful. They can swell and topple empires."

These feelings constitute the fuel that is firing the revolution that manifests itself not alone in the New Schools movement, but equally in the student revolts and in the writings of such authors as Leonard, Kohl, Kozol, Holt, Herndon, and Glasser.

The feelings are of frustration and resentment because schools are so regimented, administration so unsympathetic, teachers so hamstrung, and learning climate so sterile.

The directory issued by the New Schools Exchange lists several hundred innovative schools and educational reform groups in 28 states, the District of Columbia, and Canada. The largest number, over 100, are in California. There is also a considerable concentration in New England. (The private schools springing up in the South are not experimental in the same sense.)

A similar directory is available (for $10) from the Teacher Drop Out Center (University of Massachusetts, Amherst, Mass. 01002). This center is operated by two graduate students, Leonard Solo and Stan Barondes, who queried 400 reputedly innovative schools and published statements from 60 replies.

These replies reflect the spirit of the schools:

"We believe in the right of every individual to be free to experience the world around him in his own way."

"We encourage kids to live their own lives. Classes are not compulsory; self-government runs the school."

Reprinted by permission from Donald W. Robinson, " 'Alternative Schools': Challenge to Traditional Education?" *Phi Delta Kappan* 51 (March 1970): 374-75.

"We believe that in a loving, accepting environment in which emotional needs are met, children will feel free to grow; and that feeling free, they *will* grow, *will* follow their natural curiosity, *will* do whatever they find necessary to meet their needs."

More extreme is this statement from an Oregon school:

"Philosophy: A cross of Skinner and Neill and Leary and IWWW. The school is an integral part of a farm commune research organization crazy house. Prospectus and appropriate political material available."

Of course not all of the reform movement lies outside of the public schools, and several city systems are listed in the Drop-Out Center's directory of innovative situations. The statement submitted by John Bremer director of Philadelphia's much-publicized Parkway Program ("School Without Walls"), includes this unconventional bit:

"It is true that we teach some unconventional subjects, but the study groups are mostly small, under 10 students, and the old ways of classroom teaching just do not make any sense. So students and faculty are redefining what we mean by teaching and learning. Our faculty members teach, but when they do, it is not in a classroom; it is in the city, in an office building, in City Hall, in the street, depending on what they are teaching."

Such statements exemplify the sentiments of Solo and Barondes, whose goal is "to identify the schools—elementary and secondary, public and private—that want the unusual teacher, the teacher who believes in letting students grow into individual, alive, and aware humans, the teacher who breathes controversy and innovation." Their second goal is to locate these unusual teachers and to serve (without charge) as a clearinghouse to bring innovative teachers and free schools together. They find that the number of eager teacher applicants far exceeds the school openings. The center receives eight to 10 letters a day from teachers wanting to move to a freer school.

Still another manifestation of the freedom movement is *The Teacher Paper,* a quarterly publication produced by high school English teacher Fred Staab, assisted by his wife and a volunteer staff. *The Teacher Paper* (280 North Pacific Ave., Monmouth, Ore. 97361, $2 per year) exudes a tone of congeniality with the spirit of the new schools, though its constituency is essentially the corps of teachers who have elected to reform the public schools rather than desert them. Staab started his paper last year to provide a forum for teacher expression and to improve communication between teachers and the public. He feels that too much of the local communication about education is filtered through the administration and that even in national education journals the teacher's voice is much too muted. He claims his publication is neither anti-administration nor anti-establishment, only pro-teacher and pro-student. And indeed both the feature article in the December, 1969, issue titled "Bulletin Boards as a Guerilla* Tactic" and a foldout "Guerilla Manual" listing 162 disruptive tactics should provide a modern superintendent with more chuckles than scowls. Militant rhetoric has become part of the scene.

Staab predicts that the rapid growth of *The Teacher Paper* will continue and is seeking a part-time job so he can devote more time to making it grow. His present 1,200 subscribers in 30 states include roughly 900 teachers and 300 parents, two-thirds of them Oregonians. He is confident that circulation will expand because other journals lack style, seriousness, and bite and do not reflect teacher views.

---

*Webster spells it "guerrilla," but "free school" people tend to apply the same standard to spelling that they apply to conduct: Do your own thing.

These three voices of dissent, the New Schools Exchange, the Teacher Drop-Out Center, and *The Teacher Paper* are heralds of a protest movement that is gaining steam in its crusade to humanize education. (The founders and managers of all three are over 30.) While some educators are dedicated to extending the applications of computer assisted instruction and systems analysis, these teachers and parents are more concerned with humaneness, sensitivity, and freedom of the student to be a free, inquiring person, with human help from teachers.

The New Schools Exchange is beginning to attract attention. It has been visited by writers, foundation representatives, and government consultants, and dares to hope it may receive some grant money, while admitting that without additional support it cannot survive many more months.

Most representatives of recognized establishment groups admit that they know too little about the new schools to hazard an opinion. However, Cary Potter, director of the National Association of Independent Schools, recognizes them as one segment of the current wave of frustration with traditional education. "They represent a mixed bag," he says, "a terrific spectrum, out of which may come some useful ideas. Some of the black schools especially show something about independence which is good."

Perhaps the best opportunity to learn about the alternative schools movement is offered by the workshop conference the New Schools Exchange has planned for April 4 and 5 on a 1,200-acre ranch in Santa Barbara County, California. Director Haber invites inquiries.

Many of the conspicuous demands of the new school movement are being pushed in public schools also, but too slowly, too uncertainly to satisfy the mood of "action now." Some public schools are becoming ungraded, introducing sensitivity training, calling on parents and other adults to contribute their expertise as resource people, and even taking school completely out of the school building, as in the Philadelphia Parkway School already referred to.

One advocate of experimental schools has prepared a list of ways these "alternative schools" can relate to the public schools. The suggestions include: providing community resource specialists to supplement public school activity; giving creative parties for students from public schools; supporting radical students and teachers, if for no other reason than to let them know they are not alone, odd, insane, or whatever else the "system" might be trying to make them believe of themselves; organizing joint experimental school and public school student projects; offering student teachers practice teaching opportunities in experimental schools, and exchanging services of experimental school and public school teachers in after-hours activities.

The names of the new schools reflect the tone of the movement: Student Development Center, All Together New Free School, Alternative Foundation, School for Human Resources, Community Workshop School, Halcyon School, Involvement Education.

They represent a fairly wide spectrum of educational thought, with a heavy sprinkling of super-Summerhills. About half of them are inner-city schools. Haber estimates that approximately 80 percent are designed to accommodate students from pre-school through high school. Organization, curriculum, and financing vary widely. Some operate entirely on tuition, some rely wholly on other sources, and many combine the two.

Many of these new schools are not carefully planned; many do not survive. Haber estimates the average length of life of a new school at 18 months, after which it may die completely, merge with another school, or alter its course so severely as to cease to be a radically innovative institution.

The entire movement may prove ephemeral. But even if few alternative schools survive, the movement will have made its contribution to reform, much as third parties in our political history have forced the established parties to adopt social reforms.

If education is going to continue to be compulsory for all youngsters, and abhorred by many, why can't the public schools offer students, parents and teachers some choice in the type of school they are to attend? If an important part of learning lies in having choices about the conditions of learning, the prospects for improved learning appear bright as more options are introduced. This article suggests a kind of internal voucher system under which the student and his family are offered a variety of types of schooling, all within the public school system.

OPTIONS FOR STUDENTS, PARENTS, TEACHERS: PUBLIC SCHOOLS OF CHOICE

Mario Fantini
Donald Harris
Samuel Nash

The art of governance in a free society rests with citizen decision making. The more informed the citizen, the more capable he is of making decisions. The more options he has, the more chance he has of making a selection which is self-satisfying.

Transferring this notion to schools, the citizen as consumer should be able to decide on the kind of school his child should attend or the kind of educational environment he would like his children to have. This type of decision making would be school governance in its purest form. Making every parent the decision maker for his family's education is a significant stage beyond electing representatives to decide what kind of education makes the most sense for the majority in the locality. This is what we now have through our representative form of school governance, that is, through electing local school boards. In any majority-rule approach, significant numbers of citizens must accept majority rule in the kind of education their children receive. Therefore, diversity in education is severely restricted. Public schools then become social institutions which foster uniformity rather than diversity. Citizens who want other options must turn to private schools, if they can afford them. The private-school option is not available to many low-income citizens.

The trick is to get the *public schools* to respond to both diversity and individual rights in school decision making. However, in addition to governance, both *substance* and *personnel* are essential pillars which must be altered if genuine reform is to take place in American education. We therefore need to examine the implications of these two areas in a pattern which maximizes choice for the consumer.

A system of choice maximizes variation in both the substance and personnel of education. For example, consumers who select a school program based on a Montessori model will have important substantive differences from those who select a classical school. Choice does legitimize new programs, each of which carries with it new curriculum and new personnel.

Certainly, professionals who are attracted to a Summerhill-like school are different from those who prefer a classical school environment.

The point is that a public school system that maximizes consumer choice legitimizes new as well as old educational approaches to common objectives. The new educational

Reprinted by permission from Fantini, Harris, and Nash, "Options for Students, Parents, and Teachers: Public Schools of Choice," *Phi Delta Kappan* 52(May 1971): 541-43.

approach will be made operational by public consent. Moreover, *educators* will also be able to choose from among these educational alternatives, possibly enhancing their sense of professional satisfaction.

This choice model, therefore, tends to minimize conflict among interest groups because *each* individual is making *direct* decisions in educational affairs. Furthermore, as a supply and demand model, the choice system has a self-revitalizing capability. As the options prove successful, they will increase in popularity, thereby increasing the flow of successful programs into the public schools and generating a renewal process for public education.

Under the present system, new programs are introduced into the public schools largely through professional channels, with parents, students, and teachers having little say. However, parents, students, and teachers can actually veto any new program. Some programs, such as sex education, become controversial, especially if they are superimposed by the administration.

School systems are currently structured to present only one model or pattern of education to a student and his parents. If economic factors or religious beliefs preclude nonpublic schools as an alternative, the parent and student have no choice but to submit to the kind and quality of public education in their community. With the exception that one or two schools may be viewed as "better" or "worse" by parents and students (generally because of "better teachers" or because "more" graduates go to college or because the school is in a "good neighborhood"), the way materials are presented and "school work" is done is essentially the same in all schools on the same level. It should be possible to develop within one school or cluster of schools within a neighborhood, district, or system several different models that would offer real choices to all those involved in the educative process.

A school district might offer seven different options in its elementary schools:

Option one: The concept and programs of the school are traditional. The school is graded and emphasizes the learning of basic skills—reading, writing, numbers, etc.—by cognition. The basic learning unit is the classroom, which functions with one or two teachers instructing and directing students at their various learning tasks. Students are encouraged to adjust to the school and its operational style rather than vice versa. Students with recognized learning problems are referred to a variety of remedial and school-support programs. The educational and fiscal policy for this school is determined entirely by the central board of education.

Option two: This school is nontraditional and nongraded. In many ways it is very much like the British primary schools and the Leicestershire system. There are many constructional and manipulative materials in each area where students work and learn. The teacher acts as a facilitator—one who assists and guides rather than directs or instructs. Most student activity is in the form of different specialized learning projects done individually and in small groups rather than in the traditional form where all students do the same thing at the same time. Many of the learning experiences and activities take place outside of the school building.

Option three: This school emphasizes learning by the vocational processes—doing and experiencing. The school defines its role as diagnostic and prescriptive. When the learner's talents are identified, the school prescribes whatever experiences are necessary to develop and enhance them. This school encourages many styles of learning and teaching. Students may achieve through demonstration and manipulation of real objects, as well as through verbal, written, or abstractive performances. All activity is specifically related to the work world.

Option four: This school is more technically oriented than the others in the district. It utilizes computers to help diagnose individual needs and abilities. Computer-assisted instruction based on the diagnosis is subsequently provided both individually and in groups. The library is stocked with tape-recording banks and "talking," "listening," and manipulative carrels that students can operate on their own. In addition, there are Nova-type video-retrieval systems in which students and teachers can concentrate on specific problem areas. This school also has closed-circuit television facilities.

Option five: This school is a total community school. It operates on a 12- to 14-hour basis at least six days a week throughout the year. It provides educational and other services for children as well as adults. Late afternoon activities are provided for children from the neighborhood, and evening classes and activities are provided for adults. Services such as health care, legal aid, and employment are available within the school facility. Paraprofessionals or community teachers are used in every phase of the regular school program. This school is governed by a community board which approves or hires the two chief administrators and is in charge of all other activities in the building. The school functions as a center for the educational needs of all people in the neighborhood and community.

Option six: This school is in fact a Montessori school. Students move at their own pace and are largely self-directed. The learning areas are rich with materials and specialized learning instruments from which the students can select and choose as they wish. Although the teacher operates within a specific and defined methodology, he remains very much in the background, guiding students rather than directing them. Special emphasis is placed on the development of the five senses.

Option seven: The seventh is a multicultural school that has four or five ethnic groups equally represented in the student body. Students spend part of each day in racially heterogeneous learning groups. In another part of the day, all students and teachers of the same ethnic background meet together. In these classes they learn their own culture, language, customs, history, and heritage. Several times each week one ethnic group shares with the others some event or aspect of its cultural heritage that is important and educational. This school views diversity as a value. Its curriculum combines the affective and cognitive domains and is humanistically oriented. Much time is spent on questions of identity, connectedness, powerlessness, and interpersonal relationships. The school is run by a policy board made up of equal numbers of parents and teachers and is only tangentially responsible to a central board of education.

Distinctive educational options can exist within any single neighborhood or regional public school. The principle of providing parents, teachers, and students with a choice from among various educational alternatives is feasible at the individual school. In fact, this may be the most realistic and pervasive approach, at first. For example, in early childhood a single school might offer as options: 1) a Montessori program, 2) an established kindergarten program, 3) a British infant school program, and 4) a Bereiter-Engleman program. Again, parents, teachers, and students will have to "understand fully" each program and be free to choose from among them.

Some may ask whether a Nazi school or a school for blacks that advanced the notion that all white people were blonde-haired, blue-eyed devils and pigs could exist within the framework of a public system of choice. Plainly, no. Our concept speaks to openness; it values diversity; it is nonexclusive; it embraces human growth and development and is unswerving in its recognition of individual worth. Within these bounds, however, is an infinite spectrum of alternative possibilities in creating new educational and learning forms.

Although we have suggested several different ways in which schools might be structured under a public schools of choice system, it should be clear that there are many other possibilities. The flexibility of the concept lends itself to a whole range of options without forcing people to accept any one option they are not attracted to. The choice educational system starts where the public school system and the clients are and develops from that point. For example, we have described above what could be developed within a school district. The same variety of offerings, teaching styles, and learning environments could be presented within *one* school facility. This would permit the bulk of parents and students in our hypothetical district to continue with educational programs and activities just as they have been, but those who wanted to try different options could do so. There could be six or seven choices in the educational supply of options from which parents and students could choose.

Another application of the public schools of choice system could be implemented on the high school level in a moderate-size city.

Distinctive high school models could be integrated into the public system, providing parents and students with choices about learning style, environment, and orientation that best met the individual needs of the learner and teacher. For example, there could be a standard or traditional high school; a university experimental high school that is a learning center for students, teachers, and those who train teachers; a classical school that emphasizes languages, learning, and rigid disciplines (Boys Latin in Boston is an example); a vocational-technical complex; a high school that emphasizes independent work and personal development, where students and teachers share a joint responsibility for the program; a high school (or student-run high school supplementary program) that in some way addresses itself to the special concerns of particular students—where perhaps black students could work out questions of identity, power, and self-determination on their own terms in their own style; and, finally, a high-school-without-walls concept, such as in Philadelphia, where students utilize the resources and institutions of the city and community as learning environments.

These alternatives, and others, are not unrealistic or significantly beyond the reach of a city school system that is concerned with the quality of its public education. Although many of these ideas have been tried in isolation, they have not been incorporated into a public education system. When they are, we will have entered a new era of public education.

We have learned from our early experience with participation that the mood among the major parties of interest is tense. The lessons from our experiences with reform can be summarized as follows. A good reform proposal:

1) demonstrates adherence to a comprehensive set of educational objectives—not just particular ones. Proposals cannot, for example, emphasize only emotional growth at the expense of intellectual development. The converse is also true. Comprehensive educational objectives deal with careers, citizenship, talent development, intellectual and emotional growth, problem solving, critical thinking, and the like.

2) does not substantially increase the per student expenditure from that of established programs. To advance an idea which doubles or triples the budget will at best place the proposal in the ideal-but-not-practical category. Further, an important factor for reformers to bear in mind is that the new arena will deal with wiser use of *old* money, not the quest for more money.

3) does not advocate any form of exclusivity—racial, religious, or economic. Solutions cannot deny equal access to any particular individual or groups.

4) it is not superimposed by a small group which is trying to do something *for* or *to* others.

5) respects the rights of all concerned parties and must apply to everyone—it cannot appear to serve the interests of one group only. Thus, for instance, if decentralization plans of urban school systems are interpreted to serve only minority communities, then the majority community may very well oppose such efforts. Similarly, if plans appear to favor professionals, then the community may be in opposition.

6) does not claim a single, across-the-board, model answer—is not a blanket panacea to the educational problem. Attempts at *uniform* solutions are almost never successful.

7) advocates a process of change which is democratic and maximizes *individual* decision making. Participation by the individual in the decisions which affect his life is basic to comprehensive support.

These seven ground rules should be borne in mind, whatever options we offer, but, above all, we must offer options, through public schools of choice.

What do the kids want? How much time have you spent in your education classes considering this question? Do you feel it's more a matter of deciding for them? What better source for finding out than from the kids themselves. In this article by an unidentified high school student are several things you might want to consider in your approach to high school students.

WHAT
THE KIDS WANT

Do you want anti-establishment feelings to stop? You can't stop the war for us? That is not what I ask. I ask this:

1. *Allow and provide encouragement for students to get together intellectually for open discussions on controversial issues.* Let everyone participate. Hold these meetings after school hours, or permit students during lunch to go to the auditorium. Invite students to speak with teachers and administrators.

2. *Listen to students.* Awareness is there. Willingness is there. Thought is there. You will find them much more articulate than you ever suspected.

3. *Explain why you do things as you do.* Ask the students to do the same. Be open and honest with yourself. You do things wrong. So do we. Give the facts as they are and explain the complicated interrelations.

4. *Talk to students on their level.* Do not stand above them on the stage and speak through a microphone, but rather form informal groups of more than 10 and less than 40 and move into the group as one of them. In this way, communication will be greatly improved.

5. *Talk to them as people—men and women.* Their minds are almost completely matured intellectually by the junior year of high school. The old rules for treating us with your understanding of adolescent psychology may be dropped and forgotten, for we are individual men and women. The college "Adolescent Psychology" course only works in general. When applied to individuals, it breaks down and falls into a ruin of broken bits of misinterpreted misinformation.

A few people in my school have tried. The vast majority are having conniptions about it. A few people have also tried these approaches outside of school. The majority of parents protest because they do not realize what is happening. But the students who are involved in the action *know it is good.* One teacher is in danger of losing his job, because he has done what is suggested here. His students find a difference. So does he. Those who are screaming against it haven't noticed:

Disciplining is unnecessary when students are in his classes.

Involved students have lost apathy toward learning.

Students learn the subject faster and better in his classes than in those of any other teacher.

Students enjoy his classes.

Students have a better understanding of what goes on around them as a result of their loss of apathy.

Instead of protesting and causing trouble, students are beginning to move in channels to build up good things while phasing out poor ideas and philosophies. They have abandoned the idea that they must ruin before they can build.

Reprinted from *Phi Delta Kappan,* March 1970, p. 407.

Students do wish to cause change. At first, this may be seen by some as undesirable. But how can the "this is so" attitude prevail when all good things come through change?

Only when the school faculties and administrations realize what I have pointed out to be true can improvement of learning take place.

Further insight into the inner workings and feelings of the students and faculty at John Adams High School is provided by the following article. Can you understand and explain the reaction of the students to their newly found freedom? Do you feel education could be improved by closer and less formal relationships between teachers and students? Did the Adams staff err by not offering greater structure and direction for those students who needed it? Can you relate to the ambivalent and uncertain attitudes that many of the teachers at Adams developed? What could have been done differently which might have improved the situation measurably?

SCHOOL CLIMATE AND STUDENT LEARNING

Patricia A. Wertheimer

From the earliest days of planning of the clinical school, we assumed that school climate would play an essential part in the educational effectiveness of the school. Climate, which here means the aggregate of attitudes of members of the school institution toward each other, toward their joint efforts and objectives, and toward the constraints and opportunities they meet there, was taken to be at least as important as formal classroom instruction in the determination of student learning. Our goal was active student participation in educational decision making, both in guiding their individual progress and in shaping the school curriculum; the preconditions we assumed necessary for this participation were freedom of movement and course choice for students and close student-teacher relationships.

We saw the provision of freedom as essential in demonstrating persuasively to students that we trusted their ability to make decisions, for a student who is not free to make the decision to go to his locker or the toilet without written permission can hardly feel confident that he is trusted to make crucial decisions about his own education.

Close student-teacher relationships were also considered an essential characteristic of the kind of climate we wanted to create. The traditional position of the teacher as authority figure would have to give way to a new role: advisor to the student. Their relationship would allow for fallibility, open exchange of opinion and information, and both challenge and acceptance of differences. The teacher would be expected to maintain a position of influence with the student, but his influence would flow from competence rather than position. If active inquiry were to be fostered, students—and teachers—would perceive teachers as less than oracles, and teachers—and students—would perceive students as more than passive recipients of the truth.

The notion that student freedom and congenial relations between students and teachers were central to the establishment of a climate of inquiry was held from the earliest days of planning. How the school would look and feel, independent of the variety and quality of course offerings, the sniff of things, the "vibes"—all these were very important to us. We wanted to create a climate that was distinctly our own, that was Adams, that was full of excitement and zest generated by the cooperation of people who like and respect each other working toward the same absorbing purpose.

Reprinted by permission from Patricia A. Wertheimer, "School Climate and Student Learning," *Phi Delta Kappan* 52 (May 1971): 527-30.

As the first year of school operation got under way, it was obvious to all of us, as well as to visitors, that the atmosphere was indeed very different from that of the traditional high school. The halls were bustling with students much of the day, students called most teachers by their first names, students and teachers frequently lunched together, and a relaxed friendliness pervaded halls and classrooms.

On the other hand, it was far from clear that the bustle in the halls was purposeful, or that close relationships between faculty and students led to greater self-direction and initiative on the part of the students. While discussion seemed open enough, the intellectual content sometimes appeared scanty, and relaxation sometimes resembled aimlessness and torpor.

We knew that most of our students had not been prepared by previous school experiences for the kind of freedom that Adams allowed them. As one looked about the school, it was difficult to decide whether most students profited by this new freedom or whether it represented a chaotic ambiguity which made some uneasy and offered others the opportunity to avoid responsible goal seeking.

It was obvious that any examination of the successes and shortcomings of the school's first year should include a hard look at the school's atmosphere and an evaluation of its effects on student learning. A two-stage assessment of student attitudes was planned. The initial effort would examine students' perceptions three months after the opening of the school; a second assessment would follow in May. In December, 1969, 130 randomly selected students were asked for their views on certain aspects of the school in fairly lengthy interviews. Interviewers asked students what made this school different from others and whether or not they approved of these differences. Perceptions of relationships with other students and with teachers were explored; students discussed ways in which they had been involved in planning their own educations, how they used their free time, how much time they spent in studying, and how much they felt they were learning. They were asked how they perceived their chances of being accepted to college and their chances of succeeding in post-high school education.

The second stage of assessment of student attitudes took place in May, 1970, when another sample of 130 randomly selected students responded to questionnaires. These questionnaires, developed on the basis of responses given in the December interviews, were designed to provide a more efficient way to gather essentially the same information as had been obtained through the interviews. To insure that any possible changes in attitude revealed by the questionnaires reflected real changes over time, rather than being a result of a different instrument, interviews were readministered to 40 additional students at the same time.

Though both the interviews and the questionnaires yielded a great deal of information about student attitudes toward a variety of aspects of the school climate, for present purposes the discussion will concentrate on the students' attitudes toward the particular dimensions of climate mentioned earlier.

STUDENT FREEDOM

For Adams students, freedom was one of the most salient characteristics of the school. When asked what made the school different, almost all of them gave "freedom" as the response. This is particularly striking in view of the fact that the relaxation of rules for students was by no means the only innovation confronting them—the curriculum, school organization, grading policy, and schedule were all different in important and obvious respects from those in schools they had previously attended. And yet, out of all these, freedom seemed by far the most important way in which Adams was different.

Throughout the interviews, particularly in December, respondents returned again and again to mention freedom in the school. By far the majority of students said they approved of it, and for some it made all the difference in their feelings about the school that they were released from the irritations and humiliations of restrictions on their freedom.

A few of the comments will illustrate. "What's different about Adams?" "Freedom —that's by far the most important thing. Around here, I don't feel like I'm in jail." "At my other school, there were rules, rules, rules, rules all the time. Here it's so relaxed, and nobody nags you." "I like the freedom—I can go where I want, and I don't always have to be where somebody else tells me to go."

However, not all students were comfortable with the lack of constraints. For some, it seemed more like confusion and license than freedom. There was a tendency to blame "other students" for rowdiness, time wasting, and fighting. This represented an interesting shift in assignment of responsibility for school ills. In most schools, students identify rigid rules and authoritarian teachers as the cause. The Adams students, however, tended to blame each other. Certainly there were things wrong with the school—some classes were boring, the halls were chaotic, belongings were stolen, things weren't organized—but it was *students* who caused these problems. "There are some kids who just don't belong here—they run wild and give the school a bad name."

Since some students doubted that they had the self-discipline to force themselves to master essential but unattractive material, they wished that the teachers would demand more. Particularly toward the end of the school year, a minority fairly strongly expressed the view that the school should insist much more firmly on regular class attendance.

An interesting ambivalence was revealed on the issue of freedom. While some students worried about receiving proper preparation for college or job and thought students should be made to attend classes regularly, very few students were willing to say that there should be firmer enforcement of rules. They may have feared that their freedom was costly, but they were far from willing to give it up.

Student responses to queries about school climate showed that the school not only looked free and relaxed to adult observers, but the students felt this difference, too, and by and large were very positive in their views of it. The first hoped-for goal had certainly been accomplished.

STUDENT-TEACHER RELATIONSHIPS

Although students revealed some ambivalence about freedom, their relationships with teachers were seen almost universally as extremely positive. Indeed, many students judged their relationships with teachers as the most enjoyable part of their school experience. Like freedom, many saw close relationships with teachers as a distinguishing characteristic of the school. Unlike freedom, they saw in close relationships no possible detriment to their learning.

Getting to know teachers as "real" people was particularly important, for students formerly were not able to reveal themselves honestly and openly to their teachers. Students frequently described their teachers as understanding, nonjudgmental, and more like friends than teachers. "Teachers here aren't bossy or crabby, and they don't always yell and pressure you," said one student. "I really like calling teachers by their first names—it makes you feel comfortable with them," remarked another.

"My teachers are always willing to help me, and they're patient. They don't make me feel dumb." This comment was typical—teachers were seen as supportive, as caring about the student's academic progress, and as helpful. They did not badger or embarrass the student or pressure him.

Close relationships with teachers, and the feeling that genuine friendships could be formed, probably helped those students survive who were made anxious by the ambiguity of relaxed rules—support was there to cushion the shock of loss of clear behavioral guidelines. At any rate, even those students who wished for greater academic demands were not willing to see teachers become stricter or more authoritarian.

From all the evidence, then, it must be concluded that the second goal for the climate —close relationships between student and teacher—had been established.

INVOLVING STUDENTS IN DECISION MAKING

An important relationship exists between the first two conditions of school climate— student freedom and close student-teacher relationships—and student involvement in educational decision making. From the initial days of planning for a clinical high school, we assumed that a school characterized by greater student freedom and closer relationships with adults would do much to assure extensive student participation in shaping education. In fact, although student freedom and informal staff-student relationships were considered good in themselves, it was not so much because of their intrinsic worth that they were deemed to be essential to the clinical school, but rather because they were thought of as the necessary preconditions for student participation in processes of inquiry.

What, then, were the actual attitudes of our students toward their studies and their intellectual development? Dissatisfaction with the curriculum became more acute as the year progressed: A substantial minority said that general education was worse than courses given in other schools, and about half the students said that the curriculum should be improved if the school were to help them more. In particular, they wanted more direction from teachers, better organization of class work, and more attention to skill weaknesses. Certainly, a climate of inquiry would be one in which such complaints would be welcomed, and one in which students would feel free to make them openly. And yet these students confessed that they had done very little about making their feelings known to their teachers, nor had they approached other staff members with their concerns. Perhaps more discouraging, half of the few students who *did* try to discuss their dissatisfaction with their teachers said that nothing had come of the attempt. Far from initiating productive, collaborative dialogue with teachers, most students who were dissatisfied with classes dealt with that problem in one way: They opted out. They simply did not attend the class, choosing instead to lounge in the halls, to chat with friends, or, sometimes, to read.

Some students felt that they had become lazy or apathetic about their studies while attending Adams; some felt that they were learning less than they ever had before. And they admitted that they themselves had done very little to try to correct this; many found it impossible to overcome the temptation to simply drift. After all, nobody else seemed worried about it—the teachers kept saying it was the students' decision to make. For these youngsters, the magic had not worked—at least not yet. Freedom and close relations with teachers had not instilled in them the zeal for the examined life; on the contrary, they were more apathetic than ever.

It should be said, however, that most students claimed to be learning as much or more than they had before. Many said it was a different kind of learning—they were learning to express themselves better, and learning more about other people than they had before. They considered these to be important learnings (as did the staff), but they were less sure that they were learning as much as they had or should in "the basics."

But the fact is, or so it seems to me, that the school had failed to provide adequate accommodations for those students whose learning styles simply did not fit our picture of the good educational life. The student who wanted or needed extremely explicit direction from teachers floundered. And, although these students may have been relatively few in number, the impact of their disengagement on the school climate was serious. By spring, 1970, it appeared to many of us that the school was characterized to far too great an extent by a pervasive restlessness and lack of commitment to the effort required to achieve excellence. Migratory bands of students in search of excitement looked in on classes, only to leave if what was going on proved unentertaining. Speakers were frequently treated embarrassingly rudely, films were disrupted by chattering and rustling, and doors opened to a stream of students who entered for a quick look and departed for the next event promising diversion.

While teaching was certainly difficult under these circumstances, in some ways teachers were relieved of some of their major tasks—the alienated or dissenting students were not very often in classes, so their needs did not have to be addressed. Because classes tended to be made up of those students who either were too docile to leave altogether or who were in sympathy with classroom activities, a unanimity of opinion often prevailed in classes which impoverished rather than enhanced inquiry.

Perhaps some tentative conclusions can be drawn from these findings. Most important, it now seems questionable that a school climate can be established which, in and of itself, will lead to students' active engagement in the curriculum. Student freedom and close relationships between students and teachers may be important in bringing about responsible decision making and inquiry, but they may not be sufficient. We have some reason to believe that the curriculum offerings—even, perhaps, some of the ways in which we have tried to encourage inquiry—have affected the climate, for when students become disaffected from these offerings, the tone of the entire school can appear to be altered.

Second, it appears (though this is difficult to admit) that we recognized differences among adults—we placed great weight on the careful selection of teachers with competencies and talents which we thought essential to the accomplishment of our goals—but we did not recognize differences among students. Somehow, we assumed that with the right staff, their skills in "advising" would ensure that all students would function easily and productively within the new school environment. True, we talked of differences in learning styles, but these differences did not seem to include the need for authority, lack of interest in discussion of educational issues, or apathy. We deemed careful selection of the staff to be essential, but did *not* prefer to select our students —we wanted the school to be public and desired a widely heterogeneous student body. It now seems that many of the implications of this choice escaped us, for the picture of students we saw more closely resembled a group of Rhodes scholars than inner-city, or for that matter suburban, adolescents.

Third, many of our ideas have been successful for many—perhaps most—students, and it is too early to decide that they won't be for others. Certainly we need to provide (and have provided) much more carefully designed alternative modes of learning to our students; many students told us we needed to increase the intellectual content of the curriculum and make more demands for achievement. However, they would strenuously resist destruction of the atmosphere of freedom or the quality of student-teacher relationships.

The relationship between learning and the school climate remains an intriguing issue, particularly as we have seen it develop at Adams. It is also extremely complex and baffling to analyze. Conceivably, our climate could better foster desired educational attitudes were it not that some as yet undiagnosed factor or factors are at play, such as students' prior educational experiences, their age, their relations among each other —the list could go on almost interminably. It now seems to me that we may have viewed climate too simplistically and may have counted too heavily on its influence to solve learning problems. As we alter some aspects of the program in an attempt to find more effective ways to solve these learning problems, presumably the overall climate will also be altered. The trick is to improve the curriculum, while preserving, as much as possible, those aspects of climate valued so highly by students and teachers alike.

The Plowden Report is singled out here for its contribution to the "open classroom" movement in the United States. Many of the prescriptions offered by Paul Goodman ("Freedom and Learning: The Need for Choice") come into being in the "open classroom." Kozol in the next article points out some of the cautions to be observed in the transcendence of traditional subject-centered approaches to schooling. The Grosses, however, are convincing in their plea for institutional reform. Can you ignore them?

BRITISH INFANT SCHOOLS —AMERICAN STYLE

Beatrice Gross
Ronald Gross

"British Infant School," "Leicestershire Method," "Integrated Day," "The Open Classroom"—these names are heard increasingly among theorists and practitioners of early childhood education. The terms all refer to a new approach to teaching that discards the familiar elementary classroom setup and the traditional, stylized roles of teacher and pupil, for a far freer, highly individualized, child-centered learning experience that may hold the key to a radical reformation of primary education.

This approach—for which the Open Classroom seems the most useful label—is based on a body of new theory and research on how children do and don't learn, but its attractiveness for educators is even more directly attributable to the fact that it is highly effective under a variety of circumstances for children between the ages of five and twelve. It has spread widely throughout the British school system since World War II, and in the past five years it has been introduced in a variety of American schools, ranging from rural Vermont and North Dakota to inner-city classrooms in Philadelphia, Washington, Boston, and New York.

This year the Office of Economic Opportunity sponsored twelve Open Classroom training centers in nine cities as part of Follow Through, its program for continuing the social and intellectual growth of "deprived" children graduating from Head Start programs. The Open Classroom movement has also won the support of the Ford Foundation, which is funding several efforts to encourage its dissemination in public schools.

There are four operating principles of the Open Classroom. First, the room itself is decentralized: an open, flexible space divided into functional areas, rather than one fixed, homogeneous unit. Second, the children are free for much of the time to explore this room, individually or in groups, and to choose their own activities. Third, the environment is rich in learning resources, including plenty of concrete materials, as well as books and other media. Fourth, the teacher and her aides work most of the time with individual children or two or three, hardly ever presenting the same material to the class as a whole.

The teachers begin with the assumption that the children want to learn and will learn in their fashion; learning is rooted in firsthand experience so that teaching becomes the encouragement and enhancement of each child's own thrust toward mastery and understanding. Respect for and trust in the child are perhaps the most basic principles underlying the Open Classroom.

From the application of these principles derive the most notable characteristics of learning in such a classroom: a general atmosphere of excitement; virtually complete flexibility in the curriculum; interpenetration of the various subjects and skills; emphasis on learning rather than teaching; focus on each child's thinking and problem-solving processes, and on his ability to communicate with others; and freedom and responsibility for the children.

From the moment you walk in the door of such a classroom, the difference from the conventional procedures is striking. In most classrooms rows of desks or tables and chairs face the front of the room, where the teacher is simultaneously presenting material and controlling the class; the children are either quietly engaged by what the teacher is doing, surreptitiously communicating, daydreaming, or fooling. Even in classrooms using innovative materials, such as the Individually Prescribed Instruction, in which each student works on a math sheet prescribed for his particular level of achievement, the basic pattern is one in which all the children do the same thing at the same time, sitting at their desks with the teacher watching from up front.

But in an Open Classroom, there is none of this. There is no up front, and one doesn't know where to look to find the teacher or her desk. She is usually to be found working intensively with one or two children, or, if things are going as they should, often standing unobtrusively aside but observing each child's activities with great diligence. There are no desks and few chairs—fewer than the number of children. And the children are everywhere: sprawled on the floor, in groups in the corners, alone on chairs or pillows, out in the hall, or outside in the playground if it's good weather.

"The children are working on fractions." This kind of description of what's going on in a class, which comes so easily in a conventional situation, can never be applied to an Open Classroom. Each child uses the room differently, according to his own interests, concerns, and feelings on a particular day.

How does the day proceed? As they arrive, the students check the Chore Chart to see what their housekeeping responsibility is for the day. They take turns doing such chores as bringing up the milk, watering the plants, cleaning the animal cage, mixing new paints, sharpening pencils, taking attendance.

Many Open Classroom teachers call a general meeting after the children arrive, focusing on some interesting experiment several children did the day before, something brought from home, an unusual item in the newspaper, or a sentence she has written on the board to be corrected by the class. The children squat on their haunches or sit cross-legged in whatever area most comfortably holds the whole group.

After the meeting, children choose the areas in which they would like to begin their day. Some prefer to start quietly reading, curled up in the overstuffed chairs. Some like to get their assigned work out of the way first, but others may not have a choice if the teacher has noticed, for instance, that they have been neglecting math or need work in punctuation, and she tells them that they should start the day working with her. Soon the room is full of action, used as it will be for the remainder of the day, unless some special visitor or specialist locuses the group's attention for a special activity.

The layout of the room supports the program. An aerial view of a typical second-grade class in the middle of a morning would show that the room is divided into six sections, defined by open bookshelves that hold appropriate equipment, all of which is easily accessible to the children.

The child is free to choose but whatever choice he makes he will be confronted with a wealth of opportunities for exploration and discovery. In the math section is everything he can use to measure and figure, including the Cuisenaire rods, balance scales, rulers and a stop watch, workbooks, and counting games such as Sorry and Pokerino. Similar riches await him in the language arts section, where he can read, make a tape recording or type write, and play word-games and puzzles; or in the arts area with its paints, clay, dyes, and sand. Other corners are devoted to science, music, and blocks.

The child's freedom, autonomy, and independence—as well as his responsibility— are epitomized by the largest and most elaborate of the many charts and pictures around the room. It is the "Activity Chart," and it lists by word and appropriate picture all the possible activities in the room: from reading, typing, playground, painting, right through to visiting and gerbils. Next to each are several hooks, on which the child hangs his name tag to indicate what he's doing. A simple device, but it says much about the respect for the child and the relationship between the child, the teacher, and the room. The equivalent in the conventional classroom is the notorious Delaney Book, still widely used, which represents each student by a little card tucked in a slot corresponding to his desk position, fixing the child in a constrained position, with the teacher clearly in charge.

In the Open Classroom, each child's day is distinctive and different from every other day. To give him a sense of his progress, each child may keep a diary, which is also used to communicate to the teacher. Some typical entries indicate the flow of activity, and the frustrations and concerns of the children:

Today I read *Horton the Elephant.* I began the green series in SRA. Ollie helped me with the words in the *Horton* book. I helped John and Sara make a staircase with the Cuisenaire rods.

I played in the Block Corner most of the day. We were making a suspension bridge. We talked a lot about our water tower and how it got flooded by Jimmy and what we should charge for a tool. I'll do my math tomorrow. Okay?

We had a turtle race today. Mrs. White taught me how to break words down. I can read words, but I can't break them down. We timed the turtles with the stopwatch. They tried to climb over the side of the box.

We're making a book of fables like "How the Snake Lost His Legs"; "How the Elephant Got His Trunk"; "How José Got to Be a Genius"; "How I Got to Be Invisible."

The variety of the activities mentioned in the diaries suggests the highlights of each child's day, but many educators and most parents find it difficult to define clearly what is being learned at any one moment and are usually resistant to the idea that a relaxed and unpressured atmosphere can stimulate serious work.

The evidence that this approach does work and the reasons why were first presented to a wide public in *Children and Their Primary Schools,* a 1967 report of Great Britain's Central Advisory Council for Education. Popularly known as the Plowden Report, after Lady Bridget Plowden, chairman of the council, these fat volumes were handsomely responsive to the council's mandate to "consider primary education in all its aspects." The Plowden Report is one of those classic official documents that only the British seem capable of producing: generous-spirited, concrete, progressive, and written with charm and spirit.

The report is comprehensive in scope: some half-million words covering topics as diverse as the rate of growth in height for boys and girls, religious instruction, salaries, school building costs, sex education, the handicapped, and team teaching. But the aspect of it that has had the most impact on American educators is its portrayal and analysis of the new mode of teaching.

The Plowden Report does not just discuss the theory and marshal the evidence from various fields and disciplines. It goes the further step of showing that it can be *done,* that in fact it already *is* being done. And it is being done not just in the small private schools that have harbored such education for decades, but in the mainstream of Britain's state-supported, mass education system.

In surveying the state of British primary schooling, the Plowden Report discovered that one-third of the primary schools had already dispensed with a fixed curriculum, a teacher-dominated unified classroom, and narrowly focused one-way teaching measured by tests, and replaced them with Open Classroom techniques and practices.

To make its preference for this approach perfectly clear, the Plowden Report gives negative criteria as well as positive ones. In the schools that were found to be damaging children, administrative and teaching practices hadn't changed significantly in the past decade, creative work in the arts was considered a frill, much classroom time was spent in the teacher's teaching in ways that generated few questions from the children (and those narrowly circumscribed by the teacher), and there were too many exercises and rules, resulting in frequent punishments and many tests.

Against this paradigm of educational stultification, the report poses the ideal: emphasis on each child's interests and style, lots of gabble among the kids, an abundance of fascinating concrete materials, and a teacher who stimulates and sometimes steps back. All of this came to the attention of American educators through a series of articles by Joseph Featherstone in *New Republic* in the autumn of 1967. Featherstone was the perfect publicist for the Plowden Report. His down to earth style and modesty matched the report's manner perfectly. By speaking in a low voice, Featherstone raised a storm of interest and triggered a hegira of American educators to England. Lillian Weber, who is now the Open Classroom expert for New York City's schools, and who was virtually alone in the schools in England in 1965, could hardly elbow her way past the study teams from twenty American cities when she returned in 1969.

The theoretical basis of the Open Classroom is found in the work of the Swiss child psychologist Jean Piaget. His work began to influence many other experimental psychologists in the 1950s when his studies were published, but not until recently has his work been interpreted and popularized in the mass media.

Piaget is best known for his finding that intelligence—adaptive thinking and action —develops in sequence and is related to age. However, the ages at which children can understand different concepts vary from child to child, depending on his native endowment and on the quality of the physical and social environments in which he is reared.

But Piaget's books—*The Origins of Intelligence in Children, The Psychology of Intelligence,* and *The Construction of Reality*—based on his research on how children learn, also proved that it is a waste of time to tell a child things that the child cannot experience through his senses. The child must be able to try things out to see what happens, manipulate objects and symbols, pose questions and seek the answers, reconcile what he finds at one time with what he finds at another, and test his findings against the perceptions of others his age. Activity essential to intellectual development includes social collaboration, group effort; and communication among children. Only after a good deal of experience is the child ready to move on to abstract conceptualizations. Piaget is critical of classrooms where the teacher is the dominant figure, where books and the teachers talking are basic instructional media, and where large group instruction is the rule, and oral or written tests are used to validate the whole process. Clearly from his findings, traditional teaching techniques are ineffectual. But for children who must depend on the school environment as the richest they are to encounter, it can be downright damaging; denied a chance to grow, their minds may actually atrophy.

Can the Open Classroom approach transform American primary education as it is doing in England? To Lillian Weber, this is the basic question. As assistant professor of early childhood education at City College, she feels there is a ground swell of interest.

"When I started placing student teachers, after coming back from England, there wasn't one classroom in New York City that I could put a teacher into where she had the slightest chance of being able to apply the theories of how children learn that she was studying at the college." Now, as the result of three years of intensive effort, there are thirty-seven, mostly on the Upper West Side and in Harlem, and Mrs. Weber is swamped with requests for help in introducing these theories in more schools.

Considerable progress has also been made in Philadephia, where the reform school administration of Mark Shedd got behind this approach as one element of its attempt to "turn on the system." Under the guidance of Lore Rasmussen, eighteen teachers are using the Open Classroom approach in five schools, and twenty more are trying it on their own.

On the national level, the Educational Development Center, a nonprofit curriculum-development agency in Newton, Mass., sponsors workshops, provides advisory and consultant services, and develops materials under grants from the Ford Foundation and the federal government's Follow Through program. To spearhead the movement in this country, EDC has brought over experienced British educators, such as Rosemary Williams, who directed the Westfield Infant School, portrayed so vividly by Joseph Featherstone. Through these activities EDC advises teachers in more than 100 classrooms in eight states.

Three questions are asked most often by educators and parents first exposed to Open Classrooms in operation. What problems loom largest? Do the children do as well on standardized tests? And what about cost? Do the additional training and the wealth of materials add greatly to the cost of schooling?

The problem cited most frequently is the fad psychology of educational reform. The trajectory was documented by Anthony Oettinger in *Run, Computer, Run.* An innovation comes roaring in on a wave of rhetoric, there is a bustle to get on the band wagon, things seem to be burgeoning, and then suddenly disenchantment occurs when reality falls short of the glowing press releases.

"The biggest threat is that the approach will catch on and spread like wildfire," insists Ann Cook, who has served widely as a consultant on Open Classroom projects. "Then it would fall into the hands of faddists who are unwilling to give it sufficient time to evolve and mature. Developing the necessary talent to make this work is time-consuming, and Americans are an impatient people."

For this reason, advocates of the approach want to win their battle classroom by classroom, rather than by convincing educational administrators to install the new approach through ukase. "Careful work on a small scale," Featherstone has written, "is the way to start reform worth having. . . . The proper locus of a revolution in the primary schools . . . is a teacher in a classroom full of children."

Another common problem is the tendency to confuse the self-conscious freedom of the Open Classroom with mere "chaos" and disregard of the children. Conventional educators observing an Open Classroom for the first time are often so fixated on the children's informality and spontaneity that they fail to note the diligent planning and individual diagnoses by the teachers and the intellectual and sensuous richness of the prepared environment. These latter qualities, however, are hard-won, and to "open" the classrooms without having developed these strengths is to invite mere mindlessness and frustration.

How do the children score on standardized tests? That question is regularly asked by parents and teachers, as if it gets to the heart of the matter with hard-nosed exactness. But Open Classroom theorists refuse to accept the assumption behind the question. They insist that our new understanding of how children learn and grow makes the present standardized tests obsolete.

"In England there is never any pressure to test in Infant Schools," explains Rosemary Williams, "but since there is pressure here, someone must come up with realistic tests. We've got Princeton's Educational Testing Service at work on tests that will measure original thinking, independency, and creativity—the kind of thing our program is out to develop."

The available evidence indicates that, even measured by the present tests, Open Classroom children progress normally in reading and arithmetic scores. But an increased *desire* to read and write is also evident, and children score higher, on the average, in math comprehension. This is startling, since traditional classrooms focus principally on reading and arithmetic the first two years, while Open Classrooms accord them equal status with such activities as painting and block building.

The question of cost also arises in many people's minds when they see the richness of materials and equipment in the classroom. And indeed there are considerable start-up expenses. David Armington of EDC estimates that to fill an Open Classroom with the most elaborate equipment available in a situation where money is no object costs $1,100 to $1,200, making an initial investment of $36 per child the first year. However, roughly half the equipment is highly durable and does not have to be replaced in subsequent years, and operating costs can be reduced by using parents and older children as aides. For educational value received, its advocates argue, the Open Classroom is a bargain—but, like good buys, it can often be least afforded by those who most need it.

In the present climate of American education, the Open Classroom approach sometimes seems like a flower too fragile to survive. The demands on the schools today are harsh and often narrow. Many black parents demand measurable reading achievement and other test scores to assure that they are no longer being given short shrift. At the same time, white parents are often concerned that the schools continue to give their children an advantage in status over someone else's children.

In such a climate, the Open Classroom seems precariously based on a kind of trust little evident in education today. Teachers must trust children's imagination, feelings, curiosity, and natural desire to explore and understand their world. They also must learn to trust themselves—to be willing to gamble that they can retain the children's interest and respect once they relinquish the external means of control: testing, threats, demerits, petty rules, and rituals. School administrators, in turn, must trust teachers enough to permit them to run a classroom that is not rigidly organized and controlled but, rather is bustling, messy, flexible, and impulsive. Parents must trust school people to do well by their children, without the assurance provided by a classroom atmosphere recognizable from their own childhoods and validated, however emptily, by standardized tests.

Much recent experience suggests that the basis for trust such as this may not exist in American education at present. But perhaps the existence of classrooms where learning based on such trust is taking place will itself help create the beginnings of a new climate.

Jonathan Kozol has been a leading advocate of radical school reform since the publication of his book, Death At An Early Age *(1966), an insightful story of his experiences in the Boston public schools.*

In this brief excerpt, Kozol admonishes the free school movement for its often cited lack of direction and sense of purpose. He also questions whether teachers can and should always be facilitators of learning without ideas or convictions. Would they do a superior job as knowledgeable adults with vocal ideas and feelings?

Much of this article is reminiscent of the attacks on child-centered, progressive education in the late 1950s. Is Kozol sounding the first bell in the death of the free school movement?

FREE SCHOOLS:
A TIME FOR CANDOR

Jonathan Kozol

For the past six years free schools have almost been pets of the media. Too little of this coverage, however, has focused on the deep and often overwhelming problems that confront some of these schools: the terrible anguish about power and the paralyzing inhibition about the functions of the teacher.

The difficulties begin with a number of foolish, inaccurate, and dangerous cliches borrowed without much criticism or restraint from fashionable books by fashionable authors who do not know very much about either life within the cities or responsibilities that confront a free school for poor children in a time of torment and in a situation of great urgency and fear. It is almost axiomatic that the free schools that survive are those that start under the stimulus of a neighborhood in pain and that remain within the power of that neighborhood. Those that fail are, time and again, those that are begun on somebody's intellectual high or someone's infatuation with a couple of phrases from the latest book and then collapse after six months or a year of misery among the cuisenaire rods.

It is time for us to come right out and make some straightforward statements on the misleading and deceptive character of certain slogans that are now unthinkingly received as gospel. It is just not true that the best teacher is the one who most successfully pretends that he knows nothing. Nor is it true that the best answer to the blustering windbag of the old-time public school is the free-school teacher who attempts to turn himself into a human inductive fan.

Free schools that exist under the sledge conditions of New York, Boston, or one of the other Northern cities should not be ashamed to offer classroom experience in which the teacher does not hesitate to take a clear position as a knowledgeable adult. Neither should these free schools be intimidated in the face of those who come in from their college courses with old and tattered copies of *How Children Fail* and *Summerhill.* Many of these people, fans of John Holt or A. S. Neill though they may be, are surprisingly dogmatic in their imposition of modish slogans on the real world they enter. Many, moreover, have only the most vague and shadowy notion of what the free school represents.

Free schools at the present moment cover the full range of beliefs from the Third World Institute of all black kids and all black teachers, operated by a group of revolutionary leaders wearing military jackets, boots, and black berets, to a segregated Summerhill out in the woods of western Massachusetts offering "freedom" of a rather different kind and charging something like $2,000 or $3,000 yearly for it. The free schools that I care most about stand somewhere in between, though surely closer to the first than to the second. The trouble, however, is that the intellectual imprecision of the school-reform movement as a whole, and the very special imprecision of the free schools in particular, allow *both* kinds of free schools to advertise themselves with the same slogans and to describe themselves with the same phrases.

The challenge, then, is to define ourselves with absolutely implacable precision—and to do so even in the face of economic danger, even in the certain knowledge of the loss of possible allies. "This is what we are like, and this is the kind of place that we are going to create. This is the kind of thing we mean by freedom, and this is the sort of thing we have in mind by words like 'teach' and 'learn.' This is the sort of thing we mean by competence, effectiveness, survival. If you like it, join us. If you don't, go someplace else and start a good school of your own."

Such precision and directness are often the rarest commodities within free schools. Too many of us are frightened of the accusation of being headstrong, tough, authoritarian, and, resultingly, we have tried too hard to be all things to all potential friends. It is especially difficult to resist the offered assistance when we are most acutely conscious of the loneliness and isolation of an oppressive social structure.

The issue comes into focus in the choice of teachers and in the substance of curriculum. In an effort to avoid the standard brand of classroom tyranny that is identified so often with the domineering figure of the professional in the public system, innovative free-school teachers often make the grave mistake of reducing themselves to ethical and pedagogical neuters. The teacher too often takes the role of one who has *no* power.

The myth of this familiar pretense is that the teacher, by concealing his own views, can avoid making his influence felt in the classroom. This is not the case. No teacher, no matter what he does or does not say, can ever manage *not* to advertise his biases to the children.

A teacher "teaches" not only or even primarily by what he *says*. At least in part, he teaches by what he *is,* by what he *does,* by what he seems to *wish to be.* Andre Gide said, "Style is character." In the free school, life-style is at the heart of education. The teacher who talks of "redistribution of the wealth" yet dresses in expensive clothes among the poor and spends the Christmas holidays in San Juan gets across a certain message, with or without words, about his stake in some of the nice things privilege can offer.

In certain respects, the things a teacher does not even *wish* to say may well provide a deeper and more abiding lesson than the content of the textbooks or the conscious message of the posters on the wall. When war is raging and when millions of people in our land are going through a private and communal hell, no teacher—no matter what he does or does not do—can fail to influence his pupils. The secret curriculum is in the teacher's own lived values and convictions, in the lineaments of his face, and in the biography of passion (or self-exile) that is written in his eyes. The young teacher who appears to children to be vague or indirect in the face of human pain, infant death, or malnutrition may not teach children anything at all about pain, death, or hunger, but he will be teaching a great deal about the capability of an acceptable adult to abdicate the consequences of his own perception and, as it were, to vacate his own soul. By denying his convictions during class discussion, he does not teach objectivity. He gives, at the very least, a precedent for nonconviction.

It is particularly disabling when a strong and serious free school begun by parents of poor children in an urban situation finds itself bombarded by young teachers who adhere without restraint or self-examination to these values. Not only does such behavior advertise gutlessness and weakness to the children, it also represents a good deal of deception and direct bamboozlement. The willingness of the highly skilled white teacher to blur and disguise his own effectiveness and to behave as if he were less competent and effective than he really is provides the basis for a false democracy between himself and the young poor children he works with. The children, in all honesty, *can't do nothing*. The young man from Princeton only *acts* as if he can't. The consequence of this is a spurious level of egalitarian experience from which one party is always able to escape, but from which the other has no realistic exit.

I believe, for these reasons, in the kind of free school in which adults do not try to seem less vigorous or effective than they are. I believe in a school in which real power, leverage, and at least a certain degree of undisguised adult direction are not viewed with automatic condescension or disdain. I believe in a school in which the teacher does not strive to simulate the status or condition of either an accidental "resource-person" wandering mystic, or movable reading lab, but comes right out, in full view of the children, with all of the richness, humor, desperation, rage, self-contradiction, strength, and pathos that he would reveal to other grownups.

In the face of many intelligent and respected statements on the subject of "spontaneous" and "ecstatic" education, the simple truth is that you do not learn calculus, biochemistry, physics, Latin grammar, mathematical logic, Constitutional law, brain surgery, or hydraulic engineering in the same organic fashion that you learn to walk and talk and breathe and make love. Months and years of long, involved, and—let us be quite honest—sometimes nonutopian labor in the acquisition of a single unit of complex and intricate knowledge go into the expertise that makes for power in this nation. The poor and black cannot survive the technological nightmare of the next ten years if they do not have this expertise.

Free schools, if they wish to stay alive and vital, must learn to separate the fear of domination from the fear of excellence. If a free school were ever able to discover or train a leader with the power and vision of a Jesse Jackson or, in a different sense, a George Dennison or a Truman Nelson, I hope it would have brains enough not to attempt to dull his edge or obscure his brilliant provocations with communal indecision. "Participation" and "the will of the full group," inherently eloquent and important aspects of a democratic and exciting free school, can easily turn into the code words for a stylized paralysis of operation and for a new tyranny of will and function.

In every free school that has lasted longer than two years there is—*there always is* —some deep down and abiding power center. Free schools do not hang photographs of unremarkable individuals. They put up photographs of Malcolm X, of Cesar Chavez, of Martin Luther King, of Tolstoy, or Jose Marti. What is true in history and on the poster-photographs is also true in our own numbers: Some women and some men *are* more powerful and more interesting than others. Behind every free school that survives are the special dedication, passion, and vocation of one woman, one man, or one small and trusted group of men and women. Is A. S. Neill the "ego-tripper" or the "power center" or the "ethical fire" in the heart of his own school? Ask anyone who has ever been to Summerhill.

CASE STUDY:
FREEDOM OR CHAOS?

In the morning, the headmaster makes breakfast for his eleven pupils and staff of four. Classes begin at 9:30 a.m., but no one need attend. In the afternoon, the boys and girls and their teachers go swimming, frequently in the nude. The boys as well as the girls knit. And some of the 6- to 12-year-old pupils drink occasionally from plastic baby bottles with nipples.

To many—both in and out of the conservative world of education—all this may sound like an Ionesco play about boarding-school life. Actually, it is a brief description of life at western Nevada's Evergreen School, a deadly serious academic enterprise with a dramatically unconventional philosophy.

Western Nevada's Evergreen School is patterned on England's Summerhill, the famous hyperprogressive school founded by a Scotsman named A. S. Neill. Without compromise, Neill believes that children are best educated in an atmosphere of freedom and that school should be made to fit the child, not vice versa.

Like Summerhill, Evergreen is a loose fit. The pupils (who pay $2,400 a year in tuition and fees) attend class no more than half the time, and when they do, lessons can be chaotic. At one recent session, punctuated by laughs, burps, and shouts, a noisy debate developed over what to study: "I want geometry." "No, I hate math; let's have nouns and verbs." "I want to write a love story about goons."

If a youngster wants to swear in class (and some do), that's also permissible. In fact, little is forbidden by the school code. When one pupil started drinking water out of a baby bottle, others asked for and were given their own. According to the Summerhillian principle of self-government, children make their own rules and are judged by their peers if they break them.

In this child-centered atmosphere, headmaster Keith Crosley, 27, is just the first among equals. "Children shouldn't be forced to learn," said the boyish-looking Englishman, who taught at Summerhill for eighteen months before coming to the U.S. "Give them time. If they come to class when they're ready, they'll do better."

Crosley's chief assistant in the classroom is Gay Smith, 21, of San Francisco who teaches English, biology, and math, usually in a baggy gray sweatshirt, faded dungarees, and bare feet. "It was hard at first," Gay says of the Summerhill approach, "I had to learn myself what 'freedom' meant. Also, I wasn't used to swimming nude, but I did it to help kids feel there's nothing wrong with the body."

Despite their disheveled appearance and the lack of discipline, most of the pupils at Evergreen are bright and articulate. "The kids back in civilized land think differently," said a 12-year-old girl from Elko. "They tell sex jokes and are shocked by them." Added a classmate: "If there were schools like this all over the world, there'd be no more wars."

Such pre-adolescent optimism jibes with the Summerhillian faith in human nature. In *Summerhill,* a book on his school, the 80-year-old Neill says: "New generations must be given the chance to grow in freedom. The bestowal of freedom is the bestowal of love. And only love can save the world."

More than half a dozen schools based on Summerhillian principles have been founded in the U.S. in recent years. Besides Evergreen, which was established by three Nevada parents last October, there are four Summerhill schools in New York State as well as others in Minneapolis, Los Angeles, and Palo Alto, California. Comedian Orson Bean has had experience with free schools having operated his own in Greenwich

Village. "Because if children are inherently capable of self-regulation, then human beings are inherently civilized. It raises my hopes for the possible salvation of the world," Bean says.

Amid all the talk of salvation, some feel education is forgotten. "Education has evolved over hundreds of years," says A. Chenavix-Trench, headmaster of England's Eton. "I find it inherently impossible that any one man (Neill) could turn the picture upside down and produce a simple solution. I have a supreme distrust of a priori education. One must take the empirical approach in dealing with something as fragile as a child's education." And yet many British educators, while skeptical of the Summerhill itself, agree that Neill's educational heresies have helped unlace the tight Victorial corset that once constricted just such schools as Eton.

Schools like Evergreen ultimately will be judged less by their pedagogy than by their pupils. The important question is not how, why, or when, pupils come to class, but what they can learn once they're there.

SCHOOL
WITHOUT RULES

At Mount Rose School near Liverpool, two seven-year olds strolled into the recreation room. "Got a match?" asked one. "Sure," said the other. The boys were puffing away, when suddenly the headmaster appeared. "Hi, Bill," they said with friendly smiles. Waving back with kind disinterest, William West, M. A. (Cambridge), explained to a visitor: "Kids always smoke, and I'd rather know about it than have it done in secret."

Mount Rose is the tight little isle's loosest "freedom" school. Shunning all rules, it allows boys and girls aged 7 to 17 to smoke, swear, pet, go barefoot, stay dirty—and study only if they care to. The school looks it: a crumbling Victorian mansion with peeling ochre paint and broken windows, its front pillars alternately scrawled with "Ban the Bomb" and "Keep the Bomb." Inside is a happy jumble of paintpots, squashed toffee, dirty clothes, and unmade beds. Scribbled over the walls are drawings, poems and off messages. Sample: "I've been sick and I feel godam arful."

Founded 25 years ago, Mount Rose operates on the hopeful theory that freedom breeds responsibility, not license. This exactly suits Headmaster West, 46, a bachelor who believes that discipline dulls the spirit. The son of a professional soldier, West once aspired to be an Anglican priest, studied theology after Cambridge. When a wartime stint in the R.A.F. eroded his faith he turned his fervor to children. Eight years ago, he took over Mount Rose "to establish a community in which the individual can find out for himself the extent to which he must curb his personality so he can work well with others."

West's 40 charges are mostly the children of arty people ("We have no children of businessmen"). The school offers all the conventional subjects from art to science, French, history and math. But the students attend only classes that interest them. To hold his audience, a teacher may have to lecture while sprawled on the floor. Though most children attend regularly, and some even beg for homework, others play hooky for weeks at a time. One boy failed to appear once in two years. "I think that he must have had strong outside interests," West muses.

Each week West holds a "school meeting"—to settle behavioral problems. Typical debate: Was West right to blast a lad whose banging around at night woke him up? Consensus: No. In keeping with school spirit was the problem of children who keep hurtling about the house on bicycles, alarming pedestrians. When the practice was voted down, one nine-year-old refused to accept the decision. But he did compromise: he now rides only two days a week, which West regards as splendid evidence of personality development.

Interestingly, smoking and swearing diminish at Mount Rose as the kids get older. Unrepressed while young, says West, they simply grow out of it. Drinking is almost unknown; the kids apparently value their pocket money. As for sex, boys and girls theoretically bathe or even sleep together, but as it turns out, they only pet a little. "At my old school," explains one girl, "we talked about boys all day long. Here boys and girls mix so freely that we take one another for granted."

Energy aplenty remains for games, dancing, painting, play-acting and frequent debates. One recent subject: "Does God exist?" To West's surprise God won—by one vote.

"There is something about these children," says one satisfied mother. "There is honesty and kind directness. They don't dissemble or try to be adults. And they don't giggle." The kids themselves are passionately loyal to their offbeat school. "When I left," says one older girl, "I just couldn't find anything to talk about to other kids. They didn't think about anything."

West does not seek accreditation by the Ministry of Education, but government inspectors frequently check his school, as the law requires. Says one inspector laconically: "Parents have a right to send their children to any school they like so long as it provides adequate teaching. This is a free country."